DIALOGUES IN CUBAN ARCHAEOLOGY

DIALOGUES IN CUBAN ARCHAEOLOGY

Edited by
L. ANTONIO CURET, SHANNON LEE DAWDY,
AND GABINO LA ROSA CORZO

THE UNIVERSITY OF ALABAMA PRESS
Tuscaloosa

Typeface: AGaramond

Library of Congress Cataloging-in-Publication Data

Dialogues in Cuban archaeology / edited by L. Antonio Curet, Shannon Lee Dawdy, and Gabino La Rosa Corzo.
p. cm.
Originally presented at a symposium held at the 2002 Society for American Archaeology 67th Annual Meeting held in Denver, Colorado.
Includes bibliographical references and index.
ISBN 0-8173-1464-4 (cloth : alk. paper) — ISBN 0-8173-5187-6 (pbk. : alk. paper)
1. Indians of the West Indies—Cuba—Antiquities—Congresses. 2. Excavations (Archaeology)—Cuba—Congresses. 3. Cuba—Antiquities—Congresses. I. Curet, L. Antonio, 1960– II. Dawdy, Shannon Lee, 1967– III. La Rosa Corzo, Gabino. IV. Society for American Archaeology. Meeting (67th : 2002 : Denver, Colo.)
F1769.D53 2005
972.91′00497′0729—dc22

2005000438

To the memory of three pillars of Cuban archaeology, Ramón Dacal Moure, José M. Guarch Delmonte, and Manuel Rivero de la Calle.

Contents

Figures

Tables

Acknowledgments

Both the spirit and the reality of this project correspond to a collaborative team project. Many individuals and organizations have lent their support and enthusiasm to its inception, realization, and transformation from a conference symposium to an edited volume. The symposium and related forum out of which this volume grew took place at the 2002 Society for American Archaeology 67th Annual Meeting held in Denver, Colorado. The travel and participation of the Cuban presenters was made possible by a generous grant from the American Council of Learned Societies and Social Science Research Council's Working Group on Cuba. The sources of the funds made available were the John D. and Catherine T. MacArthur Foundation and the Christopher Reynolds Foundation. Staff member Rachel Price of the ACLS/SSRC was encouraging and helpful at every point along the way.

Cuban organizations such as the Centro de Antropología de Cuba and the Gabinete de Arqueología de la Habana also lent their logistical and financial support toward preparing travel arrangements for the Cuban participants.

The leadership and staff of the Society for American Archaeology were extremely supportive of the endeavor, offering official sponsorship of the symposium, extending hospitality to the participants, and helping to accommodate the needs of a bilingual session. SAA President Bob Kelly was particularly gracious and enthusiastic, opening the session with introductory comments in Spanish. The difficult task of real-time translation fell to Gustavo Gamez. Others participated in the round-table forum following the symposium which established a consensus and sense of urgency in support of this publication. Daniel Sandweiss of the University of Maine and Sean Britt of Earthwatch Institute made substantial contributions to the discussion.

Shannon Lee Dawdy, who organized the conference events, received logistical support from the University of Michigan's Institute for the Humanities and travel funds from the Rackham School of Graduate Students during 2001–2002. Her own trip to Cuba in 1999 that led to her friendship with Gabino La Rosa and the idea for the symposium was supported by a Latin American and Caribbean Studies pre-dissertation award from the University of Michigan's International Institute. She would not have gone to Cuba had it not been for the buoyant advising of Rebecca Scott. In Cuba, Marcos Rodríguez Matamoros and Lester Puntonet Toledo shared their knowledge of Cuban archaeology and helped set a path for this project in ways of which they are probably unaware and for which she is deeply grateful. Shannon would also like to thank her brother, Jess Dawdy, who provided childcare in Denver under some difficult, if humorous, conditions.

The editors are grateful that all of the original symposium presenters (Mary Jane Berman, Ramón Dacal Moure, Lourdes Domínguez, Jorge Febles, Perry L. Gnivecki, Pedro Godo, Gabino La Rosa Corzo, Theresa Singleton, and David Watters) agreed to submit their contributions for publication. It was clear in the early stages of the preparation of this volume that additional authors were needed in order to include a wider representation of Cuban archaeology, and the decision was made then to invite several other colleagues to contribute to this publication. The editors would like to thank these additional contributors—Marlene Linville, César Rodríguez Arce, Jorge Ulloa Hung, Roberto Valcárcel Rojas, and Samuel M. Wilson—for graciously accepting our invitation to participate in this publication. More than anything we deeply appreciate the patience, understanding, and support of all these distinguished authors during the whole process in the preparation of this volume.

The editors also express their gratitude to Judith Knight, acquisition editor at The University of Alabama Press, for her support of this project from the beginning and for her patience. José Oliver, Kathleen Deagan, and an anonymous reviewer provided valuable and important comments that strengthened the quality of the volume. We would also like to thank Tisha Smith and Louise Elinoff for their assistance in preparing the list of references cited and Daniel McNaughton for final proofreading. Jill Seagard, Scientific Illustrator of the Department of Anthropology of the Field Museum of Natural History, deserves credit for the final versions of Figures 1.1 and 4.1.

DIALOGUES IN CUBAN ARCHAEOLOGY

1 / Introduction

Shannon Lee Dawdy, L. Antonio Curet, and Gabino La Rosa Corzo

This volume evolved out of a symposium titled "Prehistoric and Historic Archaeology of Cuba: A New Era of Research, Dialogue, and Collaboration" presented at the Annual Meeting of the Society for American Archaeology in 2002. The goal of the symposium was to provide a setting for Cuban and American archaeologists to engage in a dialogue that could help thaw the state of communication between scholars from both countries, which in many ways has remained frozen in the political climate of the early 1960s. The symposium also provided an opportunity to present a retrospective on the history of Cuban archaeology, as well as results of recent research. This volume shares the aims of the symposium, but it also has the goal of raising awareness among American archaeologists about the current social, political, and academic state of archaeology in Cuba. In particular, we want to present a more precise picture of Cuban archaeology since the beginning of the Revolution in order to redress some of the misunderstandings, mistrust, and myths created by the absurdities of the Cold War and its lingering ghosts.

SOCIETY AND ARCHAEOLOGY: INTERACTION BETWEEN CUBAN AND AMERICAN ARCHAEOLOGISTS UNDER THE EMBARGO

For some time now, archaeologists and social scientists have recognized that the social, political, and economic context of their work can and does affect many aspects of research, including the questions being asked and the results obtained from their studies. In many cases, paradigms, research topics of interest, methodology, results, and conclusions are influenced by our personal and social conditions (e.g., Trigger 1989). However, these conditions can also affect the shape and trajectory of research in another way, by determining, at least indirectly, with whom we interact professionally. Social biases inevitably influence communication and interaction with other scholars, according to how our social perspective and background agree with those of colleagues. Ultimately, the terms, composition, or even lack of interaction between scholars can greatly influence the historical and intellectual development of an academic discipline. Within archaeology, few examples of how the lack of communication can affect the development of a field are more dramatic than the case of Cuban and North American archaeologists separated by the U.S. embargo.

The ongoing U.S. embargo of Cuba is an anachronism from the Cold War that affects everyone living in the island and a large number of people living in other countries. Before the 1960s, Cuba depended heavily upon products manufactured in the United States. In fact, the small island nation was one of the largest trading partners of the United States, particularly in the exchange of agricultural products (Forster and Handelman 1985). This economic interdependency was entangled with a long history of American interest in Cuba that included military interventions and significant control over the political and economic life of the island dating back at least to the 1870s. American influence was so strong that pre-Revolutionary Cuba is considered by many scholars to have been a modern colony of the United States (Pérez 1999). In 1959, Fidel Castro's Partido del Pueblo Cubano (Party of the Cuban People) came to power as a result of a revolutionary war against President Fulgencio Batista, now generally acknowledged to have been a brutal and inept dictator propped by the Eisenhower administration. Under Batista, the poverty of the Cuban people reached an all-time postcolonial low, with hunger and malnutrition widespread in 1950s Cuba (Forster and Handelman 1985:176; Wilkie and Moreno-Ibáñez 1985:79).

Within a few years of Batista's ouster, Castro began to establish a close relationship with the Socialist Party and the Soviet Union as U.S. political, military, and economic pressure mounted, including the failed Bay of Pigs invasion. A seizure of U.S. corporate assets and Cuba's growing alliance with the USSR soon led to the famous Cuban Missile Crisis of 1962. It was during this crisis that President Kennedy began the embargo of Cuba, banning the trade of all American products and businesses with Cuba, as well as travel to the island by most U.S. citizens, a move that has lasted in a modified version until the present day. For a relatively small nation whose whole industrial and agricultural infrastructure was based upon U.S. technology and designs, this sudden and severe break in economic and political relationships was devastating. For the average Cuban citizen in the 1960s, the embargo meant that basic products such as medicine, food, clothing, chemicals, fuel, and even clean water suddenly became unavailable. For the Cuban citizen of today, "El Bloqueo" means that many of these items are scarce, absurdly expensive, of poor quality, or available only sporadically. Although Cuba has survived by creating strong trade relations with other nations, the exclusion from the world's largest economy located just 90 miles away still means that the Cuban people suffer shortages in essential goods. The embargo is now perpetuated for quite different reasons than it was at the beginning, through the lobbying of Cuban exiles in the United States who are critical of the Revolutionary government, many of whom also hope to regain family property (and perhaps power) lost in the 1960s.

Despite frequent media coverage of the political tensions between the United States and Cuba and an outpouring of scholarly works on the history of Cuban-American relations, many Americans remain unaware of the economic, political, and personal impact of the embargo on everyday life in Cuba. Even less is said about how the "communication blockade" between scholars has affected the historical course of academic disciplines and scholarship in general. Communication between colleagues and the sharing of research results and ideas are critical to the advancement of all disciplines. The absence of regular avenues for scholarly exchange can slow the processes of discovery, theory-building, testing, and critique that are important to the mature development of a field. Unfortunately, the lack of communication between two generations of Cuban and U.S. scholars has led not only to a near silencing of scholarly exchange but also to a misunderstanding about the conditions underlying this silence. For example, in his review of archaeology in post-1959 Cuba, Davis (1996) argues, among other things, that this state of affairs is due to a *voluntary* isolation adopted by his Cuban counterparts. Archaeologists who have traveled to Cuba in the past few years have found this assumption to be false. Cuban archaeologists are eager, even hungry, for intellectual exchange and information on the state of the field in North America. The perception that Cuba's isolation is self-imposed rather than a condition structured by the U.S. embargo is a relic of Cold War rhetoric.

New archaeological findings and methods have been developed in many areas of study in both countries, but the gap in scholarly communication has limited the potential contribution that each side could make to the mutual benefit of theoretical and methodological discourses. For instance, greater scholarly interaction between Cuba and the United States during the 1960s and 1970s (difficult years for American archaeology and the social sciences in general) could have molded different historical trajectories of the discipline. On the one hand, Cuban archaeology could have benefited from many of the developments in American archaeology that resulted from the debate over New Archaeology and the development of Cultural Resource Management archaeology (Flannery 1973; Plog et al. 1978; Schiffer 1976). On the other hand, American archaeology could have profited from many of the early theoretical works developed in Cuban archaeology and anthropology that focused on themes such as transculturation, increasing social complexity, and the cultural impact of the African Diaspora (Ortíz 1943; Tabío and Rey 1966). This is not to say that during this time period no advancements were made or even that Cuban and American archaeologists were oblivious to developments elsewhere. Our argument here is rather that the nature of the developments and debates in the discipline could have been considerably different, and probably richer, if the channels of communication had been open at key moments in the history of archaeology.

CUBAN CONTRIBUTIONS TO ARCHAEOLOGY

It is important to point out some of the contributions Cuban archaeology has made to the study of past societies and to the discipline at large. As can be seen from the papers in this volume by Dacal Moure and Watters (Chapter 2), Berman et al. (Chapter 3), Domínguez (Chapter 4), and Linville (Chapter 5), Cuban archaeology has a long scholarly and institutional tradition that dates back to the nineteenth century. In addition to trajectories in research and education, Cuba has a long tradition in conservation and cultural resource management, as Dacal Moure and Watters point out (see also Linville, Chapter 5, on the conservation of rock art). In fact, Cuban laws for the protection and regulation of archaeological heritage appear to be stricter than those of the United States.

In terms of the Caribbean, Cuban archaeology has led the field in some areas of important research. Innovative Cuban studies of lithic and shell assemblages in a region where ceramics monopolize discussion appear as an oasis in the desert. Another example is the government-sponsored program of the Censo de Sitios Arqueológicos, which has resulted in a sizeable computerized database; it should serve as a model for recording and inventorying archaeological sites throughout the Caribbean (see Dacal and Watters, Chapter 2).

In the realm of theory, Cuban archaeologists have applied the concept of transculturation, developed for the first time by the Cuban anthropologist Fernando Ortíz (1943), to the interaction of ancient groups. Transculturation has been used successfully to explain many changes in late Archaic and Colonial times that resulted from the interaction between groups within Cuba and with those from neighboring islands (e.g., Rey 1970; Ulloa Hung and Valcárcel Rojas 2002). Cuban archaeologists have brought the issue of culture change to a higher level of discussion, especially in dealing with protoagricultural societies or with Archaic pottery-makers (see Ulloa Hung, Chapter 6; Ulloa Hung and Valcárcel Rojas 2002).

Another major contribution is in the area of historical archaeology (Domínguez, Chapter 4). In general, historical archaeology has been poorly appreciated in the Caribbean and other parts of the Americas, but the works of Cuban archaeologists dealing with topics such as the hacienda system (see Singleton, Chapter 10), slavery and escaped slaves (La Rosa Corzo, Chapter 9), and urban processes (Domínguez, Chapter 4) have in many ways anticipated developments in the North American branch of this field by a decade or more. Of special interest are recent renovation projects in Old Havana that have integrated in an exemplary manner the work of historians, architects, and archaeologists (Domínguez, Chapter 4). Although it is true that other pioneering works tied to historic renovations exist (e.g., Ricardo Alegría's work in Old San Juan, Puerto Rico), most of these have focused on architectural restoration rather than on a scholarly, multidisciplinary study of colonial urban settlements. In terms of its multidisciplinary nature, the joint project between the Cuban government and UNESCO is serving as a model for restoration of other colonial zones in the Americas.

ON INTERNATIONALISM, POLITICS, AND THE PRACTICE OF ARCHAEOLOGY

To qualify our critique of American perceptions of Cuban scholarship, we should acknowledge that in recent years archaeologists have become increasingly sensitive to the political context of their work, both intellectually and in terms of practice. Critical assessments of "nationalist archaeology" in different parts of the globe, such as those made by contributors to the volume *Nationalism, Politics, and the Practice of Archaeology* (Kohl and Fawcett 1995; see also Fowler 1987; Gathercole and Lowenthal 1990; Kohl 1998; Meskell 1998), have shown how archaeology plays a part in forming "imagined communities" (Anderson 1983) of nations and ethnic communities. A growing sensitivity to nationalist politics has put archaeologists on their guard, ready to cast doubt on research that smacks of undue boosterism or patriotism. But two problems remain unresolved by this criticism. First, the closely related problem of international politics remains relatively neglected—especially in the field of Americanist archaeology. Nations, nationalism, and nationalist archaeology do not arise in a vacuum; rather they are creations defined in part by their opposition to other nations and, we must allow, other "archaeologies." A second problem arises out of the epistemological assumptions made in critiquing "nationalist" scholarship. Critics have attacked participating scholars as "distorting the past" (Kohl and Fawcett 1995:13). They exhort that archaeological interpretation should "adhere to scholarly standards of logic and evidence" (Silberman 1995:250). But this remonstrance then begs the question: *whose* scholarly standards of logic and evidence? Who ought to decide what the priorities and standards of archaeology should be? Is it possible to reach a consensus on archaeological practice without regard to national contexts?

The dominance of North American and European funding, publication, and organizational power in archaeology would certainly favor the "standards" of archaeologists living in the West. However, there is no guarantee that just because a disciplinary culture is dominant that it is any less political. A long history of claims-making in Western academia shows that many interpretations or policies asserted to be derived from "objective" standards, or observations of the "natural" order of things, were later revealed to be anything but disinterested in their design. In working toward global standards of archaeological practice, we must be wary of unilateralism, and we must base consensus on actual conversations with colleagues from around the world.

An understanding of these two problems frames the intent of this volume, both in the spirit in which it is offered and in the model of "dialogue" that it follows. Few nations in the last 50 years have had such a constant oppositional relationship in the realm of politics than have Cuba and the United States, yet archaeologists have hesitated to acknowledge how much this tension has affected the field.

With the recent focus on nationalist archaeology, one might overlook that an earlier phase of criticism focused on the more complex question of international relations, particularly archaeology's relationship to colonialism. The rise of Marxist-influenced Social Archaeology in Cuba, Mexico, and other Latin American countries in the 1960s engaged in this critique and eventually contributed to the development of Post-Processual Archaeology in North America and Europe in the 1980s and 1990s (Oyuela-Caycedo et al. 1997; Patterson 1994). The gist of these critiques was that in the Americas much of archaeological practice (its structures of funding, labor relations, and curatorial arrangements, for example) either directly supported, or were supported by, relationships of political-economic inequality broadly defined as colonialism. Some critics went further to say that interpretations themselves were biased by colonialist perspectives. Archaeology was seen as replicating hegemonic relations in other realms, particularly between the United States and Central American countries. Although a parallel critique of anthropology's role in colonialism, galvanized by Fabian (1983), has nearly run its course and become part of the worldview of cultural anthropology, few North American archaeologists would yet agree with, or have paid any attention to, statements such as Daniel Miller's, that "Archaeology rises solely out of the colonial structure" (1980:710). A small scatter of publications by historical archaeologists does voice this view, but their critique has by and large failed to penetrate the mainstream of archaeological practice in Latin America and the Caribbean.

Archaeologists from other parts of the world have more readily acknowledged the historical reality of archaeology's relationship to colonialism (e.g., Chakrabarti 1997; Shepherd 2002). The creation of the World Archaeological Congress (WAC) in 1986 promised in part to address postcolonial conflicts arising in archaeology. One of its statutes advocates "the explicit recognition of the historical and social role, and the political context, of archaeological enquiry, of archaeological organizations, and of archaeological interpretation" (on the political history of WAC itself, see Kitchen 1998; Taylor 1988). At the 1999 WAC, the lead theme for the plenary session and symposia was "Identity, Nationalism, and Local Voices." Strangely, not one of the nearly 100 papers organized for this theme addressed the relationship of North American archaeologists to colleagues or communities in Latin America and the Caribbean. The fifth congress, held in June 2003, sponsored several new themes and sessions that addressed the international politics of archaeology, but again, among the approximately 80 papers grouped under the headings "Colonialism, Identity, and Social Responsibility," "Empowerment and Exploitation: North-South and South-South Archaeological Encounters," "Global Perspectives," and "Indigenous Archaeologies," only *one* paper—presented by Javier

Nastri of Argentina (2003)—explicitly addressed the political context of Americanist archaeology.

Most North American archaeologists seem to remain blithely unaware of the historical context of their own specialties, or they simply deny that archaeology is political. This view extends even to those reviewing the state of Cuban archaeology (Davis 1996). Their very distance from the field owing to the travel restrictions imposed by the U.S. embargo of Cuba should provide a clear clue that archaeology cannot be considered in isolation from global politics. One of the purposes of this volume is to provide a historically and politically informed review of Cuban archaeology, giving equal time to the Cuban perspective.

Although collaborative projects between North American and Latin American scholars have long existed, the dissemination of the results of these projects most often occurs through U.S.-based venues such as *American Antiquity, Latin American Antiquity,* or U.S. academic book publishers. Contributing archaeologists from other countries are expected to translate their own archaeological traditions not only into English but into terms and standards acceptable to a North American audience. As a result, institutions such as the Society for American Archaeology have had a powerful influence over the archaeology of the Americas. It could even be argued that the shadow of North American practice has stymied the development of national (not to mention nationalist) archaeological traditions in many Latin American and Caribbean countries. Not so in Cuba.

Therefore, another purpose of the volume is to expose a North American audience to another archaeological world. Because of both the successes of the Revolution and the restrictions of the embargo, Cuban archaeology has evolved since the 1960s largely without the involvement of North American institutions. As in a few other cases in Latin America (e.g., Colombia), Cuban archaeology has also evolved in the context of a culture of resistance to U.S. hegemony. North American readers may find in the work of Cuban archaeologists the reflection of a distinct disciplinary culture, as expressed in terminology, expectations, research agendas, and even methodologies. As the reviews of Cuban archaeology in this volume illustrate (Dacal Moure and Watters, Chapter 2; Berman et al., Chapter 3), the discipline has had a very different historical trajectory and context of practice over the last 40 years. We have termed this collection of papers a "dialogue" because we have tried to refrain from overtranslating Cuban archaeology into North American terms in the hopes that archaeologists on both sides of the Florida Strait can gain perspective on their own practices. The selection of papers by Cuban archaeologists was less motivated by a desire to answer pressing research questions of interest to North American Caribbeanists than by a need to present a cross-section of work by Cuban archaeologists that depicts the local interests of Cuban archaeologists. If it is true that all politics is local, then perhaps all archaeology is local as well. On the other side of the conversation, the selection of papers by North American archaeologists was determined almost entirely by international politics. So few U.S.-based scholars have worked in Cuba since the beginning of the embargo that "natural selection" narrowed this pool to the hardy few who survived the tangled system of visas, permits, and sanctioned money-laundering that comprises the barbed border between the United States and Cuba.

This border, however, has itself been evolving. In the 1990s, the U.S. government made it easier for academics to visit Cuba to conduct research. At the same time, the Cuban government seemed to be more receptive to collaborative projects. The final goal of this volume is to present the results of some of these recent collaborations and to begin a conversation, or dialogue, that can provide a foundation for future coordinated efforts. If international collaborations are based upon an awareness and mutual respect for local archaeological interests, then scholarship everywhere should be strengthened by the challenges of alternative interpretations.

Following the model of a collegial conversation, the editors will now break apart the "we" authorial voice of this introduction to discuss the particular perspectives and experiences that each of us brings to the project.

LIFTING THE EMBARGO IN ARCHAEOLOGY: THREE VIEWS

An American in Cuba, by Shannon Lee Dawdy

Since 1995, I had been eyeing Cuba across the waters of the Gulf of Mexico from my post as an archaeologist in New Orleans, Louisiana. The more I learned about my new home and its history and prehistory, the more I realized how it was intricately connected to a Caribbean-Gulf world that spanned from Mexico to Panamá, from the Spanish Main to the Greater Antilles. In the eighteenth century, a triangle of illicit intercoastal trade connected New Orleans to two port cities in particular, Veracruz and Havana. As I learned more, I realized that strong parallels, as well as connections, existed between Cuba and Louisiana: a reliance on sugar planting, a strong retention of African culture, and complex creole identities. Both places were also former Spanish colonies that had been taken over (at least temporarily) by the U.S. empire in the nineteenth century.

This intellectual curiosity combined with an admittedly personal curiosity. The fact that travel to Cuba has been virtually forbidden to American citizens for most of the last 40 years (despite the fact that this prohibition is in flagrant violation of the U.S. Constitution) makes it that much more alluring. I do not smoke cigars or drink my weight in rum, but, like many would-be tourists, I was attracted to the prohibited. I wanted to meet the people who have created some of the most moving music in the world. I wanted to see the landscape that inspired Cubans to become chronic revolutionaries. The irony was that I would have to surmount a host of artificial barriers put in place since 1959 in order to make the same journey that was so natural in 1759. Even if successful, I could not engage in trade, although smuggling seems to be as active as ever, at least for certain commodities.

When I applied to graduate school in 1998, I proposed exploring the connections between Louisiana and Cuba further. I was fortunate to find at the University of Michigan Rebecca Scott, a historian who had been doing just that over a multiyear project. Dr. Scott is renowned for her ability to build worldwide networks of colleagues and to forge new scholarly collaborations infused with her own enthusiasm. I was soon swept into this exciting atmosphere and was on a plane bound for Cuba during my first spring break at Michigan in 1999.

During that week, we traveled to Cienfuegos, a sugar-planting region in south-central Cuba. My license to travel to Cuba had been approved by the U.S. Treasury Department because I was contributing a poster to a historical exhibit at the municipal museum. Another of my objectives on this trip was to seek out local archaeologists and to learn about possibilities for research there. I soon learned that Dr. Scott's personal networking skills reflected, or were compatible with, a very Cuban way of doing things. An informal discussion with my hosts at the house where I was staying led me to the town architect, who in turn referred me to a young man associated with the museum who was an archaeology enthusiast. The curator then introduced me to another gentleman who was a scholarly amateur archaeologist. This gentleman spent many hours with me that week (despite the glares of his higher-ups in the government office where he worked), telling me about the history of archaeological research in the region. He also gave me the names and phone numbers of professional archaeologists elsewhere on the island, particularly at institutions in Havana. Ever since our meeting, he has periodically sent me postcards, which often take several months to make it over the 90-mile stretch between Cuba and Florida.

The list of names and phone numbers made for me by my Cienfuegos friend became very important when I returned that same summer for a two-month stay to explore research possibilities. If I were to write an entry in an archaeological travel guide to Cuba, I would emphasize the incredible hospitality and generosity of our Cuban colleagues. I, a North American student of unknown credentials, dropped in out of nowhere on archaeologists at the Centro de Antropología (similar to the anthropology branch of the Smithsonian) and the Gabinete de Arqueología in Havana, the city archaeology office. At the Gabinete, Roger Arrazcaeta and his colleagues gave me a full day's tour of the center's facilities and its active excavation sites. I was impressed.

Before traveling to Cuba, I had a lot of hubris—a typical American trait and, I am afraid, a typical trait of American archaeologists. I had imagined that because of the isolation of the embargo and the supposed "freezing" of Cuban society in the Revolutionary moment of 1959, urban archaeology would be unknown or underdeveloped on the island. Or I assumed that if it were practiced, it was done without the advantages of zooarchaeology, ethnobotany, or even updated ceramic typing. My intent was to propose a collaborative effort where I would offer these technical aids (and training) in exchange for access to sites and assistance in excavation.

Although I found Cubans themselves to be self-effacing about their field methods and equipment, I was utterly humbled by what I saw in Havana. The archaeology of New Orleans was primitive by comparison. We had nowhere near the same staffing or support; we had done nowhere near the same amount of research or excavation on the city's key historical sites. It didn't really matter that they used mechanical transits rather than fancy laser total stations. Further, our archaeological projects had nowhere near the same visibility on the public horizon. As Lourdes Domínguez describes in her paper for this volume, archaeological investigations of Havana have been ongoing for several decades in conjunction with historic preservation and renovation projects. Archaeology and historic preservation play prominent roles in the national identity of contemporary Cuba and in the civic reinvention of Havana as an exhibition space for the best the Revolution has to offer. As a result, archaeologists have the power to halt construction projects wherever they perceive a threat to important deposits. Archaeologists are also seen as participants in the urban renewal of Havana, where previously privately owned residences in Old Havana (the original colonial town) are being adapted into multifamily units for poor families in a way that restores their historic beauty. In Revolutionary Cuba, archaeology is part of social progress. In the United States, it is viewed as a gnatty impediment to progress or at best an irrelevant amusement.

I found that rather than the politics of the Revolution hindering archaeological research, in my subfield they had stimulated it. Cuban archaeologists have been given carte blanche to pursue their research in the historic district of Havana in a way unimaginable in our "free," capitalist society, where scholarly pursuits are actually quite restricted by private property rights and profit orientation. Certainly, much of Havana's urban archaeology is motivated by the pride of Cubans in their heritage. It also serves explicitly nationalist narrative-building by the Cuban government, but one should not be too quick to disparage the outcomes of nationalist or civic-minded archaeology. Were there more of it in the United States, I suspect we would be able to fill in a lot of nagging research gaps, not to mention be able to block the destruction of prehistoric mound sites, colonial forts, and historic cemeteries by the private developer's backhoe.

The incommensurability of the state of urban archaeology in New Orleans and Havana was one of the reasons I decided to abandon my ambition for a comparative project in the form of a dissertation. I needed first to get archaeology up to snuff back home (which itself may take a revolution, at least in the way public money is allocated in Louisiana). The second reason was perhaps more predictable. The prickly bureaucracies of both countries, built on a history of mutual fear, resentment, and downright pettiness, made me worry that permitting hang-ups could prolong the completion of my degree interminably. I imagined being left forgotten in a jail cell somewhere, all because of some paperwork peccadillo. I had slipped into Cuba during a period when regulations were being loosened for research travel in the late Clinton era. The election of George W. Bush in 2000, I feared, would have a cooling effect on Cuba-U.S. relations.

This has indeed happened on the diplomatic front with a war of words exploding between the U.S. and Cuban governments soon after September 11, 2001. In May 2004, the Bush administration imposed new travel and humanitarian aid restrictions on U.S. citizens traveling to Cuba. Recently, the U.S. Treasury has even attempted to restrict the exchange of ideas by prohibiting U.S. publishers from editing or marketing works by Cuban authors, a condition which has delayed the publication of this very volume. There is no more salient reminder of how international politics can affect scholarship, even in an area as seemingly benign as archaeology. Still, the openings created by scholarly exchanges in the 1990s and the proliferation of electronic communications have created a stronger bond between Cuban and American scholars, both personally and professionally. On the personal and scholarly front, relations between Cuban and American scholars have become warmer and stronger due to improved communications. Travel can still be complicated for both sides, but conditions are certainly better than they were during the Cold War era.

Although my personal exploration of Cuban archaeology did not lead to an immediate field project, it did lead to collaboration, one that has expanded far beyond my original ambitions. One of the archaeologists who gave me such a warm welcome in Havana was Gabino La Rosa Corzo. As we sat and talked for the first time at the Centro de Antropología over shots of black, sweet coffee, we discovered we shared a mutual curiosity about the state of archaeology in our respective countries and a mutual lack of information. Talking, we excitedly began to satisfy this curiosity but realized that a lot more talking, by a lot more people, was needed to bridge the communication gap imposed by political conditions. We thus formed the idea of a joint Cuban and American session on Cuban archaeology and the possibilities for collaborative work. From there, the session at the 2002 Society for American Archaeology meeting came to be. As the session co-organizer, I myself adopted the Cuban style of informal networking that demands combining sociability with scholarship. The Cuban approach is infectious. Through it, I met Antonio Curet, who then decided to take this collaboration to a new level by transforming it into a publication.

Ultimately, this book is a gift born out of Cuban hospitality, a welcoming gesture that I hope American scholars will return in kind. They may need to adopt the Cuban style of networking through friendship rather than official channels in order to form meaningful collaborations, but I can assure them that gestures of friendship will be genuinely reciprocated.

Cuban Archaeology: The View from Inside, by Gabino La Rosa Corzo

Just as it is difficult for Cuban scientists, as a consequence of the embargo, to stay abreast of the latest research findings published in the United States, North American scholars are limited by their lack of access to the results of our work, and today they know little about archaeology in Cuba. However, archaeologists are a stubborn breed, and they are mutually interested in improving relationships of collaboration. A success story resulting from these efforts was the participation of four Cuban archaeologists, including myself, who represented several generations of professionals at the 2002 Annual Meeting of the Society for American Archaeology held in Denver. The focus and scale of representation in this event were a first for the Society for American Archaeology.

This collaboration allowed Cuban archaeologists an opportunity to meet many of the central figures of contemporary archaeological theory. It also provided an opportunity to become familiar with the concepts, research methods, and viewpoints characterizing the field today. Our perspective on theoretical currents was enriched and expanded by this experience. Equally, the opportunity to present our own research allowed us to discuss issues with high-caliber specialists and educated us in how to apply emerging concepts to our work.

To provide some background on Cuban archaeology, on February 20, 1962, one of the first laws passed by our new government created the National Commission of the Academy of Sciences of Cuba. It included an Archaeology Section (later renamed the Center of Archaeological Investigations), and today it oversees the discipline at the national level. It can be argued that scientific archaeology in Cuba was established in 1962 with the institutionalization of archaeology through this act. At that time, the knowledge accumulated and the research methods used were similar to the ones used in other Latin American and Caribbean countries. However, during the last 40 years, Cuban archaeology has made significant achievements that can be used as a standard for many countries in the Western Hemisphere in which archaeology is still being conducted by the colonial superpowers.

As archaeology was institutionalized in Cuba, investigations developed out of the interests of a number of archaeologists who had devoted their spare time to looking for indigenous sites and artifacts or studying colonial architecture. The 1960s was an era of collection building. Any scientific focus was superseded by a museological interest, although a few excavations and interpretive syntheses of indigenous occupations in the interior of the island were undertaken by some Cuban and North American archaeologists.

In order to promote the discipline, one of the first duties of the Archaeology Section was the creation of a group of professionals with the financial support necessary for the development of research projects. The training of young scholars focused on centralizing and cataloguing Cuba's archaeological collections, both those created by earlier generations and those being created by new investigations. In terms of scientific applications, two important methodologies were applied to Cuban excavations: the use of stratigraphy and absolute radiocarbon dating. These methods produced a reevaluation of the objectives, methods, and results known up to then.

During the first decade of institutionalization of Cuban archaeology as a science, the country's archaeological heritage was preserved and recovered by field projects, priorities for future research were established, and a core group of field professionals was trained. The following decade saw the continuation of the development of excavation and recording techniques, while our knowledge of the island's indigenous cultures grew considerably. The 1980s marked the beginning of an expanding process of self-evaluation on the limitations of the scientific approach and suggestions that the discipline needed a paradigm shift.

During these years, archaeological investigations centered on two foci related to the specific needs of Cuba. One was the creation of technical manuals on the classification of archaeological evidence to make the field accessible to students, and the other was the development of historical syntheses of native peoples in the Cuban archipelago that helps inform contemporary Cuban identity. Advancements made in the area of artifact classification motivated some specialists to publish monographs intended to teach or validate classification systems. Also during the 1980s, investigations developed by several Cuban archaeologists were made accessible to the scientific community through the publication of excavation results, artifact analysis, and studies of collections. Many of these specialists also offered historical syntheses and interpretations of the communities they studied. One of the most important social results of Cuban archaeology during recent decades has been its contribution to national identity and to the preservation of our archaeological heritage. Cuba can proudly point to accomplishments in these fields, but they respond more to the needs of Cuba than to current archaeological problems in the wider field.

The 1990s, certainly the most fruitful years for Cuban archaeology from a scientific perspective, were also a period of questioning and hardship. These were the years during which global socialism collapsed and the U.S. embargo of the island was reinforced. Despite the many difficulties produced by this situation, most Cuban archaeologists continued to work with dedication. Although we are far from feeling completely satisfied because we have so many goals yet to fulfill, we have been able to expand greatly the scope and profile of Cuba's national register of archaeological sites, creating a database and a preservation program far beyond what most Third World countries are able to attain.

During this period of economic difficulty, resources for projects were rationalized by establishing three-year plans, with an emphasis on projects with high viability. As a consequence, ceramic collections were restudied, extensive excavations were closely regulated, and more attention was paid to activity areas and surface archaeology. In terms of research questions, we also shifted emphasis from the study of egalitarian to nonegalitarian societies and focused more on settlement patterns. In addition, information was collected on historical societies not reported by the European colonizers. In the area of rock art, simple morphological analogies gave way to the search for other essential relationships and meanings. Excavations and studies of indigenous cemeteries from both the preceramic and the ceramic periods progressed from simple recording to theoretical discussions. Also, successful excavations on underwater and submerged sites have caused scientists from other parts of the world to pay new attention to the largest island of the Greater Antilles (Calvera et al. 1996; Jardines and Calvera 1999; Pendergast 1997, 1998; Pendergast et al. 2001, 2002). These projects, in particular, have demonstrated the importance of collaborative fieldwork. In another subfield, historical archaeology projects in Cuba have been conducted with a keen sense of social responsibility by ensuring that historic districts and restored architectural zones benefit the community. This field of the archaeological sciences in our country is one of the best examples of what archaeology can contribute to heritage, culture, and the economy. The investigations developed in Cuba at sites of slave resistance outside the plantation as yet have few equals; perhaps only the work of Orser and Funari in Palmares, Brazil, offers a comparison (Funari 1995; Orser 1994).

Historians and archaeologists such as Louis Pérez, Jr., Rebecca J. Scott, Kathleen Deagan, Theresa Singleton, Betty Meggers, Susan Kepecs, David R. Watters, Dan Sandweiss, and Shannon Dawdy, who have either worked in Cuba or have collaborated with Cuban specialists, have proven the advantages of establishing a collaboration based on mutual respect, remote from the old attitudes of servility on the one side, and colonialism on the other.

The articles gathered here make accessible to the English-speaking archaeological community the papers presented at that historic meeting of Cuban and American archaeologists in 2002. Some papers have been added to cover additional topics in Cuban archaeology. It is hoped that this publication will stimulate broader exchange and mutual understanding.

A Puerto Rican Mediator? by L. Antonio Curet

When Shannon Dawdy contacted me in the summer of 2001 to ask me to be the discussant for the symposium she and Gabino La Rosa Corzo were organizing on Cuban archaeology at the Annual Meeting of the Society for American Archaeology in Denver, I did not hesitate to say yes. This was a great professional honor, as well as an opportunity to interact and learn more about the ancient history of this island that I knew only from readings of archaeological works such as those by Tabío, Guarch, La Rosa Corzo, Domínguez, Dacal, Rivero de la Calle, and others. Needless to say, this was a naive and innocent approach to a large responsibility that I was taking on. It was not until months later that Shannon confided to me that more than just a discussant, she chose me as a cultural mediator between the American and Cuban archaeologists. As a Puerto Rican who, owing to the colonial situation of our island, both is and is not an American, she thought I would be a good person to be this mediator, capable of navigating a new academic dialogue they hoped to develop. In other words, I was, and at the same time was not, an insider. At that time I did not know if I should have felt flattered or frightened by the unwanted burden that I had agreed to take. This last sensation did not hit me in reality until I started receiving the papers before the meetings. It was then that I realized that I was not so much a mediator, as Shannon put it, but more stuck in the middle.

Because I work in the Caribbean, I know more about Cuban archaeology than the average American archaeologist, yet because of my training and working conditions, I know more about American archaeology than the average Latin American archaeologist. But after reading the papers, I decided not so much to concentrate my discussion on the content of the papers per se, since they were self-explanatory and significant contributions, but instead to contribute to the dialogue that Shannon and Gabino had started by organizing the symposium. After reading many of the papers and reading the meager American literature available on Cuban archaeology (e.g., Davis 1996), I began to sense that there were considerable misunderstandings and misconceptions about the realities of the discipline in the "other" country. It seemed to me that the majority of these misconceptions had resulted either from a lack of communication between archaeologists from the two countries or from political and social biases produced by more than 40 years of Cold War propaganda generated from both sides—or a combination of these factors. It was in addressing some of these misunderstandings that I saw an opportunity to act as a mediator. Ironically, while it took me weeks to come to this realization, Shannon probably had this idea from the beginning. Owing to the complexity of the issues, it is difficult to discuss all of these misconceptions in detail, but I can present a few examples. I begin first with misunderstandings that I think may be more prevalent among American archaeologists.

Because of the scale and geographic coverage of American archaeology, it is difficult to have a sense of what opinion an average American archaeologist has about Cuban archaeology, or if one would have an opinion at all. Also, Americans working in the Caribbean have a different perspective than American archaeologists working elsewhere. Thus, opinions and conceptions about Cuban archaeology in the United States can be highly diverse. However, judging from a review published by Davis (1996), who is a Caribbeanist, and the experience of many Cuban colleagues who have interacted with American scholars, one of the most common myths held by some American archaeologists is the belief that Cuban archaeology is frozen in time and that its practitioners have worked in relative isolation since the Revolution of 1959. While this view is in itself a fallacy, what makes this misconception more striking is that this presumed isolation is usually seen as resulting from a *voluntary* decision by Cuban scholars arising from their allegiance to the Marxist orientation of the Cuban establishment. According to this view, Cuba's self-imposed isolation has created some problems in the theoretical and methodological approaches of Cuban archaeologists, reflected in the quality of their work (Davis 1996). To support this argument, Davis has pointed to the lack of participation of Cuban scholars in international meetings and their limited publication record in other countries. Although it is true to some extent that internal social factors and needs have affected the trajectory taken by Cuban archaeology, those presenting the isolation argument often ignore the historical and sociopolitical situation not only of Cuba but also of the United States and the rest of the hemisphere. At the level of international politics, it was the United States that isolated Cuba from the rest of the Americas by placing pressure on many neighboring countries to shun Cuba diplomatically.

The U.S. economic embargo has also contributed to this imposed isolation. The ban on exports and even regular international mail service has prevented books and scientific journals from crossing the border in any reliable manner. The embargo at the same time has contributed to ongoing economic problems that make international travel by Cuban scholars prohibitively expensive, not a unique problem within the developing world but perhaps more absurd given the short 90-mile distance between the island and the U.S. coastline. The cost of professional memberships in organizations such as the Society for American Archaeology, even at discounted rates (currently $50), represents an astronomical sum to Cuban archaeologists with little access to U.S. currency.

However, what is most important to point out is that the impression that Cuba remains in total isolation is in many ways a fallacy; it is a myth created by a lack of communication specifically between U.S. and Cuban archaeologists. For decades, Cuban archaeologists have been interacting with their counterparts from many other countries, such as the former Soviet Union, Mexico, Dominican Republic, Venezuela, and, more recently, England and Spain. They have also done their best to overcome the blockade of U.S. scholarship. As an anecdote, it was intriguing for me to see that some of our visiting Cuban colleagues wanted to be introduced to several well-known archaeologists such as Lewis Binford and Colin Renfrew during the annual meeting in Denver. They had read and used many of their publications but had never had the chance to meet them in person.

But perhaps the clearest counterargument to the myth of isolation is the role of the Smithsonian Institution and Betty Meggers in Cuban archaeology. This institution, represented by Meggers, has played a significant role in financial and moral support for Cuban scholars today and in influencing their theoretical and methodological approaches (e.g., see Berman et al., Chapter 3; Ulloa Hung, Chapter 6). Meggers has also contributed articles to Cuban publications and exchanged correspondence, publications, and information with Cuban colleagues. The Smithsonian has financially supported certain aspects of archaeological research in Cuba by funding radiocarbon dates or other types of analysis. In this sense, a dialogue between U.S. and Cuban archaeologists has been present for decades in the person of Betty Meggers.

Turning to the other side, misconceptions are also present in the views that many Cuban archaeologists have of American archaeology. Perhaps the main misconception, which in my experience is common throughout Latin America, is that American archaeology is still characterized by the New Archaeology, with its emphasis on high-tech methodologies and simplistic ecological perspectives. Although I cannot deny that there are some American archaeologists who still follow this path, I do not think this is an accurate depiction of American archaeology today. It is now more theoretically and methodologically diverse than ever, thanks in part to communication with other disciplines and with scholars from other countries. As can be seen from a quick survey of any recent meeting program of the Society for American Archaeology, North American members approach the field with diverse theoretical backgrounds and are interested in a wide variety of issues. Methodologically, American archaeology still promotes the application of new techniques to our research, some of them "high tech." However, the integration of technology into archaeology is approached from a different and more refined perspective than during the heyday of the New Archaeology. Technology is seen as a tool to help archaeologists reach their goals, not as an aim in itself. Further, American archaeology has become more international. By this I mean that fewer American archaeologists are working in foreign countries on the old colonial model and more are engaging in true collaborations and dialogues with international colleagues.

Besides interacting with my Cuban colleagues in the symposium and the discussion forum, I had the opportunity to spend considerable time with them over the course of the 2002 meeting. During the four days that we were together, I started noticing changes in the attitudes that both American and Cuban archaeologists held about the practice of the discipline in the other's country. It was then that I realized that my discussion in the symposium may not have even been necessary, because what was really helping to debunk some of the misconceptions and stereotypes was the direct exchange between scholars.

During this time, I had long and interesting conversations about a variety of topics, including the impact of the embargo, the invasion of the Bay of Pigs, and Cuban, Caribbean, Puerto Rican, and American archaeology. On most occasions, it was an amazing, humbling experience to listen to my Cuban colleagues and to exchange views and information. Sometimes we also had our disagreements. These mixed results continued during our work as editors of the volume, especially when trying to reconcile different publishing traditions. However, our most important aim was accomplished: to stimulate what we hope will be a sustained international dialogue and spirit of collaboration.

NEW DIRECTIONS IN COLLABORATION

Our stated aim of stimulating collaboration is not intended to suggest that we are pioneering a thoroughly vacant (or abandoned) territory. Since the mid-1980s, there has been a gradual reopening of communication between Cuban archaeologists and those from other parts of the Caribbean and North

America. Many times these collaborations have been done in informal ways at the personal or lower institutional levels. For example, Cuban archaeologists have gone to Puerto Rico to teach courses and work on projects, and Dominican archaeologists have established strong links with their Cuban counterparts with results such as the publication of the journal *El Caribe Arqueológico.* There have also been some earlier efforts to improve contacts between Cuban and North American colleagues, including exchange visits sponsored by the University of Florida, the translation of *The Art and Archaeology of Pre-Columbian Cuba* by Dacal Moure and Rivero de la Calle into English by Watters and Sandweiss (1996; see also Sandweiss and Watters 1993; Watters 1997; Watters and Dacal Moure 2002), as well as a highly successful project conducted at the submerged site of Los Buchillones by a joint Canadian/British and Cuban team (Calvera et al. 1996; Jardines and Calvera 1999; Pendergast 1997, 1998; Pendergast et al. 2001, 2002).

While these examples make it clear that some lines of friendship and communication have breached the embargo, in most cases efforts have been at lower levels of collaboration without having a lasting impact on knowledge and practices. For example, the awareness that the average North American archaeologist has of Cuban archaeology is still nil or ill founded. One way of correcting the misconceptions that archaeologists of one country might have about the other is to increase the rate of communication through publications. It is true, as Lourdes Domínguez points out in her chapter, that Cuban archaeologists are neither read nor cited by American archaeologists, but it is also true that Cuban publications are not readily available in the United States. Some national and international journals that have started to deal with this problem are *Latin American Antiquity* in the United States (e.g., see La Rosa Corzo 2003a) and *El Caribe Arqueológico* published by Casa del Caribe in Cuba. Further, university presses recently have begun to publish work by Cuban archaeologists, including the University of Pittsburgh Press (Dacal Moure and Rivero de la Calle 1996), the University of North Carolina Press, which is publishing a translation of La Rosa Corzo's book on escaped slaves (La Rosa Corzo 1991b, 2003b), and the University of Alabama Press with this volume.

THIS VOLUME

The symposium and discussion forum that led to the publication of this volume were originally organized by Shannon Dawdy and Gabino La Rosa

Corzo. Shannon handled arrangements stateside, including a successful grant application to the Social Science Research Council's Cuba Program, which made the event possible. Gabino handled the often-complicated permission and visa arrangements in Cuba and served as a liaison for the group. The original participants included four visiting Cuban colleagues (Dacal Moure, Domínguez, Godo, and La Rosa Corzo) and four American archaeologists who had worked in Cuba or collaborated with Cuban archaeologists (Berman, Gnivecki, Singleton, and Watters).

One conclusion reached during the discussions in both the symposium and the forum was that our goals would be best served by publishing the resulting papers. Soon thereafter, Curet, La Rosa Corzo, and Dawdy agreed together to edit the volume and the University of Alabama Press expressed an interest in publishing it. In order to provide a broader sampling of Cuban archaeology for a North American audience, additional authors were invited to submit articles, leading to the contributions of Roberto Valcárcel Rojas, César Rodríguez Arce, Jorge Ulloa Hung, and Marlene Linville. Jorge Calvera, Juan Jardines, and David Pendergast were also invited to contribute the results of their research in the submerged site of Los Buchillones but had to decline because of previous commitments. Samuel Wilson was asked to write an afterword. Our intention in selecting the final set of papers was not to attempt to cover the whole range of archaeological research being conducted in Cuba (Figure 1.1) but to select a relatively representative sample that demonstrates the variety of research questions and regional foci of archaeologists working on the island.

The volume is divided into two sections. Part I focuses on the history of Cuban archaeology as a discipline and practice. The papers by Dacal Moure and Watters (Chapter 2) and Berman et al. (Chapter 3) deal with the general history of Cuban archaeology, the former from an institutional and legislative perspective, the latter from a political and intellectual view. Domínguez's article (Chapter 4) reviews Cuba's accomplishments in historical archaeology, emphasizing the research and restoration work undertaken by the Oficina del Historiador de la Ciudad (Office of the City Historian) in Old Havana. Linville (Chapter 5) recounts the long and important history of research and conservation of Cuba's rich collection of rock art manifestations.

The second section presents substantive findings of recent archaeological research on the island. The first three articles focus on pre-Hispanic times, and the last two papers deal with the archaeology of slavery in the colonial period. Within the Caribbean, Cuba has one of the longest known prehis-

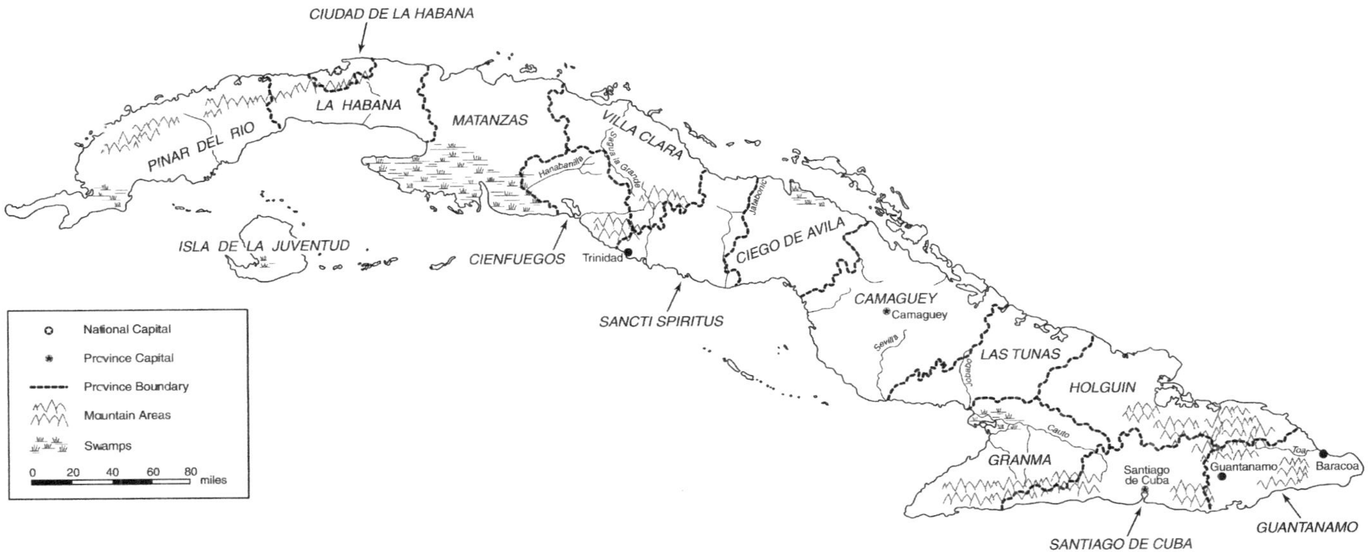

1.1. Map of Cuba

toric sequences. There is strong evidence that the peopling of the island began by at least 4,000 B.C., and there is tantalizing evidence that cultivation and the invention of pottery arose there independently (see Ulloa Hung, Chapter 6). Cuba's early ceramic groups are commonly called *protoagrícolas* or *protocerámicos* in Spanish. Sometime between A.D. 600 and 700, ceramics stylistically related to assemblages from Hispaniola began to appear in eastern Cuba. Traditionally, this shift in material culture has been interpreted to be an indicator of migrations by horticultural Arawak groups from Hispaniola to Cuba. Although originally the societies that produced these wares were seen as carbon copies of their counterparts in Hispaniola, now it seems that these new populations emerged through social and cultural processes that resulted in diverse types of social formations, including social hierarchy and inequality. The article by Valcárcel Rojas and Rodríguez Arce (Chapter 7) presents a case study in the site of Chorro de Maíta. Besides domestic units and remains, this site contained a cemetery from which a large number of burials were excavated, many having a variety of funerary offerings made of ceramic, stone, shell, and metal including gold, gold alloys, and copper, some of them possibly exotic in nature. In their article, Valcárcel Rojas and Rodríguez Arce argue convincingly that Chorro de Maíta was considered a special religious, social, and political location and that the distribution of artifacts in the cemetery is clear evidence for the presence of social differentiation and inequality in eastern Cuba. Godo's article (Chapter 8) summarizes several of his studies on the symbolic meaning of decorative designs present in the ceramic assemblages in Cuba. Using archaeological, ethnohistoric, and ethnographic evidence, he conducts a structural analysis of various repetitive themes by relating them to mythological stories recorded in the early chronicles.

The last two articles in this section represent two important papers on historical archaeology in Cuba. Gabino La Rosa Corzo (Chapter 9) examines the diet of escaped slaves, or *cimarrones,* from remains found in cave sites suspected to have been used by Cuba's well-documented maroon communities who survived in the rough terrain of central Cuba. Interestingly, the results show that escaped slaves' diets combined wild and domestic resources, the latter probably obtained from raiding nearby ranches (*haciendas*). The diet and health of maroons appears to have been much better than that of slaves still held in bondage. The paper by Theresa Singleton (Chapter 10) reports and interprets some of her findings on a walled slave village on a coffee plantation in the interior of Cuba. Her research indicates that slaves in Cuba were engaged in many of the same activities as enslaved Africans in other parts of the

Americas. However, the walled enclosure was a constraining device not as common in other slave communities that restricted their use of space and interaction with people from the outside, including cimarrones. Both of these articles report parts of larger research projects (La Rosa Corzo 1991b, 2003b; Singleton 2001b) that are helping to reshape our views of slave and maroon life previously obtained from biased historic documents written by slave owners and government officials.

In translating and editing the papers presented in this volume, we felt it was our moral and professional duty to maintain the accuracy of the meanings and connotations of the texts as much as possible. It was a difficult task, not only because we ran the risk of losing much in translation but also because we had to reconcile two very different discursive traditions in archaeological writing. We strove to respect the style and publication tradition of the respective Cuban and American authors, but at the same time we tried to weave some common threads into the format of the articles.

We hope that publishing this volume will encourage further exchange, debate, and communication between American and Cuban archaeologists. It is our sincere belief that this process has already been started by recent publications in the United States (Kepecs 2002; Dacal Moure and Rivero de la Calle 1996; La Rosa Corzo 2003a, 2003b) and by the collaborative work of American and Cuban archaeologists exemplified in this volume (e.g., Berman et al., Chapter 3; Singleton, Chapter 10). These research efforts, combined with honest and respectful professional relations, will benefit the discipline in both countries. It is through such interaction and direct cooperation that American and Cuban archaeologists can best make strides toward the main goal of archaeology as a discipline—to describe, explain, and understand the variability and commonality of past human behavior.

EDITORS' NOTE

After submitting our manuscript to the University of Alabama Press for its review, we received the unfortunate news that Ramón Dacal Moure had passed away in December 2003. Needless to say, this news filled us with great sadness, and our prayers and thoughts are with his family. We feel proud and honored that we had the opportunity to include in this volume a contribution of such a distinguished Cuban archaeologist.

Part I
History of Cuban Archaeology

2 / Three Stages in the History of Cuban Archaeology

Ramón Dacal Moure and David R. Watters

The periodization used in this work, as in any other, is a somewhat arbitrary form of analysis, in this case employed to bring out elements important for contextualizing Cuban archaeology. As history consists of a continuous interrelationship of factors, alternative periodizations could be defined from other points of view (see Dacal Moure and Rivero de la Calle 1996:27–31).

FIRST STAGE: LOCAL ANTIQUARIANISM (1841–1898)

In the first stage, Cuban archaeology could not yet be considered a formal discipline since it consisted almost exclusively of the study of historical documentation and occasional discoveries. The chronicles of the Indies were the main source of information, and the accounts of aboriginal peoples they contain were used to extend Cuban history back prior to the Spanish conquest. Writers described material evidence of the island's prehistory in forms as diverse as novels, poems, and scientific articles on new discoveries. The discoveries of John L. Stephens (1841) in the Mayan area in October 1839 spurred dreams of greatness about the pre-Hispanic past on the part of Cubans. In prose and verse, the Cuban Indian served as the symbol of an emerging nationality, as seen in the works of José Fornaris y Luque and Juan Cristóbal Nápoles Fajardo. José Fornaris Luque (1827–1890), an attorney, poet, and professor, wrote several books including *Cantos del Ciboney.* Juan Cristóbal Nápoles Fajardo (1829–?), a self-educated scholar, was one of the first students of rural popular song and author of *Rumores del Hórmigo.* Both writers praised the virtues of the Cuban natives as part of the Movimiento Siboneyista.

The Sociedad Arqueológica de la Isla de Cuba was founded on July 26, 1877, and was active up through 1895. It provided a forum where topics of Antillean and world archaeology were debated. Actual archaeological fieldwork and artifactual studies took two directions: the research of Cubans such as Eusebio Jiménez, Luis Montané, and Carlos de la Torre, and the activities of the Spaniard Miguel Rodríguez Ferrer, who can be considered the first professional archaeologist to work in Cuba. Rodríguez Ferrer, who began working in Cuba before 1868, came to consider the island his homeland. He had a broad knowledge of European archaeology and had been a curator of a museum in Vitoria, Spain.

For the most part, the early projects consisted of exploration and excavation of archaeological sites on the island from three different perspectives. Jiménez was an avid collector, Montané had an anthropological orientation supported by an excellent formal education, and de la Torre was one of the most renowned Cuban naturalists. They had in common an enthusiasm to dig deeper into the indigenous past, and they shared a lack of training in excavation techniques. In the case of Rodríguez Ferrer, we see a practice closer to that of modern archaeology. Although he never conducted well-documented excavations, his detailed book *Naturaleza y civilización de la grandiosa Isla de Cuba* (1876–1877) was praised by the renowned anthropologist and intellectual Fernando Ortiz: "The historic work of Rodríguez Ferrer, in its totality, may still be today the most valuable and original one ever produced in Cuba. It has a philosophical sensibility and an objective base; it is, however, among the most forgotten. The reasons for this are perhaps the few numbers of publications and, certainly, the fact that its tenor did not agree with the separatist values of Cubans at that time, nor with peninsular absolutism" (Ortiz 1935:84). This book was the result of the first archaeological research conducted on the island, and it included information about Rodríguez Ferrer's fieldwork in 1847 and his study of the chronicles. The sites discovered by Rodríguez Ferrer and the evidence collected, including human remains, marked the onset of a new scientific discipline in the country. Thus, taking into consideration the nature of the studies and the information included, this publication can be considered the first true archaeological book published in Cuba.

Antiquities Law during the First Stage

During the first stage, the legal framework for archaeology was limited to the application of the Spanish Civil Code effective in Cuba from November 5,

1889, until July 16, 1987. In two of its titles, the code stipulated that hidden treasures and portable objects abandoned on private property belonged to the owner of the land where they were found. But if the discovered objects were of interest to the sciences or the arts, the state had the authority to acquire them. None of the earlier Spanish or Republican codes addressed archaeological issues.

SECOND STAGE: CUBAN AND NORTH AMERICAN ARCHAEOLOGISTS (1898–1959)

Cuban archaeology began in earnest during the second stage, characterized by two central trends that had their beginnings in the earlier period. These trends, consisting of a North American and a European influence, mixed and intertwined for several years.

The first consisted of a serious North American interest in the island that began with E. G. Squier's visit to Cuba (Squier 1860). Although most of his contributions belong chronologically to the previous stage, his thoughts and discoveries influenced Cuban archaeologists well into this second stage, including scholars such as Montané, Cosculluela, and Felipe Pichardo Moya. S. Culin (Culin 1902) and W. H. Holmes (Holmes 1894), who came in search of Moundbuilders, were interested in etiological issues (issues of origin) and had a perspective akin to Historical Particularism.

Luis Montané Darde initiated the second significant trend, in the form of a European influence, by introducing the ideas of Paul P. Broca, founder of French anthropology. Interestingly, the anthropology program at the University of Havana, which extensively influenced the development of archaeology in Cuba, was created by an act of the U.S. occupational government, but it had Luis Montané as its first program chair (Rangel Rivero 1994; Vasconcellos Portuondo 2001). Montané had returned from France in 1874. From that moment, interest in Cuba's past grew noticeably, especially following the fortuitous discovery of archaic sites. The best example is the discovery of the site Guayabo Blanco in the Ciénaga de Zapata, which Montané excavated and which was written up by its discoverer, Juan A. Cosculluela. Guyayabo Blanco has played a prominent role in the study of Cuba's indigenous populations. It represented the first discovery of nondeformed skulls on an archaeological site in Cuba. The physical anthropology aspect was the focus of Montané's research (see Alvarez Conde 1956:93–98; Ortiz 1935:56–60). His work, which adhered to high methodological and theoretical standards of the time, was widely distributed. Another important feature of the site was the internal structure of the deposits, with six well-defined layers that indicated the construction of an artificial funeral mound as described by Montané: "In conclusion, two or three times we have found mixed with the stone artifacts and the already mentioned skeletons, voluminous clay masses, colored and hardened, and we have asked ourselves if they do not represent what people have been calling altars" (Montané 1918:140). These interpretations were based on his knowledge of the mounds of North America, in part influenced by the ideas of Squier (1860), as well as discoveries of funerary mounds in other parts of the Caribbean.

The notion of archaeology as an avocation and a collector's hobby, which dominated the first stage, changed in the first half of the twentieth century. Academically trained individuals in various organizations throughout the country created an increasingly greater degree of professionalism in archaeology, often working in concert with local avocational archaeologists. García Feria in Holguín, creator of a collection with the same name, is a good example. The Grupo Humboldt in Santiago de Cuba, the Sociedad Espeleológica de Cuba, and the Grupo Guama in Havana are other representative groups. At the margins of academic archaeology, several private individuals interested in archaeology made valuable contributions, including Orencio Miguel Alonso in Banes, Antonio González Muñoz in Cienfuegos, and Pedro García Valdes in Pinar Río (see Dacal Moure and Collado López 1975).

During this period, several North American institutions sent outstanding archaeologists to the island. One of the first was Mark R. Harrington, who eventually published *Cuba Before Columbus* in 1921. Cornelius Osgood (Osgood 1942) and Irving Rouse (Rouse 1942) were two other important investigators in Antillean studies. The former outlined a detailed methodology for work on the island while the latter created an analytical system for the study of Antillean ceramics that he developed during his work in Haiti in the summers of 1934 and 1935; it is still relied on today in Caribbean archaeology. Harrington, Osgood, and Rouse had a significant influence on Cuban archaeologists who later became the main actors in the development and promotion of Cuban archaeology.

Other distinguished scholars from this period were Carlos García Robiou and Rene Herrera Fritot, who studied in North America and worked in the Museo Antropológico Montané; Felipe Martínez Arango of the Universidad de Oriente and Felipe Pichardo Moya, who produced studies on precolumbian Camagüey; and the influential Fernando Ortiz, whose great knowledge of anthropology and Cuban folk culture was influenced by the functionalism of Malinowski. During the middle of this stage, the Junta Nacional de Arqueología y Etnología was created on September 17, 1937. It published twenty volumes of its journal from August 1938 to December 1961. Also, so-called colonial archaeology (see Domínguez, Chapter 4) was developing out of investigations related to the architectural restoration of palaces, fortresses, churches, and coffee plantations. Still, during these years, Cuban archaeology was not strongly affiliated with any of the archaeological schools of the time, because the institutions of higher education in Cuba offered limited opportunities to develop well-defined theoretical frameworks. Archaeology was being professionalized, but the process was evolving slowly.

As happened throughout the world, Cuban objects ended up in North American museums. Harrington, in particular, removed a great deal of material. The government eventually placed some restraints on him by appointing a professor of the Universidad de La Habana to accompany him on occasion. Cuban collections acquired by other North American archaeologists also turn up in North American museums. In 1994, J. M. Weeks and P. J. Ferbel reported in *Naciente Caribbean* the presence in a North American museum of a previously unknown collection of aboriginal materials from western Cuba that had been taken out of the island in 1931, which came as a surprise to many Cuban scholars.

Antiquities Law during the Second Stage

In the late 1930s and early 1940s, a number of legal and regulatory initiatives were enacted to provide better protection for Cuban antiquities. On August 7, 1937, it was decided that cave or land exploration undertaken with the purpose of creating archaeological collections to be taken out of the country would require executive authorization. That same month, the Comisión Nacional de Arqueología was created. Its aims were the conservation and study of precolumbian and colonial monuments; the conservation and critical analysis of precolumbian objects located on sites or in stratified deposits; the conservation and study of precolumbian human remains; the formation of a national archaeological map; and contributions to the development of the Museo Arqueológico Nacional.

In addition, the Constitution of 1940 made the state responsible for regulating the conservation of the nation's cultural treasures through the creation of laws. In 1941, the Junta Nacional de Arqueología (later the Junta Nacional de Arqueología y Etnología) was established to review and authorize all archaeological explorations. Toward the end of the period, on February 18, 1958, the Junta Nacional de Arqueología y Etnología was replaced by the Instituto Cubano de Arqueología and the Comisión Nacional para la Preservación de Monumentos Históricos y Artísticos, maintaining the same objectives under separate research and regulatory branches.

THIRD STAGE: POST–NORTH AMERICAN ARCHAEOLOGY IN CUBA (1959–2000)

The beginning of the third phase coincided with profound changes in Cuban society that led to the foundation of the Department of Anthropology of the Academia de Ciencias de Cuba in 1962. Four individuals played a central role in its founding. The first, Antonio Núñez Jiménez, president of the Academia de Ciencias, was a Ph.D. dedicated to geographical studies and, to a lesser extent, archaeology. The second, René Herrera Fritot, was a professor of anthropology and conservator of the Museo Antropológico Montané, with a long record of archaeological investigations and an independent position. Ernesto Tabío was an outstanding amateur archaeologist who had collaborated with Herrera Fritot and the Grupo Guama. As a meteorologist, he worked in the Organization of Civil Aviation of the United Nations in Lima, Peru, where he collected objects and visited multiple archaeological sites. He brought his experiences from this work and a strong influence from North American archaeology, including the concept of settlement patterns. The fourth influential figure is Dr. Estrella Rey, a professor of history, whose work focuses on the study of indigenous societies.

Although it was titled Department of Anthropology, in reality this organization was dedicated for the most part to archaeology. At the time, archaeology did not have a strong enough position within the disciplines of the Cuban sciences to occupy an independent place in the Academia de Ciencias. This situation changed with the publication of *Prehistoria de Cuba* by department members E. Tabío and E. Rey (1966). The first author contributed an overview of the culture history of the island influenced by North American conceptions, and the latter wrote an ethnohistorical study, based on Marxist historiography. In addition, the department conducted its own educational effort to train archaeologists, culminating in the year 1970, when it granted the first and only archaeology degrees to R. Dacal, J. M. Guarch, R. Payares, and M. Pino.

In 1975, the Reunión de Teotihuacán began to shape the scholarly movement known in Latin America as "Archaeology as a Social Science" or "Latin American Social Archaeology." This term serves as an umbrella that covers different materialist views of indigenous societies, some of which include cultural ecology blended with Marxist ideas. Some of the influential individuals of this movement are Lumbreras in Peru (1974), Bate (1978) and Lorenzo (1976) in Mexico, Sanoja and Vargas (1974) in Venezuela, and Veloz Maggiolo (1976–1977) in Dominican Republic. The original meeting grew out of the ideas published by Luis G. Lumbreras (1974), who aimed "to bring back the essence of what V. Gordon Childe outlined in *Archaeology as a Social Science* (1947), by advocating to conduct archaeology with a historical sensibility, by clearly distancing from a colonialist archaeology, and by situating archaeology in a field that makes its existence comprehensible and real: in other words, using historical materialism" (Lorenzo 1976:6). The work group that considered these questions in the Reunión de Teotihuacán consisted of José Luis Lorenzo, Luis G. Lumbreras, Eduardo Matos, Julio Montané, Mario Sanoja, and others not mentioned in the publication.

Several of the archaeologists affiliated with the Social Archaeology movement, such as José Luis Lorenzo, Luis G. Lumbrera, Mario Sanoja, Iraida Vargas, and Marcio Veloz Maggiolo, visited the island and exchanged ideas with Cuban archaeologists. However, the influence of this "school" of thought in Cuba ended abruptly in 1978, when the senior Cuban archaeologist Dr. Ernesto Tabío published an article in which he wrote, "Recently we have had the opportunity of reading some publications by Latin American prehistorians that present some 'Marxist' theoretical formulations that we cannot in any way accept within a Marxist-Leninist perspective" (Tabío 1978:7). His main concern was that the "social archaeologists," especially Sanoja and Vargas (1974), were taking particular modalities (or lifeways) of several groups and elevating them to the level of a mode of production without considering the relations and means of production. This approach led to a proliferation of supposedly distinct modes of productions that in reality share similar relations of production. For example, Sanoja and Vargas proposed the hunting mode of production, the marine-gathering mode of production, and the tropical mode of production. According to Tabío, all of these actually belonged to the mode of production called primitive communism because the means of production were communally owned and the societies lacked class divisions and a state-level political system. Tabío's criticism was directed most strongly at the so-called theocratic mode of production that, according to Sanoja and Vargas, included the presence of an inherited position of leadership, a clear contradiction of the principles of primitive communism. Tabío's orthodox article resulted in the formal abandonment of the Social Archaeology movement in Cuba.

Meanwhile, Cuban archaeologists continued to pursue their own local research interests and seek out new collaborations. The results of studies by Dr. Antonio Núñez Jiménez on indigenous pictography and petroglyphs were published in several books (Núñez Jiménez 1975) that can be characterized as descriptive, similar to many European works on the topic. He also established zones for these features in the Cuban Archipelago. In the later part of this period, an interest in use-wear analysis led several Cuban archaeologists to conduct studies in St. Petersburg. Excavations were conducted in Cuba with Russian specialists, and Cuban archaeologists went to Siberia to work in the field (Domínguez and Febles 1981). Cuban archaeologists also attended Russian universities. E. Tabío, E. Rey, and J. M. Guarch defended their doctoral dissertations at the Institute of Ethnography of the USSR Academy of Sciences. Polish specialists in chipped stone visited Cuba, leading to a mastery of Bordes school techniques (Kozlowski 1975).

During this period, Historical Archaeology became a specialized area of study focused on the colonial past, as demonstrated by the works of Lourdes Domínguez (1988), one of the central figures in this field. Historical Archaeology has played an important role during this stage, especially after the Gabinete de Arqueología de la Oficina del Historiador de la Ciudad de La Habana was created on November 14, 1987. A variety of specialists work at the Gabinete, and this office continues to host courses and seminars by Cuban and foreign professionals. Underwater archaeology has also developed in this period in Cuba from the efforts of multiple organizations, including the Academia de Ciencias, the Banco Nacional, and the Ministry of Finance. These efforts resulted in the formation of an enterprise called Carisub, Inc., which during the last 20 years has conducted investigations in the archives of Cuba and Spain, gathering information on approximately 1,600 shipwrecks in the territorial waters of the island. To accomplish its purpose, Carisub owns the appropriate ships, underwater equipment, laboratories, and warehouses, all attended by specialists in the field. Moreover, staff members have published their research and attended international congresses. Carisub has mounted a large number of their best pieces in an exhibit in the museum of the Castillo de la Punta, at the entrance of the Bay of Havana.

Museology, as a complement to archaeological investigations, has led to the creation of several site museums ranging from the Laguna del Tesoro in the Ciénaga de Zapata, the subject of archaeological research undertaken at the beginning of this stage, to the Museo del Chorro de Maíta in Lomas de Maniabón. At the latter, a group of archaeologists from the province of Holguín headed by the late Dr. José M. Guarch excavated a cemetery and then re-created it for public interpretative purposes, making it one of the most important archaeological museums on the island (see Valcárcel Rojas and Rodríguez Arce, Chapter 7).

Advances have also been made in the field of site registration and information technology through the Censo de Sitios Arqueológico de Cuba conducted by the Departamento de Arqueología of the Ministerio de Tecnología y Medio Ambiente and a computerized database of archaeological objects in Cuban museums, which at the moment is updated continuously by the Consejo de Patrimonio Cultural of the Ministerio de Cultura.

Other efforts during this period have been directed toward an improved understanding of methodologies used in the investigation of artifacts and animal remains, ceramic analysis, and the application of chemistry to living surfaces (see Davis 1996 for a more detailed discussion of this topic). Cuban archaeologists have published several studies and guides intended to standardize methods and systems of analysis. The first attempt was *Método Experimental para el Estudio de Artefactos Líticos de Culturas Antillanas No Ceramistas* by Ramón Dacal, which in 1968 inaugurated the *Serie Antropológica* of the Cuban Academy of Sciences. In 1975, this series was followed by a book published by the Museo Montané of the University of Havana titled *Técnica de la Talla y Tipología de los Instrumentos Líticos* by Janusz K. Kozlowski and Boleslaw Ginter (1975) with a preface by Ramón Dacal. Three years later, the Museo Montané published *Artefactos de Concha en las Comunidades Aborígenes Cubanas* by Ramón Dacal Moure (1978). In 1987, José Manuel Guarch wrote *Arqueología de Cuba: Métodos y Sistemas,* which included his recommendations for field and laboratory techniques that should be employed in archaeological investigations. Manuel Rivero de la Calle published in 1985 *Nociones de anatomía humana aplicadas a la arqueología.* In 1988, Jorge Febles Dunas presented his book *Manual para el Estudio de la Piedra Tallada de los Aborígenes de Cuba,* published by the Academy of Sciences.

During this period, master's degrees in archaeology have been awarded to several archaeologists, and a small group possesses the doctorate in historical sciences. These individuals with degrees do not include the whole range of archaeologists working in the discipline, who either come from other disciplines or are conducting important work in national and municipal museums.

In spite of efforts directed at the development of methods and analytical systems, Cuban archaeology has continued to suffer a persistent problem—the lack of a degree-granting archaeology program having a rigorous curriculum, professors with strong theoretical backgrounds, and one or more ambitious personalities to lead it. Nevertheless, in 2001, a master's program in archaeology began to be offered by the Departamento de Arqueología, of the Centro de Antropología del Ministerio de Ciencia, Tecnología y Medio Ambiente, with the approval of the Minister of Higher Education. It is expected that the program will address this lacuna in archaeological training.

Recently, Cuban archaeologists have collaborated in several ways with various North American colleagues. Ramón Dacal Moure and the late Manuel Rivero de la Calle worked closely with Daniel Sandweiss and David Watters (Figure 2.1) in translating and editing *The Art and Archaeology of Pre-Columbian Cuba,* the first book summarizing Cuban archaeology to be published in English in many years (see Sandweiss and Watters 1993; Watters 1993, 1997; Watters and Dacal Moure 2002). Theresa Singleton has collaborated on historical archaeology projects (Chapter 10) and Mary Jane Berman on prehistoric research (Chapter 3). David Pendergast of the Royal Ontario Museum exemplifies collaborative work with Canadian institutions. Cuban archaeologists have become increasingly involved in archaeological projects elsewhere in the Caribbean, including Aruba, Dominican Republic, and Puerto Rico. The Social Archaeology of Latin America, represented by some of its original proponents, has also made a comeback and attained a special prominence in Cuban archaeology. After the death of Dr. Ernesto Tabío, Latin American archaeologists who had attended the Reunión de Teotihuacan visited Cuba several times, and their publications have since been widely distributed, especially those by Mario Sanoja and Iraida Vargas from Venezuela (1974) and Marcio Veloz Maggiolo from Dominican Republic (1976–1977). Presently, *El Caribe Arqueológico* is an important publication that has on its editorial and advisory boards several scholars of this school and is financed by Taraxacum, S.A., located in Washington, D.C. Another recent journal, *Boletín Gabinete de Arqueología,* published by the Oficina del Historiador de la Ciudad de La Habana, focuses on urban archaeology but dedicates some space to other areas. For the first time, Cuba now has two regular archaeological journals.

Antiquities Law during the Third Stage

This third stage began with the reestablishment of the Junta Nacional de Arqueología y Etnología on April 25, 1959, with the same duties and power. On

2.1. Work group translating and editing the book titled *The Art and Archaeology of Pre-Columbian Cuba* by Dacal Moure and Rivero de la Calle: (*left to right*), Daniel Sandweiss, Dave Watters, Ramón Dacal Moure, and Manuel Rivero de la Calle

April 19, 1963, the Junta was incorporated into the Comisión Nacional de la Academia de Ciencias de la República de Cuba, taking over its activities. In February 1976, the Constitution provided for the defense of Cuban cultural identity and its protection through conservation of its cultural heritage, a function delegated to the Ministry of Culture. In 1977, a law titled *Protección al Patrimonio Nacional* and its regulations considered the products of archaeological excavations and discoveries as commodities. Also that year, the law *Monumentos Nacionales y Locales* created the Comisión Nacional y Provinciales de Monumentos. Its regulations specify that the approval of the commission must be obtained to conduct excavations and archaeological investigations and that the results of such investigations have to be reported. It also established that objects obtained in excavations conducted by official archaeological institutions would be conserved by the institutions until the conclusion of their study, after which the commission and the Dirección de Patrimonio Cultural del Ministerio de Cultura determine their final location.

In 1987, the Penal Code was revised to state that a person who conducts archaeological explorations by excavations, removal of soils, or other means without the authorization of the pertinent state body incurs a sanction of jail for three months to one year or a heavy fine. More recently, in 1996, two laws were promulgated, the first establishing mechanisms to control the exportation of archaeological objects and the second stating that a permit approved by the pertinent entity is required to perform research expeditions and visits of a scientific-technical nature to areas of sensitive ecosystems. Finally, the Environmental Law of 1997 regulates the Sistema Nacional de Areas Protegidas, making archaeological review mandatory.

CONCLUSION

To conclude, we would like to address two issues briefly. First, we are sure that members of the Society for American Archaeology, whose professionalism and working conditions have seen remarkable advances in these last forty years, understand that although international collaboration is sought, Cuban archaeology cannot go back to conditions prevalent in similar relations in 1931. Although the work of past U.S. investigators, such as Cornelius Osgood and Irving Rouse, are good models for future studies in the sense that we should always have as the main purpose the improvement of our understanding of the human past, we also have to realize that social and academic conditions in Cuba have changed markedly since the 1930s. Therefore, any scholarly collaboration and exchange will have to take a considerably different path determined by the developments achieved by professional archaeologists from each country and current national laws.

Second, as Cuban society strengthens and protects its indigenous culture with an eye on tourism, it needs the discipline of archaeology and an appropriate interpretative theory to support these efforts. This theory, however, cannot be imposed or influenced by advances in the other disciplines and sciences. Independent of their complexity, importance, and specificity, archaeometric approaches can contribute only new tools and not the main aims of archaeological research. This volume may help Cubans approach this task.

3 / The Organization of Cuban Archaeology

Context and Brief History

Mary Jane Berman, Jorge Febles, and Perry L. Gnivecki

In this chapter we provide a brief descriptive organizational and social history of Cuban archaeology beginning with its nineteenth-century foundations and leading up to the present. We examine the means by which Cuba's prehistoric past has been researched, theorized, and interpreted by looking at where archaeology has been situated ideologically and administratively within Cuba's scientific, cultural, and political agendas. We consider private and public support for archaeology, its practitioners and their backgrounds. We also touch upon the ways in which the project of archaeology has contributed to nation-building and how it was and is *organized* as a nationalist archaeology (*sensu* Trigger 1984).

This work emerges from the premise that the practice of archaeology, including its organization, can best be achieved by understanding the context in which it takes place. Numerous archaeologists such as Patterson (1995) and Trigger (1984:88 and elsewhere) have written extensively about the interconnectedness and interdependency of political ideology, cultural climate, social context, and archaeological practice. Oyuela-Caycedo (1994), Oyuela-Caycedo et al. (1997), and Politis (2003) recognize that political views and regimes profoundly affect archaeology in Latin America. We argue that similar relationships exist for all areas of intellectual life in Cuba, a country not covered by recent archaeological overviews of Latin America. We suggest, therefore, that the organization of Cuban archaeology has always been dependent upon these factors, and thus we look at how it has been produced and fashioned by changing sociopolitical and economic contexts.

3.1. Welcome sign, a billboard in central Cuba. Photograph by Mary Jane Berman.

In Cuba, archaeology is conceptualized as belonging either to prehistory or to the historic era (Fernández Leiva 1992). The division is temporal and is structured by the kinds of questions asked and the methods employed for each period. Broadly defined, prehistoric archaeology begins with the earliest peopling of the island and ends with Spanish colonization, and historical archaeology is concerned with the Spanish colonial period, which extends to the late nineteenth century. We focus here on the practice of prehistoric archaeology, although some methods associated with it, such as zooarchaeological analyses, have recently been extended to the archaeology of the historic period (Kepecs 2002:47). Two texts in English (Dacal Moure and Rivero de la Calle 1996; Davis 1996), and numerous Cuban works (e.g., Tabío and Rey 1979) address contemporary Cuban archaeology's method and theory and current reconstructions of its culture history. While Cuban site reports typically include osteological data, we will not discuss how physical anthropology is conducted in Cuba; the reader is referred to Blakey (2001), Goodwin (1978), and Wienker (2001).

In Cuba, as elsewhere, past cultures live in the public and commercial imagination. Throughout the countryside, roadside billboards depicting idealized views of Native American and African communities welcome travelers to today's communities (Figure 3.1). The Taíno chief, Hatuey, who some call the "first Cuban rebel" and the first martyr for Cuban independence, has been immortalized and popularized by serving as the logo for Hatuey beer. As all Cubans know, the Spanish captured him and burned him at the stake on February 2, 1512. The Rey del Mundo-Taíno, one of Cuba's most expensive cigars, features a picture of a Taíno Indian. A popular tourist hotel located in Guama features a reconstructed Amerindian village. These figures and images, associated with contemporary economic production, are very much a part of Cuban identity. As viewed by Fernando Ortiz, materials such as tobacco and sugar are "highly complex metaphorical constructs that represent at once material things and human actors" (Coronil 1995:xxvii). Prehistory, though represented through these popular but highly symbolic and ideologically rich images, is taken seriously in Cuba. The work of archaeologists has supported the revolutionary agenda by contributing significantly to the construction of the country's history through the lens of Marxism and Historical Materialism.

THE FOUNDATION OF CUBAN ARCHAEOLOGY

The Nineteenth Century

Interest in archaeological remains was well established in Cuba prior to the Revolution and can be viewed as a long-standing expression of pride in national heritage that is also reflected in the works of numerous nineteenth-century writers such as José Martí, the Cuban national poet. As Fernández Leiva (1992) and Davis (1996) have pointed out, a strong sense of *patria* (fatherland) and curiosity about the archaeological history of the country existed before the Revolution. This earliest work was highly descriptive and speculative and was performed by schoolteachers, engineers, and doctors, who pursued their interests as an elite avocation. During the later part of the century, the study of the past began to become more scholarly. While archaeology had not yet become a formally recognized science, several scientific papers were published that brought local findings to the attention of scholars outside of Cuba. Excellent summaries of these early works can be found in Ortiz (1922a) and Fernández Leiva (1992). Fewkes (1904) and Rouse (1942) both provide overviews in English. Rouse's summary relates specifically to the history of archaeological investigation in the Maniabon Hills area in north-central Cuba.

Fernández Leiva (1992:33) regards the work of Andrés Poey as marking the beginning of archaeological study in Cuba. Poey's 1847 discovery of a fragment of a human mandible at a prehistoric site on the south coast of Camagüey set in motion the study of prehistoric people, as well as their physical remains. In 1855, he presented his findings to the American Ethnological Society in a paper titled "Cuban Antiquities: A Brief Description of Some Relics Found in the Island of Cuba." By 1891, archaeology had become a recognized science (Fernández Leiva 1992). Soon thereafter (1902), the Montané Anthropological Museum was established, named after Montané Dardé, who had conducted the country's first major archaeological excavation in the Maisí region and had studied the skeletal remains from the Cienaga de Zapata. In the same decade, archaeological artifacts were exhibited at other museums, such as the museum of the Academy of Science on Calle de Cuba and a museum in Baracoa (the Santiago Museum) (Fewkes 1907). In 1913, the government created anthropology courses for University of Havana students and a chair of Anthropology and Anthropometric Exercises was established (Rivero 1994:61).

The National Commission for Archaeology (Comisión Nacional de Arqueología) was created in 1937. In 1941, its name was changed to the National Board for Archaeology and Ethnology (Junta Nacional de Arqueología y Etnología) and its scope broadened to include ethnological studies. Laws for the preservation and restoration of historical monuments were promulgated (Dacal Moure and Watters, Chapter 2; Fernández Leiva 1992:36). The council's research was published in the *Revista de Arqueología y Etnología.* Between 1937 and 1962, the council published 20 volumes. By 1943, sufficient data had been amassed that Fernando Ortiz could write a synthesis of Cuban archaeology (Davis 1996:163).

Prior to the formal professionalization of archaeology after the Revolution, archaeology was conducted by groups of highly dedicated avocational archaeologists such as the Grupo Guamá (Havana area), Grupo Humboldt (eastern Cuba), Grupo Arqueológico Caonao (Banes area), Grupo Yaravey, and the Speological Society of Cuba (Sociedad Espeleológica de Cuba) (Dacal and Watters, Chapter 2; Davis 1996:164; Fernández Leiva 1992; Linville, Chapter 5). The Grupo Guamá, founded in 1941, consisted of medical doctors, engineers, mathematicians, lawyers, and university professors. Some notable members included the writer Felipe Pichardo Moya, the natural scientist and political leader Antonio Nuñez Jiménez, César García del Pino, Manuel Rivero de la Calle, René Hererra Fritot, Oswaldo Morales Patiño, Antonio García Valdés, García Castañeda, Martínez Arango, García Robiou, and Roberto Pérez de Acevedo, among others. Their articles and monographs were published in *Revista de Arqueología y Etnología* and *Revista Nacional de Arqueología.*

American Involvement before the Revolution

U.S. archaeologists have had a lengthy but sporadic involvement in Cuban archaeology. For example, Squier, who with E. H. Davis published *Ancient Monuments of the Mississippi Valley,* the first volume in the series of *Smithsonian Contributions to Knowledge,* was the first U.S. professional archaeologist to bring Cuban archaeology to the attention of North Americans. On a train trip in 1860, he noted elongated 3–6 foot mounds between Bemba and Unión, which he reported in "Discovery of Ancient Tumulí in the Island of Cuba" in *The Century,* June 1860 (Harrington 1921:51; Ortiz 1922a:16). Although, he did not conduct work in Cuba, Daniel Brinton (1919), who introduced the four-field approach to American archaeology (Urbanowicz 1992), published "The Archaeology of Cuba" in *American Archaeologist* 2(10) in 1898. This work summarized and reviewed the contributions of Poey, Ferrer, García, and others.

Brinton was the first North American archaeologist to recognize that a tradition of archaeological study existed in Cuba. Reflecting a general national ideology that knowledge about the world was in the country's best interest and should apply everywhere, U.S. archaeological interests extended to the Caribbean in the early part of the twentieth century. Through capitalist philanthropy and nationally sanctioned efforts, projects were undertaken throughout the Antilles. During the late nineteenth century and the early part of the twentieth, American anthropology was interested in discovering the origins and antiquity of prehistoric groups in order to link them with contemporary natives (Parezo 1987:19). Meltzer (1985:252; see also Parezo ibid.) notes that this goal and the associated method of the direct historical approach formed one of the major paradigms of American archaeology at this time. Thus, in 1901, the University of Pennsylvania Museum sent Stewart Culin (Fane et al. 1991) to Cuba to investigate reports of surviving Indians in Oriente. During his visit, Culin acquired a small collection of artifacts (Culin 1902:225). Culin's work also reflected another dominant paradigm of the time—salvage ethnography, the idea that native peoples were disappearing and it was anthropology's mission to study them before they became subsumed by Western culture. Anthropologists considered it their moral duty to collect as much as possible from the groups that they perceived to be on the brink of extinction.

Through the Platt Amendment, the United States acquired Guantanamo Naval base and was granted the right to intervene in Cuban affairs whenever it was determined necessary (Pérez 1995). In 1902, the chairman of the National Research Council suggested that American anthropology should "follow American interests overseas" (MacCurdy 1902:534, cited in Vincent 1990: 134). U.S. expansionist policies allowed for new areas of research (Hinsley 1981; Patterson 1995:41; Vincent 1990). The acquisition of the Philippines, Guam, Puerto Rico, and Guantanamo Bay from Spain opened up previously uninvestigated areas for scientific exploration. In 1904, the Bureau of American Ethnology sent Jesse Walter Fewkes to Puerto Rico to "investigate the aboriginal economy of the island and to report just how America could use her new acquisition" (Noelke 1974:175, cited in Vincent 1990:134). Fewkes went to collect data and specimens that "would shed light on the prehistoric inhabitants" of Puerto Rico (Fewkes 1907:17), but it was necessary to visit other islands and obtain collections to attain comparative insight into the origins and spread of Antillean cultures. Thus, he visited Cuba and in 1904 published an *American Anthropologist* article titled "Prehistoric Culture of Cuba." The work described a small collection of artifacts he purchased from Nipe Bay (Fewkes 1904:395–396). The purchase of collections was not unusual at this time, and many major museum collections, such as the Smithsonian's, were created this way (Parezo 1987).

In February 1914, Theodore de Booy of the Museum of the American Indian–Heye Foundation visited Cuba. In the fall of 1914, he returned and conducted several excavations in the province of Baracoa (northeastern Cuba). His enthusiasm about the abundance of sites prompted Mark Harrington's trip in 1915. During this visit, which lasted almost a year, Harrington concentrated his efforts in the Baracoa area. For two months in 1919, he returned for a brief stint in Baracoa and then conducted some preliminary work in Pinar del Rio, Cuba's westernmost province. He presented his findings and interpretations in two volumes, *Cuba Before Columbus* (1921).

In 1932, Herbert Krieger, curator of ethnology at the National Museum of Natural History, went to Cuba, but he never published his findings and they remain in the Smithsonian's files, now accessible on the Internet (Krieger 1933). The following year Yale University established its Caribbean program "as an attempt to improve the methodology of archaeology through intensive research in a particular area, as well as to resolve the historical problems of the aboriginal populations of the West Indies and related peoples in North and South America" (Osgood 1942:5). Under the program, archaeological research was conducted throughout the northern Antilles. In 1936, during America's Great Depression, the U.S. Congress established the Division of Cultural Relations to establish links with Latin America (Patterson 1995:78).[1] This office established and funded the Institute of Andean Research, which oversaw archaeological research in South America and the Caribbean. The institute supported Rouse's archaeological work in the Maniabon Hills of northeastern Cuba and Osgood's work at Cayo Redondo in Pinar del Rio. Their investigations resulted in two publications: Cornelius Osgood's *The Ciboney Culture of Cayo Redondo, Cuba* (1942) and Irving Rouse's *Archaeology of the Maniabon Hills, Cuba* (1942). These works represent the last published U.S. research effort in Cuba until the 1990s. Their work, and that of their U.S. predecessors, influenced several generations of Cuban archaeologists and continues to be referenced by contemporary Cuban archaeologists.

ARCHAEOLOGY AFTER THE REVOLUTION

Nationalization

The study of history was an important concern from the onset of the Revolution. The Revolution drew upon the historical conditions that had created and perpetuated social inequities, inequities that had also threatened Cuba's national identity (Pérez 1999). Jorge Domínguez (1993:96) notes that the linking to Cuban history was critical in the forging of a new Cuban national identity distinct from the regime of Fulgencio Batista (*batistato*). According to Pérez, "Fidel Castro, the 26 of July Movement, which he led, and other revolutionary forces that had participated in the revolutionary war, sought to affirm Cuban nationalism. In the *symbols used and histories evoked,* in the problems diagnosed and solutions proposed, there was a *strong emphasis on enabling Cubans to take charge of their history*" (Pérez 1995:315, italics added). Pérez also notes that "by attacking the past that had created these hardships, the revolutionary leadership struck a responsive chord that initially cut across lines of class and race and served to unite Cubans of almost all political persuasions. It aroused extraordinary enthusiasm for *la revolución* and, as ambiguously defined as it was, it could mean all things to all people. Aroused too was a powerful sense of nationalism, one summoned by the revolution and soon indistinguishable from it" (Pérez 1995:315).

Respect for and pride in the past were clearly evident in early postrevolutionary government proclamations. In 1959, the Cuban government created the National Commission for Historical Monuments, which is housed in the Ministry of Culture. In 1966, the government created the Council of State of the Republic of Cuba and the National People's Assembly. The first two laws that were approved by the assembly were for the protection and restoration of historical monuments. The Department of Museums, which oversees the country's museums, is also situated in the Ministry of Culture.

With the creation of the Cuban Academy of Sciences (CAS) in 1962, organized along the lines of the Soviet Akademia Nauk (Suchlicki 2001:4), archaeology, like other scientific disciplines, became formally recognized and funded by the government. The Academy of Sciences, which replaced the Academia de Ciencias de La Habana, was established once the "necessary conditions for an increased development of science were created" (Statutes of the Academy of Sciences of Cuba 2001). The CAS is responsible for the coordination and implementation of scientific and technical research. Archaeologist Ernesto Tabío, who returned to Cuba after years of self-exile in Lima during the Batista regime, participated in the formation of the CAS and founded and directed its anthropology department (Oyuela-Caycedo et al. 1997:366).

On April 16, 1961, Fidel Castro proclaimed Cuba a socialist country (Pérez 1995). Social scientists adopted a historical materialist perspective and archaeologists modeled their work after Soviet archaeology. According to Domínguez (1991:9), the goal of archaeology is to define and explain Cuban history, to promote a materialist understanding of Cuba's history, and to provide temporal depth to that history. While many of Fidel Castro's speeches acknowledge the role of history (after the Spanish conquest) in shaping the present day, at least one speech recognizes the role of prehistory. Lourdes Domínguez (1991:9) cites a 1968 speech given by Fidel Castro (published in 1975) in 1968, in which "he says that we have the duty to undertake the investigation of our oldest history, as a fitting imperative for the discovery and analysis of the heritage of our country [cuando nos dice que debemos abordar la investigación de nuestro pasado más antiguo como la tarea justa de ahondar y profundizar en las raíces históricas de este país]." The unique character of the Cuban national identity that emphasizes themes of struggle and resistance extends these notions to prehistory, as memorialized throughout the country at highly visible public sites associated with archaeology and history. A statue of a young Cuban Indian woman stands outside the entrance of the Capitolio (Figure 3.2), which houses the Academy of Sciences. She represents liberty and the Cuban republic (Baker 1997:264). Not far from the Capitolio is the Fuente de la India Noble Habana, a fountain surmounted by a marble statue of The Noble Havana, the Indian woman for whom the province is named; tourist guides describe her as an Indian queen (Baker 1997). A famous statue of Hatuey stands in Baracoa's Plaza Independencia, facing the cathedral.

Education and Training

Pérez (1995:358) and others have noted that the most notable achievements of the Revolution have been in the areas of education, nutrition, and health

3.2. The Capitolio, Havana. Photograph by Mary Jane Berman.

services. Soon after the Revolution, the government created new educational opportunities and expanded existing ones. In 1959, there were three university centers: the University of Havana, the University of Oriente, and the University of Las Villas. By the 1980s, there were 40 universities and centers of higher education (Pérez 1995:360). During this period, archaeological training at the university level was offered in Cuba for the first time. The formal study of archaeology (often followed through a "historical sciences" curriculum) was made possible by the social and political changes that made education accessible to people of all class backgrounds, including women, who traditionally had been excluded from higher education. Significantly, the first person to receive a doctorate in archaeology was a woman.

Archaeologists, like academicians in other disciplines, doctors, and people involved in technological fields, were encouraged to study in the USSR (Pérez

1995). Scholarships and other educational support were made available. Estrella Rey was awarded a doctorate in historical sciences from the Institute of Ethnography (Miklujo Maclay) of the USSR's Academy of Sciences in 1968 and thus was the first student of prehistory to have a Ph.D. in Cuba. Ernesto Tabío received his doctorate in historical sciences from the same institution shortly after Rey. His dissertation was published by the Cuban Academy of Sciences and is considered a landmark work. Tabío and Rey's coauthored work, *Prehistoria de Cuba* (first published in 1966, then reissued in 1979), played a role in the formation of a movement in Latin America known as Latin American Social Archaeology (Dacal and Watters, Chapter 2; Fernández Leiva 1992; McGuire 1992; Oyuela-Caycedo et al. 1997:366). The advocates of this approach saw the practice of archaeology as "a way to link their revolutionary politics with archaeological practice" (McGuire 1992:65). José Guarch, another notable scholar, also received his doctorate from the USSR Academy of Sciences. In 1987, Jorge Febles, a former barber, received his doctorate from the Institute of History, Philology, and Philosophy of the Siberian Branch of the Soviet Academy of Sciences. Numerous others received master's degrees from the USSR prior to the 1990s.

During the period of close relations with the Eastern Bloc, archaeologists from these countries were welcomed and both independent and joint research encouraged. The Polish archaeologist Janusz Kozlowski published his findings in Cuba (Kozlowski 1972, 1975) and Poland (Kozlowski 1974). A set of papers, based partly on collaborative work among archaeologists from the Siberian branch of the Soviet Academy of Science's Institute of History, Philology, and Philosophy, was published in Russian (Vasilievski 1986). The bulk of the work focused on artifact analysis, although one study examined prehistoric crania (Alexeiev 1986). During this time, the Poles and Russians supplied microscopes and other equipment to support technical analyses. Radiocarbon samples were submitted for dating and a series of dates published (Panichev 1986). Collaboration with the Siberian Branch of the Soviet Academy of Science also allowed Cubans to do archaeology in Siberia. Three Cuban archaeologists, Lourdes Domínguez and Jorge Febles (in 1980), Alfonso Córdova and Jorge Febles (in 1986), and Jorge Febles (in 1987) participated in the joint Cuba-USSR Archaeological Excavations in Western Siberia between 1980 and 1987.

The system of training archaeologists instituted during the early days of the Revolution remains today. Archaeology is taught in the Faculty of Marxism and History and the Faculty of Historical Sciences at the University of

Table 3.1. Licentiate in History Curriculum, University of Havana

The history of mankind: prehistory; archaeology of the world
Social and economic formations: primitive communism, slavery, feudalism, capitalism, socialism, communism; the Middle Age, modern history, and contemporary history (including the classic revolutions of France, England, and Russia)
History of Cuba
History of every country in America, Europe, Asia, Oceania, and Africa, and their liberation movements (including the First and Second World Wars)
History of Philosophy
Marxism-Leninism (dialectic materialism and historic materialism)
English language
Methods for research in the social sciences
Statistics
Archaeology of Cuba

Table 3.2. Curriculum for Students Specializing in Archaeology, University of Havana

History of World Archaeology
History of Cuban Archaeology
Marxist philosophy applied to archaeological research
Fieldwork
Interdisciplinary sciences applied to archaeological research
Physical Anthropology
Study of food remains*
Computer techniques for archaeological analysis
Study of aboriginal technology: lithics, pottery, shell, wood, cordage, basketry, metal, and textiles

* Primarily, dietary reconstructions based on zooarchaeological analyses

Havana. One can earn a Licentiate in History (Table 3.1) that entitles the holder to conduct research. Cuban universities do not grant degrees in archaeology, but students can specialize in it. The licentiate takes five years to complete. Students who specialize in archaeology must take courses that include artifact analysis, zooarchaeology, Marxist philosophy, physical anthropology, computer analyses, history, and philosophy (Table 3.2). Fieldwork is required to complete the program. In 1987, Lourdes Domínguez (Figure 3.3) became

3.3. Dra. Lourdes Domínguez, with her husband standing to her right and her mother to her left. Photograph by Mary Jane Berman.

the first archaeologist to graduate from the University of Havana with a Ph.D. in historical sciences. Attempts to create a separate Department of Archaeology here, at some of the Higher Pedagogical Institutes, and at the other university centers have been unsuccessful. The Ministry of Higher Education has granted several notable individuals, such as Ramón Dacal Moure, Milton Pino, Alfredo Rankin, and César García del Pino, the Master of Science degree in recognition of their commitment and contributions.

In addition to offering courses in archaeology, several universities have museums where collections are curated and exhibited. The Montané Museum of the University of Havana (Figure 3.4) is the oldest and most widely known. The University of Oriente and the University of Holguín both have active archaeology programs and museums. Other institutions such as the Universities of Villa Clara, Pinar del Rio, Ciego de Avila, Camagüey, Sancti Spiritus, and Cienfuegos are working to develop museums.

During the 1990s, several people, many of whom are represented in this book, received their doctorates in history from the University of Havana. Pedro P. Godo was awarded his Ph.D. in 1995 for the dissertation "The Study of Use-Wear Traces in the Tool Kit of the Aborigines of the Fishing-Gathering Phase and Its Application on Ethnohistorical Reconstruction." Others include Ricardo Sampedro for "The Study of Use-Wear Traces in the Tool Kit of

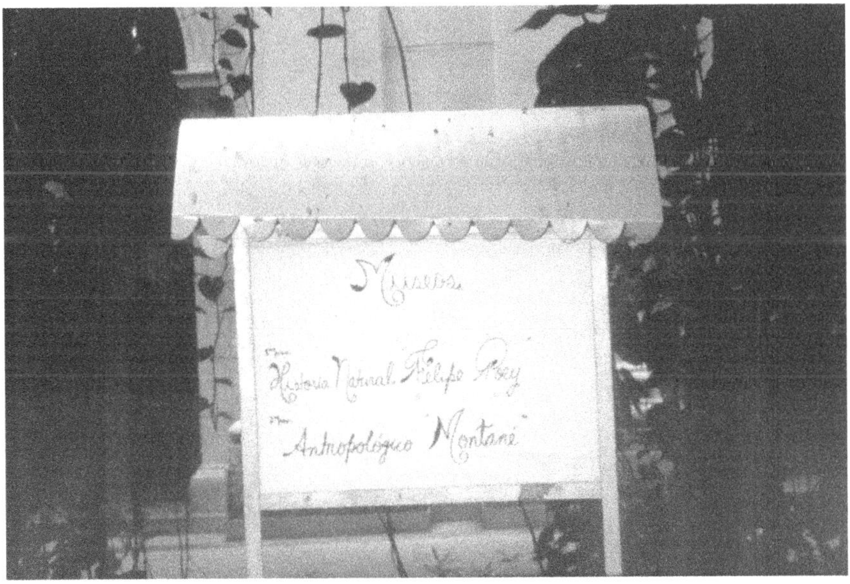

3.4. Entrance to the Montané Museum, Havana, Cuba. Photograph by Mary Jane Berman.

the Aborigines of the Protoagricultural Phase and Its Application on Ethnohistorical Reconstruction"; Gabino de La Rosa for "The Palisades of the Eastern part of Cuba: Chase and Resistance"; Enrique M. Alonso for "The Real Origin of the So-Called Guanahatabey of Cuba"; and Jorge A. Cabrera for "The Aborigines of the Cunaqua Cultural Variant: An Ethnohistorical Reconstruction." Many of these studies reflect the influence of Soviet thought and method.

While cultural and educational exchanges between Cuba and the United States were at a standstill for the most part from 1959 onward, the Smithsonian's Latin American Archaeology program, administered by Dr. Betty J. Meggers, provided Cuban scholars intellectual and other forms of support throughout this period (Politis 2003:117). In recognition of her scholarship, commitment, encouragement, and personal contributions to the field of Cuban archaeology, Meggers was awarded the Medalla de "La Periquera" from the Museo Provincial de Holguín in 1997.[2]

Publications

Archaeological reports and essays are published in journals that come out of the Institute of Historical Sciences, the Center of Anthropology, the Society of Historians, the Montané Museum, the Casa del Caribe, and the speleological societies. Each year the Provincial Speleological Committee (Comité Espeleológicos Provinciales) produces scientific papers with a section devoted to archaeology (Fernández Leiva 1992:39). Archaeological discoveries are reported in the newspapers *Granma, Juventud Rebelde,* and *Bohemia* and on radio and television. In April 2002, for example, the discovery of artifacts from Villa Clara (north central Cuba) was reported by Radio Havana (2002) and posted on the Internet, thus expanding the means by which the official news service is communicating archaeological information to Cuba and beyond.

Archaeology within the Government Administrative System

The various agencies that administer government policies are overseen by a Board of Ministries. Archaeology is administered by the Ministry of Culture and the Ministry of Science, Environment, and Technology. The Center of Anthropology (Figure 3.5), along with the Center of Historical Sciences, Institute of Linguistics, and other institutes of social and biological research, is located administratively in the Ministry of Science, Environment, and Technology. The Center of Anthropology consists of regionally based archaeology departments in Havana and Holguín and the Department of Ethnology. The Department of Archaeology (Havana) has offices in Pinar del Rio and Matanzas and collaborates with other institutions. The National Commission of Patrimony, situated in the Ministry of Culture, grants permits to conduct archaeological research (Fernández Leiva 1992:38). Archaeologists must submit a report upon finishing a project. The National Commission oversees the laws that protect and preserve sites and the administration and management of the 15 provincial museums. These museums were created as a result of a 1966 law that provides that all the municipalities must have at least one museum. There are over 100 municipal museums in addition to the provincial counterparts. Many of both kinds of museums contain archaeological collections and exhibits. Fernández Leiva (1992:39) notes that, as a result of these efforts, today's elementary schoolchild knows more about the prehistory of Cuba than the majority of educated people did before 1959.

Museums devoted specifically to archaeology also exist. Some notable examples are the Montané Museum of the University of Havana (mentioned in numerous contexts throughout this paper) and the University of Oriente's Museo Arqueológico in Santiago de Cuba. The Museo Indocubano in Banes is famous for a thirteenth-century gold figurine and for murals painted by the noted muralist José Martínez depicting Taíno life. The Museum Chorro de Maíta, situated on the site of Bani, is believed to be the largest aboriginal

3.5. Entrance to Centro de Antropología, Havana, Cuba. Photograph by Mary Jane Berman.

burial site thus far excavated in the Caribbean and is a national monument. Trinidad's Museo de Arqueología y Ciencias Naturales, located in an elegant old mansion on the southwest corner of the main plaza, contains taxidermy examples of Cuban flora and fauna and exhibits that chronicle the evolution of Cuba's aboriginal cultures. There is a Museo de Arqueología in Sancti Spiritus. Formally trained archaeologists staff these institutions. Many municipal museums whose missions are more general also have formally trained professionals. For a period of time the Capitolio housed the Cuban Academy of Sciences, but it was closed in 1996. Its re-creation of the famous Punta del Este cave that featured depictions of the pictographs painted by artist José Martínez were removed.

Avocational groups located throughout the country contribute significantly to the work of professionals (Fernández Leiva 1992:38). Their involvement further reflects the democratization of archaeology. Once perceived as an elite avocation, today everyone has the potential to participate in recovering and constructing the nation's patrimony and to assist professionally trained archaeologists. Avocational archaeologists have recorded the location of many sites and provided data about site size and occupation. Much of these data were incorporated into the compilation of archaeological censuses (e.g., Febles 1995). Many avocational archaeologists are members of the country's speleological societies that have played key roles in the discovery and description of rock art sites (Linville, Chapter 5). There is a speleological society in every province, and each has an archaeology section (Fernández Leiva 1992:38). The Escuela Nacional de Espeleología offers courses in archaeology.

Archaeology during the Special Period and Onward

The withdrawal of the USSR in the early 1990s significantly impacted the infrastructure of Cuban life, including academic research and the dissemination of scholarly findings. Opportunities to study in the Eastern Bloc evaporated, and archaeologists have not gone there to study since the onset of what Cubans call the "special period," nor has any Eastern Bloc archaeologist undertaken any scholarly work in Cuba. Attempts to maintain contact with Russian and Eastern Bloc colleagues have met with little or no success. The shortage of supplies such as paper and ink and the loss of parts for printing presses account for a reduction in the frequency of newspaper and magazine publications, a decrease in the number of pages per publication, and the delayed printing of new books and journals (Johnson 1988; Pérez 1995:386). Thus, reports and articles written during the height of Soviet influence may never see their way to publication in Cuba, while some editors have sought and attained publication through European presses. For archaeologists, the shortage of other critical materials, such as fuel, has been particularly frustrating, because it has reduced mobility and access to field sites, museum collections, and libraries and archives outside of one's home institution.

The Cuban scientific and intellectual community, including archaeologists, has responded pragmatically and innovatively to these obstacles, however. Much of their response is directed to connecting in various ways to the West, particularly North America. First, scientific collaborations between the Center for Anthropology and North American institutions have been actively sought and encouraged. Since 1997, the Royal Ontario Museum has collaborated with the Ministerio de Ciencia, Tecnología, y Medio Ambiente (CITMA) in Ciego de Avila on the excavation of Los Buchillones, a submerged site that has yielded a wealth of wooden and other organic objects (Collazo 1998; Harrington 1999; http://www.rom.on.ca/digs/belize/cuba.html; Pendergast et al. 2001). At the end of the 1999 field season, the project's base of operation moved to the Institute of Archaeology (IOA), University College, London (Graham et al. 2000). Project oversight is shared between the Cuban and British institutions; codirectors are David Pendergast (IOA) and Jorge Calvera (CITMA), and subdirectors are Elizabeth Graham (IOA) and Juan Jardines (CITMA).

Throughout the 1990s, attempts were made (and continue to be made) to create collaborative projects with U.S. museums and universities. In the early 1990s, an agreement between the Montané Museum and the Carnegie Museum of Natural History resulted in joint fieldwork in Pinar del Rio and the publication of an elegantly illustrated book on the prehistory of Cuba by the University of Pittsburgh Press (Berman 1999; Dacal Moure and Rivero de la Calle 1996; Gnivecki 1998). Other collaborators (the authors included) sought grant funds in the mid-1990s to conduct research in central Cuba, but U.S. policy, which expanded the scope and severity of its sanctions after 1995, intensified the amount of paperwork involved in obtaining visas and licenses, making it nearly prohibitive to undertake projects there.

On a more positive note, the return of human remains to a Taíno community in Caridad de los Indios (eastern Cuba) in January 2003 is bringing new meaning to archaeological collaborations between Cuba and the United States. Following six years of discussion between Smithsonian and Cuban archaeologists and the Cuban government, Cuban Taíno remains, believed to be from seven individuals, were returned and reburied in a ceremony attended by Cuba's Taíno descendants, staff from the National Museum of the American Indian (Smithsonian), representatives from several U.S. Indian tribes, and Taíno descendants living in the United States (Bauzá 2003). Cuban archaeologists are now requesting the return of artifacts collected by Harrington, but the Smithsonian's policy is to return artifacts to native communities, not to universities or museums. According to the NMAI repatriation coordinator, the Cuban Taínos themselves must claim these in order to begin repatriation proceedings (Bauzá 2003).

Another response on the part of Cuban archaeologists has been to organize international conferences to connect with scholars from other countries and intellectual traditions, which may also bring much-needed U.S. dollars and other forms of Western currency to the island. Numerous meetings brought North American, European, Latin American, and Cuban scientists and avocational archaeologists together to discuss rock art, physical anthropology, colonial archaeology, and prehistoric archaeology during the 1990s. Other conferences such as the Sixth Iberian-American Symposium of Terminology, held in Cuba in 1998, included papers by archaeologists. The proceedings of this conference were published in Portugal (Correia 2002) owing to the difficulty of publishing in Cuba.[3]

An additional means by which Cuban archaeologists have sought to engage with colleagues from other countries has been to offer their services to archaeologists outside the island. Archaeologists have recognized the unique expertise of several Cuban investigators and incorporated them into their projects: Dacal Moure (Rostain and Dacal Moure 1997) has worked on the study of shell tool production at the Tanki Flip site on Aruba and Jorge Febles on stone tool production and edge wear analyses on sites in Puerto Rico. A few Cuban archaeologists have also contributed to recent international publications. For example, José M. Guarch's chapter (2003) titled "Paleoindians in Cuba and the Circum-Caribbean" appears in Jalil Sued-Badillo's book (2003), *UNESCO General History of the Caribbean,* Volume 1, *Autochthonous Societies.* In addition to his work in Cuba, Jorge Ulloa (see Chapter 6) has participated in archaeological research in the Dominican Republic and has published in Dominican journals.[4] In 1995, Febles completed a CD-ROM titled *Taíno, Arqueología de Cuba.* His efforts to distribute it internationally to secure funds to support the work of the Centro de Antropología did not yield the much-needed and desired financial results. In 1999, Febles applied for and received a John Simon Guggenheim award to complete the database he had established with the CD-ROM.

In order to disseminate their work outside the country, Cuban avocational and professional archaeologists are beginning to publish their findings on the Internet. A recent paper by Racso Fernández Ortega and José B. González Tendero (2001b) from el Grupo-arqueológico Don Fernando Ortiz is an excellent example. Jorge Ulloa published an article in a special 2002 issue of the electronic journal *KACIKE: Journal of Caribbean Amerindian History and Anthropology.* While reducing publication costs, such papers provide outlets to the international community. This example is not typical, however, because few Cuban archaeologists own personal computers, but it is our hope that we will see more Cuban archaeologists publishing their work in this manner. Time will tell if the Internet proves to be an effective means of dissemination of information.

With the shortage of fuel and high costs that make travel prohibitive, many archaeologists are redirecting their efforts from fieldwork to the reexamination of collections housed in museums and repositories. Some are applying insights gained from their Soviet and Eastern Bloc experiences, as well as new interpretive models inspired by their more recent contacts with U.S. and Canadian archaeologists. In December 2003, the scientific publication *Journal of Trace and Microprobe Techniques* devoted a whole issue to the work of archaeologists engaged in the analysis of prehistoric and colonial period pottery (*majolica*) using instrumental neutron activation analysis (INAA) and electron probe X-ray microanalysis (SEM-EDX) analyses.[5] Three Cuban archaeologists, including Pedro Godo (Chapter 8), are featured in this volume, which will be republished in the 2004 edition of *Information Science and Technology.* Nevertheless, such analyses are difficult to undertake, since the parts for the Soviet-manufactured equipment needed to conduct this work are several decades old and hard to replace. Last, but not least, Cuban archaeologists are reaching out to North American archaeologists by marketing their national and regional conferences, which they continue to organize, in professional media. Such calls for papers and invitations to conferences appear frequently in *Anthropology Newsletter* and *SAA Archaeological Record,* which supplanted *SAA Bulletin.*

SUMMARY

Cuba's precolonial, prehistoric past has been studied for more than 150 years. Throughout this period, Cuban investigators have adopted, incorporated, and developed numerous methods and interpretive programs that reflected and contributed to the construction of their national identity. In the nineteenth century and much of the twentieth, Cubans interested in archaeology used Western European and North American models to frame questions, recover artifacts, and construct explanations. For the most part, archaeology lacked formal institutional organization and recognition. While the work of these archaeologists lacked a unifying model, their dedication reflected the profound sense of *patria* that shaped Cuban history. At the turn into the twentieth century, the work of avocational archaeologists, many of them professionals drawn from the sciences and humanities, was making significant contributions to knowledge and expanding the understanding of Cuban prehistory. In the first half of the twentieth century, North Americans conducted research as an extension of U.S. foreign policy, although it is likely that these archaeologists (like other scientists who were sent to Latin America during this period) did not realize that their work was part of a larger agenda and that it would ultimately be seen in this light. The practice of historical materialism in archaeology and the social sciences after 1962 paralleled Cuba's broader conception of struggle and resistance. Because it diverged from U.S. models, it was an affirmation of nationalism and a proclamation of Cuba's unique sovereignty. As Pérez (1995:ix) has noted, the history of Cuba is a "chronicle of a people locked in relentless struggle against the byproducts of their history: against slavery and racism, inequality and injustice, and uncertainty and insecurity."

The professionalization of archaeology through formal education was recognition of its value in the construction of a national identity that incorporated a precolonial past. At the same time, the work of avocational archaeologists, their acknowledged role in the production of knowledge, their inclusion in research, and provisions for their training speak to the democratization of education throughout the country. Today, university-trained archaeologists and their avocational colleagues, faced with reductions of resources and other impediments, have responded with unflagging dedication. Today the sciences, lacking in resources and technology, are driven by what James (2000:7) refers to as "cultural optimism." For Cuban archaeologists, too, a sense of purpose, guided by love of country and a defiant national spirit, continues to be their driving force.

ACKNOWLEDGMENTS

Much of the information presented here was acquired when Berman and Gnivecki traveled to Cuba in the summer of 1995 on a study trip supported by a Wake Forest University Pew Spires grant awarded to Berman. The authors thank Wake Forest University's Department of Anthropology and Program for International Studies (now the Center for International Studies), particularly Dr. Richard Sears, for helping to support Jorge Febles's trip to the United States in fall 1996. Dr. Candyce Leonard of Wake Forest University translated several passages from Spanish to English. Special thanks go to Linda Arcure of Wake Forest University's School of Medicine, Department of Biomedical Communications, and Miami University's M.C.I.S., Area 351, Advanced Resources for Educational Applications, for imaging production, and to Claudia López-Monsalve, Center for American and World Cultures, Miami University, who helped with Spanish and Portuguese translations. As always, José Oliver's reading of the manuscript was useful and constructive. His numerous insights and suggestions reflect well on his undergraduate education at Miami University, an institution with which we are now proudly affiliated. Finally, we acknowledge and thank our Cuban colleagues who have taught us about strength of spirit, survival in the face of difficulty, and unwavering commitment to knowledge that transcends politics.

NOTES

1. Patterson (1995:77) states that Congress created the Division of Cultural Relations to "implement Pan-Americanism at a time when private U.S. investments in Latin America had declined and investments from other capitalist countries were increasing in the area." He thus attributes economic motives to the establishment of this office and its programs.

2. See http://www.si.edu/intrel/internat/south.htm; http://www.mnsu.edu/emuseum/information/biography/klmno/meggersbetty.html).

3. See http://www.iltec.pt/publicacoes/livros/livro9.html.

4. See http://www.kacike.org/UlloaEnglish.html.

5. See http://www.dekker.com/servlet/product/productid/TMA.

4 / Historical Archaeology in Cuba

Lourdes S. Domínguez

Compared to many other countries, Cuba was early to adopt Historical Archaeology as a significant subfield within the discipline. I had the honor of playing a part in its humble beginnings. My first work was in the Casa de la Obrapía in Old Havana in 1970 (Domínguez 1980, 1981), the first controlled and systematic excavation conducted in the colonial part of the city. That same year, I conducted a study on the majolicas from this and a few other sites in Old Havana, the first study on Spanish majolicas since the work of Goggin (1968) and Fairbanks (1972) from the University of Florida. It was because of our studies on these ceramics that Kathleen Deagan visited the island in 1970 to examine our collections. Eventually, these collections were mentioned in her book on early Spanish ceramics in the Caribbean and Florida (Deagan 1987).

Later, I had the opportunity to work on the slave cemetery of the Ingenio Taoro, in the town of Cangrejeras (Province of Havana), to the best of my knowledge the first cemetery of its kind excavated in the Caribbean. Between 1972 and 1974, I worked on the ruins of *cafetales* (coffee haciendas or plantations) in the hilly region of Pinar del Río, west of Havana. Interestingly, because of the influence of plantation owners fleeing the Haitian revolution, these sites have architectural features distinct from those of others found in Cuba. Some lack slave quarter areas because slaves apparently lived in their own houses scattered throughout the property.

During the more than 30 years that I have been working in Historical Archaeology, this discipline has evolved markedly, to where it is now an inte-

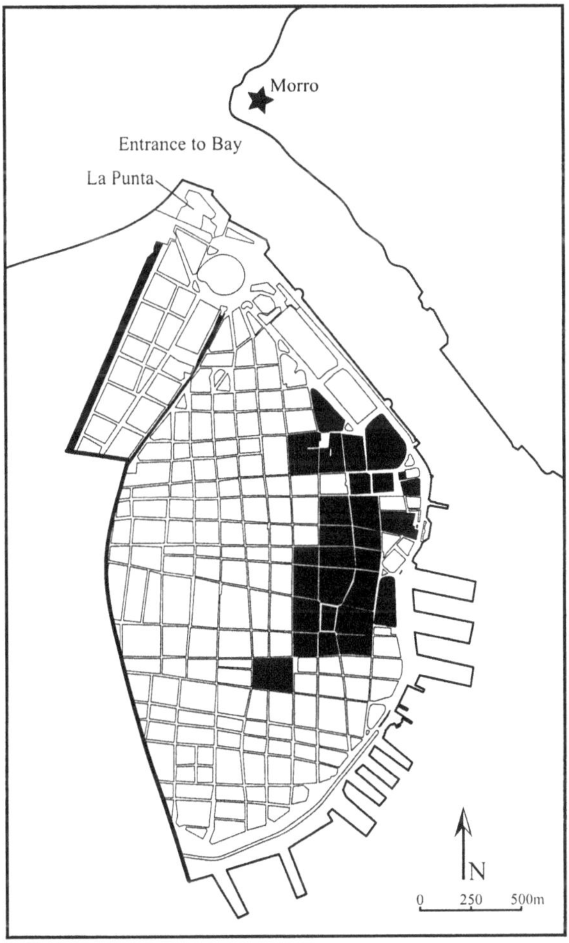

4.1. Map of Old Havana showing the areas restored by the Oficina del Historiador de la Ciudad de la Habana

gral part of the discipline of archaeology in Cuba. This chapter presents a critical review of one aspect of the development of Historical Archaeology as a scientific discipline on the island. Particularly, it focuses on advancements made through salvage projects and investigations in Old Havana (Figure 4.1).

In Cuba, Historical Archaeology forms part of the country's developing archaeological program, which tries by all possible means to be current with the most recent concerns of the field, either theoretical or empirical, when they overlap with our interests. On each project, we adapt the latest techniques, to the point that we can say today that the sites are well controlled and that we have and use the most appropriate methodologies. Cuba, like the rest of Latin America and especially the Caribbean, has been a testing ground for various disciplinary experiments carried out by investigators from many parts of the world. However, in most of the writing on this region, accounts of Cuban excavations are missing, nor is reference made to the work carried out by Cuban specialists, who are respected professionals in their areas of expertise with distinguished careers. Even worse, sometimes as a result of a serious lack of ethics or sensitivity, the work of Cuban scholars, especially if written in Spanish, is neither alluded to nor cited in bibliographies, even when Cuban sites are the subject of the publication.

Since about 1983, Latin Americanists started to conduct multiple projects in their own countries on historical sites, in some instances subsidized by governmental entities and in others by North American and European universities. The resonance of Latin American Social Archaeology (Arqueología Social) in our countries has given new vigor to this specialization. For this reason, there is a timely need to analyze Historical Archaeology from the perspective of Latin America (Rovira 1991).

This chapter is not involved in the debate on the scientific/humanistic character of Historical Archaeology. For decades now, this archaeological specialization has been practiced in the New World under different titles but in all cases with the same aim, the historical reconstruction of the lifeways of people who lived after the discovery of the Americas. The subfield has been assigned a series of names or meanings over time, all of them having connotations determined by different theoretical orientations. We could say that initially it was known as Colonial Archaeology or the archaeology of colonial sites in the New World (La Rosa Corzo 1995). Out of this simple chronological orientation, other specializations developed, such as Contact Period and Industrial Archaeology (La Rosa Corzo 1995). But in Europe, this type of archaeological work has been named according to a specific socioeconomic stage, that is to say, Medieval or Post-Medieval, Modern, Contemporary, etc. In Latin America, current appellations for the practice of Historical Archaeology include Colonial Archaeology, Archaeology of Colonial Levels, Historic Archaeology, Urban Archaeology, "Novohispana" Archaeology, Archaeology of the Recent Past, Archaeology of Recent Capitalism, and Archaeology of Imperialism, among others. Definitions of these categories depend upon two criteria, the particular focus of study and the time period (Funari 2000). Historical Archaeology is a social science as much as any other branch of the discipline of archaeology, and it is clear that, while young and able to accommodate a variety of interests, it is a well-defined field with particularities that make it truly multidisciplinary. Historical Archaeology is, in fact, the study of the modern world and especially the capitalist context, from its establishment to its expansion, embracing a wide chronological range.

The "Letter of Venice," produced by a UNESCO-sponsored meeting in 1964, states that restoration of historical features requires archaeological treatment. As a result, restoration-sponsored archaeology became an officially endorsed policy throughout the world (Centro Nacional de Cultura–Restauración de Monumentos 1984). Historical Archaeology is closely linked to restoration, but as a social science it goes beyond the mere location, excavation, and collection of artifacts from a site; it demands much more. One agenda is to describe particularistic tendencies from a historicist perspective, considering archaeological sites as reference works or case studies. The most important contribution of this type of research is reconstructing past lifeways of various social groups for whom the documentary record is limited. This type of work is called *traspatio* (backyard) archaeology, and it is generally conducted on patrimonial properties (Rovira 1985). Another approach addresses how general sociocultural processes operated in particular times and places, contributing to the development of the modern world. Examples include archaeological studies of Indo-Hispanic contact (Domínguez et al. 1994). When the scientific method is mentioned in the context of Historical Archaeology, it refers to a model in which theory and method drive research toward a desired objective. Predictive modeling makes it possible to evaluate regularities and variability in the archaeological record, sometimes combined with ethnoarchaeological studies. Following this method, we can arrive at complex inferences and perfect interpretative process that can be of great assistance to other documentary and historical studies.

My intention in the rest of this chapter is to offer a brief review of how Historical Archaeology has developed in Cuba. As mentioned, before the 1960s, investigations were initially conducted under the rubric of Colonial Archaeology or the archaeology of colonial-phase sites. Examples of this work appeared between the 1940s and 1950s in articles in the *Revista de Arqueología y Etnología,* published by the Junta Nacional de Arqueología y Etnología de Cuba (see Dacal and Watters, Chapter 2). This was the prestigious institution that regulated national patrimony in Cuba at the time. These articles should be required reading for anyone studying Cuban archaeology.

The works of our predecessors, such as professors Prat Puig, Boytel Jambu and Martínez Arango, Guarch, Payares, and Elso, have served as standards for our current efforts. These researchers also serve as role models for the work on buildings in Old Havana and in the historical core of Santiago de Cuba, as well as coffee plantations in the Sierra Maestra. Their work has undoubtedly been related to the process of restoration and on some occasions conducted from a preservationist perspective. Many of Cuba's Spanish colonial cities have since been recognized by UNESCO as World Heritage sites because of their excellent preservation.

Since the 1940s, some of the archaeological projects sponsored by the Junta Nacional de Arqueología in Cuba could be considered investigations in Historical or Colonial Archaeology. Until well into the 1960s, archaeological work concentrated primarily on Contact-period sites, isolated standing structure sites of different periods, coffee plantations, and *ingenios* (sugar haciendas). But in 1968, intensive work began on major sites in Havana, such as the Palacio de los Capitanes Generales under the direction of Eusebio Leal Spengler and, in 1970, in the Casa de la Obrapía under the direction of Rodolfo Payares and the author. Before 1968, projects in Historical Archaeology were few, sporadic, and accidental, without a cohesive plan. After that date, projects were systematic and organized efforts coordinated by the Comisión de Patrimonio Nacional and the Academia de Ciencias de Cuba. It is between 1960 and 1980 that one can truly say that the specialization became well established with thorough and systematized investigations undertaken throughout the country (La Rosa Corzo 2000).

After the 1960s, as the specialization of Historical Archaeology became widely recognized as a social science and its archaeological/historical discourse became established, Cuba kept pace with the discipline, rigorously applying it to the study of different social events and complex historical processes, as, for example, the process of transculturation or the early urbanization of the first European settlements in the sixteenth century.

One of the national duties Cuba attended to most carefully was the development of professionals. Education and professionalization had the necessary legal and state support. Institutions created for this end were given the economic support they needed, resulting in the organization and systematization of archaeology at a national level. It is important to mention that this landmark transition in 1960s Cuba is clearly reflected in the scientific work produced. It was during this same period that Historical Archaeology took off. Perhaps errors were made during this rapid development. Some projects lacked theoretical positions, or even a scientific vision to deal with some of the problems. But over the course of time these limitations have been addressed, and the important result is that we can see today how much significant work has been accomplished.

The most concrete achievement of Historical Archaeology in Cuba is the systematic work carried out in Old Havana. This work can be divided into two stages: 1968 to 1987, and post-1987, when the Gabinete de Arqueología de la Habana was inaugurated and made responsible for all archaeological work conducted in this city. The archaeological potential of Old Havana is incalculable. The integrity of its buildings and urban spaces built over several centuries makes it unique in the world. It will take several generations of scholars to make available all of the knowledge derived. Likewise, the integrity of its subsurface deposits makes this city the dream of any historical archaeologist.

One result of the early pioneering excavations in Old Havana was to make systematic subsurface study an integral part of an ambitious rehabilitation plan for Havana's built heritage. This work began by selecting buildings with high heritage value and expanded in such a way that it became necessary to establish a methodological procedure to tackle—in an orderly and efficient manner—the growing need for archaeological work in the city. It was then established that all work of restoration should be preceded by an archaeological investigation. In many cases, this situation created the sense that archaeological objectives were subordinated to the restoration projects. But priorities depended on the terms and strategies of construction, as well as a ranking of the historical value of the sites once architectural needs for stabilization were determined.

In general, the main objective of these archaeological studies was to rescue our built heritage. An example is the work in Old Havana, sponsored first by the Museo de los Capitanes Generales and then by the Oficina del Historiador de la Ciudad, which carries it on to the present. The treatment given to the city of Havana, a principal Spanish colonial city and gateway to the New World, is a real testimony to the efforts carried out by almost two generations of serious investigators who at different times have contributed their efforts and their lives to this mission.

Havana, as a representative museum of Caribbean cities, surpasses even its counterparts in Santo Domingo and Puerto Rico in terms of its chronological diversity owing to its exceptional preservation. The architectural restoration and archaeological research activities are centered in Old Havana, a district that belongs to all Havanans. It cannot be forgotten that Old Havana is an ancient but living city where thousands of families still reside, though it has been designated a museum. In 1982, the city was declared a World Heritage site, which carried with it an economic contribution that Cuba accepted, and Cuba met all the responsibilities the law required. Archaeological work in the city has never stopped, even during difficult times.

San Cristóbal de La Habana, the original and official name of the city, retains a wide spectrum of architectural elements from the sixteenth through the nineteenth centuries. It has examples of almost all variants of domestic, civil, military, ecclesiastical, and commercial architecture. To this we can add extensive artifactual deposits that allow a detailed study, unparalleled in the Caribbean.

Thanks to the dedication of the Oficina del Historiador de la Ciudad, we have been able to establish an arrangement of unusually cooperative teamwork between restorers and archaeologists. The professional development of those who took on leadership positions in these investigative tasks never lost its importance. It often came about on the ground, with a good deal of self-education resulting from trial and error, then trying again and carrying on (Domínguez 1998).

When a research project is conducted in Historical Archaeology, it should be done, as in any other scientific discipline, with a precise definition of the objectives and parameters of the work. We should not dig for the sake of digging, without an objective defined ahead of time and an already-established purpose to ensure that the results are in agreement with the aims of science. It is necessary to prove first that the archaeological resources can address the questions posed, and then the project can be expanded. The project will then be able to supplement and correct existing records and define what future steps are needed.

In Old Havana, the specialization of Historical Archaeology has been applied in this way, taking the necessary steps toward its mature development. As the result of this focused strategy, excellent information has been obtained from Havana's sites. Before the excavations of 1968, nothing was known about the city's archaeological deposits. Only then, when the city's anthropogenic subsurface began to reveal its secrets, did we fully realize the need for systematic, stratigraphic studies. We concluded that each archaeological site should be approached starting with a careful methodology that developed what we call a map of archaeological probability. This map gives a clear image of the limits of the old city against the modern urban backdrop.

Historical Archaeology in Old Havana has always aimed beyond simple architectural history or the identification of recovered materials. It rather tries to pull together all archaeological analyses for the sake of a larger objective: the revitalization of Old Havana through knowledge of its archaeological past. This should be achieved following the premise that each building will be rehabilitated according to the period in which it was erected or to the time when irreversible and lasting transformations were conducted. This idea applies especially to properties located within the city walls, whose history can be defined with the help of archaeology and its methods. Archaeology can study this history in a focused manner without having to depend on overused documents or preconceived architectural classifications (Leal Spengler 1886, 1995).

In the course of accomplishing this task, several landmark excavations have taken place during the archaeological study of Old Havana. Salvage archaeology and the rescue of any at-risk buildings was the prevailing strategy of the 1960s. This strategy was necessary to face immediate challenges. The young science of Historical Archaeology, with its uncertain methodologies and theoretical weaknesses, was quickly put into practice. Timely projects such as the Parroquial Mayor and La Casa de la Obrapía played an important role in developing the subfield in Cuba, while also providing an invaluable contribution to the identification and dating of artifacts obtained from the buried deposits of Havana. These were the first projects conducted in the city. The results provided representative, baseline samples for the region. These projects are classic examples of the particularist approach in Historical Archaeology that could be considered among the first such studies in the Caribbean and, perhaps, in Latin America. Beginning with the creation of the Gabinete de Arqueología in 1987, new standards were set for the practice of Historical Archaeology.

The two initial projects, Capitanes Generales and La Casa de la Obrapía date back to 1968 and can be considered the first archaeological case studies of Old Havana where archaeological research was conducted prior to the restoration process, with a particular interest in recovering relics. These objects may have been the first ones recovered from a religious context in Cuba using a stratigraphic approach. Later projects conducted in the area pursued the reconstruction of colonial lifeways of social and regional groups. An example of this is El Convento de Santa Clara de Asís, a type of project normally called backyard archaeology. However, the investigations of this project went well beyond simple construction details; it accomplished a detailed study of an entire religious community.

Within the walls of the old city, domestic contexts are those best studied since many of these sites ranked high in historical value and were destined to house the Museos del Complejo de la Oficina del Historiador de la Ciudad in Havana (Suárez del Portal 1997). Numerous excavations have been conducted within Old Havana, especially after 1990, when excavations were conducted at the houses of Reveros de Vasconcellos and Condes de Santovenia. The topics addressed by these two studies have ranged from diet to their significant ceramic assemblages. In addition to the pioneering work at Convento de Santa Clara and La Casa de la Obrapía, there are many other examples of investigations at religious sites, among them the Convento de San Francisco de Asís or Basílica Menor, which are representative. An extraordinary finding during the structural excavations was that the pendentives (triangular architectural features formed by the intersection of a dome and its supporting arches) of the central nave were filled with glazed ceramics of the first third of the eighteenth century. Other examples of religious sites are the Capilla del Loreto of the cathedral of Havana, the Capilla de la Fortaleza de la Cabaña, the Convento de Belén, and the Iglesia y Hospital de Paula (Vasconcellos Portuondo 2001).

Military contexts have also been the subject of several historical, architectural, and archaeological studies. The first restoration work of this type was conducted in the Castillo del Morro de Santiago de Cuba, but it is in Havana that the greatest number of projects have taken place, such as the Garita de la Maestranza. There were discovered the oldest *cubilotes* (an oven for the second smelting of iron) in Cuba, as well as foundry molds for artillery pieces. Significant archaeological studies have also been executed within the large fortification complexes that flank the entrance to Havana's bay. Two of these are the Cortina de Valdés in the Fortaleza del Morro and the foundations of the Baluarte de San Tomás, a bastion. In recent years, the Castillo de la Punta has been excavated, with the use of the most modern technology, as well as the oldest fortress of the Americas, called Castillo de la Fuerza Real de La Habana, and the Fortaleza de San Carlos de la Cabaña (Romero 1995).

From a regional perspective, the contribution represented by the study of Old Havana arises from the fact that the city walls define a time-space context in which a sociocultural process has been developing up to the present through a continuous occupation. This is what makes La Habana Vieja an intriguing area for research. As a scientific discipline, Historical Archaeology in Old Havana is not subordinated to the process of restoration; rather, both aspects are united and complement each other. It has resulted in a valuable symbiotic relationship. While not without errors, the results of all these efforts have been significant. It is everyone's responsibility to face Havana's future challenges as this city of wonder and mystery rediscovers its past, just as it is everyone's responsibility to face the future challenges of the people who inhabit it and dream of it.

5 / Cave Encounters

Rock Art Research in Cuba

Marlene S. Linville

Rock art has been found in nearly every country of the world (Bahn 1996). With over 700 examples, Cuba is no exception. Images painted, pecked, incised, or carved onto rock are among the most distinctive remains left by the early inhabitants of the Cuban archipelago. Since the mid-nineteenth century, intriguing paintings found on cave walls have fascinated not only the Cuban people but others who have contemplated both the makers and the meanings of these human creations left to embellish the natural landscape. Researchers from diverse disciplines, from Cuba and elsewhere, have sought answers to the same questions in the paintings, as well as in petroglyphs and other sculpted images: Who made the images? How did they do it? When? Why? What do they mean?

More than 130 rock art sites have been recorded in Cuba (Núñez Jiménez 1990:425). Generally located in caves, grottoes, or rock shelters, most are associated with "dark zone locations" of underground limestone caverns which, Greer suggests, "were specifically selected for special use throughout the island's occupational history for several thousand years."[1] For the past six decades, detailed data have been collected for these sites as a part of intensive efforts by researchers to document the speleological features of the Cuban landscape. This extensive set of data continues to fuel analyses of the nation's rock art.

Various techniques used to produce rock art have been identified in Cuba (Núñez Jiménez 1990:425), including both additive and subtractive processes. In addition to applying pigments to produce paintings (pictographs) on flat surfaces, prehistoric artisans also produced sculptural pictographs that incorporate the physical shape of the rock as a design element. The images depicted in Cueva de Ramos, located on the north coast of the Sancti Spiritus Province, provide an unusual example of painting that overlays incised imagery (Dacal Moure and Rivero de la Calle 1996:37). Smoke was used to create some images on cave walls, and at times smoked areas also contain incisions.

Two colors (black and red) occur most frequently in the images. Two others (grey and white) are rare (Núñez Jiménez 1990:425). Analysis of the mineral pigments used to produce some of the pictographs indicate that the red images were produced with iron oxides and the black ones with manganese (Dacal Moure and Rivero de la Calle 1996:37).[2] In addition, researchers have identified the use of organic substances, including vegetal carbon, oils, and fibers, in some pictographic media (Guarch Delmonte and Rodríguez Cullel 1980:55). Early Cuban painters produced a wide variety of images, ranging from simple, abstract or geometric images to figurative and apparently narrative scenes.

Petroglyphs (motifs carved into rock) and engravings produced by incising occur with less frequency in the Cuban archipelago than do pictographs. As with painted images, most of the petroglyphic images are located in caves and may incorporate natural cave formations (frequently stalagmites) (Núñez Jiménez 1975, 1985).

Analyses of prehistoric rock art in Cuba may also involve artifacts no longer found in situ (Núñez Jiménez 1985) but are museum pieces of known provenience. Other engraved or sculpted stone artifacts are sometimes considered in the context of rock art analyses, particularly when they share elements of style with the images found in caves (Núñez Jiménez 1985).

EARLY ROCK ART DISCOVERIES

Perhaps because most Cuban rock art sites are located deep inside caves, early discoveries were sporadic (Núñez Jiménez 1980:97). The earliest historic account of Cuban cave art appeared in 1839 in *Sab,* a novel by the Cuban poet Gertrudis Gómez de Avellaneda, who relates her discovery of the pictographs of the Cueva de María Teresa, in the province of Camagüey (Dacal Moure and Rivero de la Calle 1996:27). During that same year, these pictographs were also featured in the first published report of Cuban rock art, which appeared in *Memorias de la Real Sociedad Patriótica de La Habana* (Núñez Jiménez 1967:ix–x). Geographers of the era described the images as "the richest of Indocuban pictographs" (Núñez Jiménez 1990:128). While this suggests that other examples were known, record(s) of these have not survived. More than a century later, researchers rediscovered the cave, which contains an extraordinary petroglyphic mural measuring 10 m long (along with both prehistoric and colonial ceramic remains) at the base of Cerro de Limones (Núñez Jiménez 1990).

Two other pictograph cave sites discovered in the mid-nineteenth century have not since been relocated by modern investigators. One is in the hills of Tapaste. The other, in Banes, was first discovered during population census activities of 1846. These two pictograph sites were reported by Colonel Fernando García y Grave de Peralta and by Don José María De La Torre, respectively, and were documented in the *Faro Industrial de La Habana* of April 16, 1847 (Núñez Jiménez 1975:507).

More than 40 years later, in 1889, a priest named Antonio Perpiñá published a reference to aboriginal drawings in the hills of Cubitas, Cerro de Tuabaquey, in the province of Camagüey, in the cave now known as the Cueva de Pichardo (Núñez Jiménez 1967; Perpiñá 1889; Rivero de la Calle 1960). Unlike previous discoveries, this one emerged in the midst of the scientific debate surrounding Upper Paleolithic cave paintings in Europe. Sanz de Sautuola had by then achieved the conceptual leap that led archaeologists to question the relationship between Upper Paleolithic deposits in caves and the art found on their walls. However, his ideas would not gain widespread acceptance until they were sanctioned (in 1902) by the archaeological establishment (Bahn and Vertut 1997:22). Thus, as in other parts of the world, scientific studies of cave art and the body of useful theory that they would engender did not yet exist in Cuba in the nineteenth century. Indeed, more than six decades would pass before archaeologists would begin to investigate Perpiñá's discovery (Rivero de la Calle and Núñez Jiménez 1958).

In his 1910 publication, *A través de Cuba,* the French writer Charles Berchon described the chance discovery by a North American doctor, Freeman P. Lane, of a cave with pictographs at Punta del Este, Isla de Pinos (Isla de la Juventud) (Núñez Jiménez 1967:x). This discovery, too, went largely unrecognized in Cuba until 1922, when the noted Cuban ethnohistorian Fernando Ortiz reported the site to the president of the Academia de la Historia de Cuba (Herrera Fritot 1939:10). Ortiz also published a reference to the cave, announcing at that time his intention to produce a detailed report of the site (Ortiz 1922b:37). Although this report "never materialized" (Alonso Lorea 2001:45), Cuban researchers have recently located the unpublished notes of

Ortiz. As these were produced by the only researcher to study the pictographs before they were subsequently altered by both natural and cultural forces (Alonso Lorea 2001:47), these documents are an invaluable resource, particularly because this site, which Ortiz dubbed the "Sistine Chapel" (Alonso Lorea 2001), remains the most celebrated rock art site in Cuba.

EARLY RUPESTRIAN ARCHAEOLOGY IN CUBA

While the unpublished notes of Ortiz reveal that he was the first Cuban researcher to study pictographs in the archipelago, rupestrian archaeology in Cuba actually predates this work. In 1915, Mark Harrington and his Cuban research team discovered petroglyphs in the area of Maisí, in the context of archaeological investigations concentrated in eastern Cuba.[3] Among the rock art images they identified in the "Cueva Zemi," currently known in Cuba as the Cueva de los Bichos (Caverna de La Patana) (Núñez Jiménez 1975), is a large petroglyphic sculpture carved from a stalagmite. This sculpture, the "zemi" or idol for which the site was named, which weighs more than 900 pounds (Ortiz 1935), was extracted from the site and is currently in the collection of the Museum of the American Indian, Heye Foundation, the institution that sponsored Harrington's research (Harrington 1921).

Harrington recorded these petroglyphic discoveries in his 1921 two-volume publication, *Cuba Before Columbus,* which documents his extensive research in eastern Cuba in 1915 and 1916, as well as his preliminary study in 1919 of Pinar del Río, in western Cuba. In an effort to establish a cultural affiliation for the petroglyphic images, Harrington evaluated other cultural remains in the cave, inferring from these that both Taínos and their predecessors likely occupied the cave. Yet the name he chose for the site which, he suggests, may have been selected for "cavern worship" (Harrington 1921:273), indicates that he attributed the petroglyphic images to the "Tainan culture" (Harrington 1921:272).

Harrington's 1921 publication, now a "classic" work in the archaeology of Cuba (Rouse 1942:36), was generally influential among Cuban researchers, both when it first appeared, and particularly in 1935, when it was published in Spanish together with a second edition of Ortiz's publication (1922b) *Historia de la arqueología indocubana.* The history of rock art research in the archipelago suggests that the work also served as a catalyst that focused attention on a fertile, if largely untapped, source of knowledge on early Cuban inhabitants. It also established a precedent for a religious interpretation of

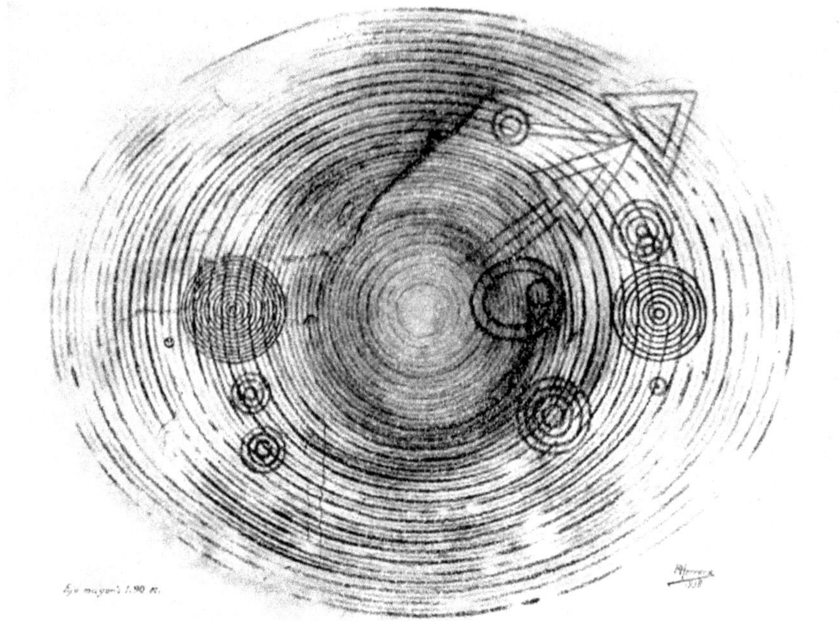

5.1. Drawing of the "Motivo Central" of Cueva No. 1, Punta del Este, Isla de Juventud (from Herrera Fritot 1939). Published with permission of the Museo Antropológico Montané de la Universidad de La Habana.

rock art images produced in caves throughout Cuba.[4] The first archaeological report to analyze and interpret pictographic images in Cuba was published in 1939 by René Herrera Fritot (La Rosa Corzo 1994). The report documents the 1937 expedition he led to Punta del Este, Isla de Pinos, to investigate the Cueva del Humo (Cueva de Isla), now known as Cueva No. 1, the same cave studied fifteen years earlier by Ortiz (Herrera Fritot 1939:11). In addition to mapping the site and collecting artifacts to establish a cultural association for the images, Herrera Fritot meticulously recorded the red and black, and largely geometric, images painted on the walls and ceiling of the cave through photographs and drawings.[5] He identified 112 pictographs during this expedition, among them the "Central Motif," the most frequently illustrated example of Cuban rock art (La Rosa Corzo, personal communication, 2002). A drawing made by Herrera Fritot of this motif is reproduced here in Figure 5.1.[6]

Despite finding in the cave only artifacts associated with preceramic "Ciboney" peoples in Cuba, Herrera Fritot did not attribute the drawings to these early inhabitants.[7] Instead, he suggested that the Ciboney lived in the cave "without religious biases" and that the Taíno later replaced them, painting the images (but leaving no other remains) in the cave they used exclusively as a temple (Herrera Fritot 1939:31–32). This conclusion was based in part on perceived stylistic similarities between the images and Taíno ceramics studied by de Booy (1915, 1919), as well as with petroglyphs studied by Harrington in Cuba and by Huckerby (1914, 1921) in Grenada and Saint Vincent islands.[8] This interpretation was also clearly influenced by the preliminary assessment provided by Ortiz. However, although Ortiz had indeed suggested that the cave functioned as a "Precolumbian Temple," his evaluation of surface finds at the site led him to infer that the images were probably produced by "Ciboney" peoples (Ortiz, May 24, 1922, recorded in Herrera Fritot 1939: 10). This sparked a cultural attribution debate among Cuban archaeologists, one that extended beyond Punta del Este to question the association between rock art and other cultural remains found in caves throughout Cuba.[9] It would be more than 30 years before the accumulation of archaeological data and development of archaeological thought in Cuba would settle the debate and credit those who left other cultural remains in Cueva No. 1 with also producing the images that embellish its walls (La Rosa Corzo 1994).[10]

ANTONIO NÚÑEZ JIMÉNEZ AND THE SOCIEDAD ESPELEOLÓGICA DE CUBA (SEC)

The "Petroglyphs and Pictographs" subheading in the Cuba section of the bibliographic work *Ancient Caribbean* (Weeks and Ferbel 1994) is telling. Although it by no means provides a comprehensive listing of the relevant published works on the topic, the three works listed were all produced by the same researcher. That person, who more than anyone else has contributed to the study and dissemination of knowledge of rock art in Cuba, was Antonio Núñez Jiménez. If, indeed, Ortiz is synonymous with the island of Cuba (Pérez Firmat 1989), Núñez Jiménez is synonymous with the cave art of the archipelago. The list of his extensive publications on rock art alone spans nearly half a century, a long period of time during which he tirelessly spearheaded the intense efforts of a diverse group of scientists to increase their understanding of the geology, geography, speleology, prehistory, and, indeed, all aspects of the Cuban landscape.

The long and distinguished career of Núñez Jiménez began on January 15, 1940, when, at just sixteen years of age, he founded the Sociedad Espeleológica de Cuba (SEC), an organization dedicated to the fundamental goals of investigating the "speleological features" of the Cuban nation and contributing to the better understanding of the national archipelago, as well as to the study and dissemination of Cuban natural sciences (Núñez Jiménez 1961:313). Research expeditions were a mainstay of the organization. In 1946, SEC members discovered two more pictograph cave sites at Punta del Este, Isla de Pinos. Four years later, Núñez Jiménez discovered yet another pictograph site on this island (now known as Isla de la Juventud), the Cueva de Finlay in Caleta Grande (named in honor of the Cuban who discovered the insect transmitter of yellow fever) (Rivero de la Calle 1966). During the 1950s, SEC participants also discovered pictographs in the Caverna de las Cinco Cuevas site (Martínez Gabino 1990), where they located the first complete drawings of concentric circles to be identified in the La Habana province.

Although political upheaval disrupted SEC efforts in the capital between 1955 and 1959, the group was able to continue in other areas. The group explored petroglyphs in the Sierra de Quemado in Pinar del Río and discovered petroglyphs in eastern Cuba, in the Cueva del Jaguey, a large cavern adjacent to the Cueva de los Bichos ("Zemi") site described by Harrington (Núñez Jiménez 1967).

In 1955, SEC researchers confirmed the pictograph discovery first reported in the nineteenth century by Perpiñá (Rivero de la Calle and Núñez Jiménez 1958). As Figure 5.2 reveals, Núñez Jiménez's study of these pictographs (in the Cueva de Pichardo) included drawing or tracing of the images in order to preserve them for future study, a standard procedure for all SEC rock art studies. The image represented in Figure 5.2 has been interpreted as a "large mask, idol, or zemi" of the Taíno peoples of Cuba (Dacal Moure and Rivero de la Calle 1996:47). Ethnohistoric records provide the basis for the interpretation, while the representational style it shares with associated remains in the cave support its cultural attribution (Dacal Moure and Rivero de la Calle 1996:47).

Among the SEC's most distinguished researchers was Manuel Rivero de la Calle (Figure 5.3). Although best known for his expertise as a physical anthropologist, Rivero de la Calle made many important contributions to pictograph research in Cuba. In January 1961, he, along with Núñez Jiménez and Silva Taboada, discovered new pictographs in the Cueva de García Robioú in La Habana province (La Rosa Corzo 1994). Later that same month, he discovered two concentrations of pictographs on Isla de Pinos. One was a group of five red figures conserved in the western part of the island in a rock shelter located in the cliffs of Puerto Francés, near a cave that served as a freshwater source for prehistoric peoples. The other paintings were located in a cave near the city of Nueva Gerona, on the eastern outskirts of the Sierra de Casas, just

5.2. Rolando T. Escardó (*left*) and Antonio Núñez Jiménez studying pictographs painted in red in the Cueva de Pichardo, Sierra de Cubitas. Photograph by Manuel Rivero de la Calle, 1956. Published with permission of Daniel Rivero de la Calle.

north of a house where José Martí once lived. The cave had long been known as the Cueva del Indio, having yielded human remains, the discovery of which was recorded by local officials on May 5, 1911 (Rivero de la Calle 1966).[11] The remains may have been those of indigenous people who had been buried in the cave, but the report does not clarify this view. Rivero de la Calle and Gilberto Silva discovered in this cave a drawing of five concentric circles similar to those recorded at Punta del Este, which extended the distribution of this motif on the island beyond the southern zone (Rivero de la Calle 1966:96).

Of Rivero de la Calle's many contributions to rock art research in Cuba, perhaps the most significant is the discovery that he and Mario Orlando Pariente Pérez made in August 1961 of pictographs in the Cueva de Ambrosio,

5.3. Manuel Rivero de la Calle delivering a speech to the Sociedad Espeleológica de Cuba. Published with permission from Daniel Rivero de la Calle.

on the Hicacos Peninsula, Varadero, Matanzas.[12] With 71 pictographic images, this cave is among the most intensively decorated of all Cuban cave sites, second only to Cueva No. 1, Punta del Este. Although the Cueva de Ambrosio contained no deposits with which to establish a cultural association for the images, Rivero de la Calle included his discussion of these pictographs in a chapter titled "Non-ceramic Groups: Guanahatabeyes and Ciboneys" (Rivero de la Calle 1966:67–99). He clearly favored their attribution to preceramic peoples of Cuba, although he also suggested that some may be associated with Arawakan (i.e., Taíno) creation myths about the sun and the sea (Rivero de la Calle 1966:96). While the presence of the concentric circles motif led him to relate these pictographs to images in the Punta del Este site, he also noted that some of the images in the Cueva de Ambrosio were stylistically distinct from any others known for the island (Rivero de la Calle 1966:98).

It has been suggested that during the first two decades following the Revolution "most Cuban archaeologists studiously avoided the cultural 'superstructure' altogether" (Davis 1996:179). However, publications by Cuban rock art researchers generally do not confirm this statement. Rivero de la Calle's 1966 publication, for example, provides a historic overview of research on the island that devotes considerable attention not only to rock art but also to other artifacts that potentially reflect mythic, religious, and artistic expressions of prehistoric peoples. Publications by Núñez Jiménez during this period (e.g. Núñez Jiménez 1967, 1975) also include observations on the symbolic importance of rock art found in caves in the Cuban archipelago. Also during this time, Guarch Delmonte focused attention on a variety of prehistoric manifestations of the "superstructure" (Guarch Delmonte 1972, 1973, 1974). Among them are petroglyphs, which he specifically describes as "symbolic artifacts of ritual use" (1973:9). Consistent with Harrington (1921) and Rouse (1942), Guarch Delmonte also refers to their cave locations as "ceremonial" sites (1972:49–50).

The history of the SEC reveals that the society never wavered in its efforts to accomplish its goals. Sponsored trips, celebrations of discovery, the promotion of a museum and library, and the publication of a magazine were all designed to cultivate and promote "speleological science and its natural relationship with geography" (Núñez Jiménez 1990:10). As always, the goals of the organization included efforts to understand not only the physical locations of rock art, but also the social context of its production.

In 1975, Núñez Jiménez marked the thirty-fifth anniversary of the SEC with the publication of his monograph *Cuba: Dibujos Rupestres,* widely recognized as a landmark achievement in Cuban rock art research (Dacal Moure and Rivero de la Calle 1986; Guarch Delmonte 1987; La Rosa Corzo 1994). The volume summarizes much of the research carried out by members of the organization, which included the discovery and investigations of more than 750 rock art images located in caves of the Cuban archipelago (Núñez Jiménez 1975). Table 5.1 reproduces his summary (1975:504–507) of the primary rock art data collected by SEC researchers.[13] Among the data presented are principal motifs, which include geometric or abstract images, anthropomorphs, zoomorphs, and a wide variety of depictions of objects (these based primarily on iconographic interpretations). For each site, the table also includes available data on rock art technique, color, associated artifacts, burials, distance from the sea, culture, and age. Although researchers (Núñez Jiménez among them) would subsequently augment the available data for rock art in the archipelago, the 1975 data set (Table 5.1) continues to provide the foundation for others who have attempted to analyze cave art images in Cuba.[14]

Table 5.1 Table of Cuban Rock Art. Note: Data translated from Núñez Jiménez (1975), cave numbers added by author.

#	CAVE	TECHNIQUE	COLOR	NO.	PRINCIPAL MOTIFS	ASSOCIATED ARTIFACTS	HUMAN BURIALS	DISTANCE FROM SEA	CULTURE	DATE
1.	No. 1 Punta del Este	Pictograph	"Red, Black"	213	"Circles, cruci-forms"	"Shell gouges, plates, and hammers"	√	≤1 km	Guayabo Blanco	1100 BP
2.	No. 2 Punta del Este	Pictograph	"Red, Black"	10	"Circles, anthro-pomorhs, serpent forms"	"Shell gouges, plates, and hammers"	√	≤1 km	Guayabo Blanco	1100 BP
3.	No. 3 Punta del Este	Pictograph	"Red, Black"	11	Circles	"Shell gouges, plates, and hammers"		≤1 km	Guayabo Blanco	1100 BP
4.	No. 4 Punta del Este	Pictograph	Red	1	Cruciforms	"Shell gouges, plates, and hammers"	√	≤1 km	Guayabo Blanco	1100 BP
5.	De Lázaro	Pictograph	Red	1	Circle			≤1 km	Guayabo Blanco	1100 BP
6.	De Finlay	Pictograph	"Red, Black"	14	Circles			≤1 km	Guayabo Blanco	1100 BP
7.	Solapa No. 2 de Caleta Grande	Pictograph	Black	1	Circles			≤1 km	Guayabo Blanco	1100 BP
8.	Solapa No. 3 de Caleta Grande	Pictograph	Red	2	Circles			≤1 km	Guayabo Blanco	1100 BP
9.	De los Alemanes	Pictograph	Black	1	Circles			≤1 km	Guayabo Blanco	1100 BP
10.	Solapa No. 1 de Puerto Francés	Pictograph	Red	5	Circles			≤1 km	Guayabo Blanco	1100 BP

11.	Del Indio	Pictograph	Red	2	Circles		√	4 km	Guayabo Blanco	1100 BP
12.	De la Pintura	Petroglyph		1	Anthropomorph	"Shell gouges, plates, and hammers"		2 km	Guayabo Blanco	
13.	De Mesa de la Gran Caverna de Santo Tomás	Incision		27	"Anthropomorph, zoomorphs, geometric forms"	"Shell plates & picks, chert"	√	22 km	Guayabo Blanco	
14.	Del Garrafón	Pictograph	White		Net-forms			15 km		
15.	De los Matojos	Pictograph	Black	8	"Anthropomorphs, zoomorphs, circles"			18 km		
16.	Del Toro	Pictograph	Black	8	"Anthropomorphs, zoomorphs"			18 km		
17.	Del Aguacate	Pictograph	Black	11	"Anthropomorphs, zoomorphs"			18 km		
18.	De la Jía	Pictograph	Black	1	Net-forms			18 km		
19.	De los Muertos	Pictograph	Black	13	"Circles, net-forms"			18 km		
20.	De Paredones	Petroglyph		4	Anthropomorphs	Shell gouge		18 km		
21.	De los Idolos	Petroglyph		1				11 km		
22.	De la Virgen	"Pictograph, Scratch"	"Red, Black"	13	"Anthropomorph, zoomorphs, "X-rays", hands"		√	≤1 km		
23.	De las Cinco Cuevas	"Pictograph, Scratch"	Black	5	"Cruciforms, circles"	Shell gouges & plates		2 km	Guayabo Blanco	
24.	De García Robiou	"Pictograph, Natural sculpture"	"Red, Black"	19	"Anthropomorph, zoomorphs, "X-rays", geometric forms"			25 km	"Ciboney, etc."	

#	CAVE	TECHNIQUE	COLOR	NO.	PRINCIPAL MOTIFS	ASSOCIATED ARTIFACTS	HUMAN BURIALS	DISTANCE FROM SEA	CULTURE	DATE
25.	Pequeña de Diago	Pictograph	Black		Anthropomorphs			25 km	Ciboney	
26.	De la Ayúa	Pictograph	Red	5	Horseshoe forms			25 km	Ciboney	
27.	De la Pluma	Pictograph	"Red, Black"	23	"Banner forms, horseshoe forms, sun"	"Hammerstone, Shell vessel"		2.8 km	Ciboney	
28.	De Simpson	Pictograph	Black	1	Geometric forms	"Gubias, plates, hammers, etc."	√	≤1 km	"Guayabo Blanco, etc."	
29.	De Ambrosio	Pictograph	Red	71	"Circles, labyrinths, geometric forms, anthropomorphs, spectacle forms"			≤1 km		
30.	De Colón	Pictograph	"Black, Red"	5	"Net-form, tri-angle"			≤1 km	Cayo Redondo	
31.	De las Conchas	Pictograph	Black	27	"Zig-zag, castle form"	Shell	√	≤1 km	Cayo Redondo	
32.	De Ramos	"Pictograph, incision"	Black	71	"Leaf-forms, an-thropomorph, spectacle form, zoomorph, castle form, geometric forms"			≤1 km	Cayo Redondo	
33.	Del Lago	Pictograph	Black	1				≤1 km		
34.	De los Chivos	Pictograph	Black	2	"Dagger-forms, net-forms"			≤1 km	Cayo Redondo	

35.	Del Pirata	Pictograph	"Black, Red"	15				≤1 km	Cayo Redondo	
36.	De los Dibujos	Pictograph	Black	17	Zoomorphs			2 km	Cayo Redondo	
37.	De los Generales	Pictograph	"Black, Red"	36	Leaf-form	Ceramics	√	14 km	Ciboney	400 BP
38.	De Matías	Pictograph	"Black, Red"	31	"Anthropomorphs, zoomorphs"			30 km	"Ciboney, etc."	[≤]4000 BP
39.	De las Mercedes	Pictograph	Black	26	"Anthropomorphs, triangles, hands"			30 km	Ciboney	
40.	De María Teresa	Pictograph	Red	39	Zoomorphs			24 km	Ciboney	
41.	De Pichardo	Pictograph	Red	2	Anthropomorphs	Ceramics		26 km	Ciboney	
42.	De Waldo Mesa	Pictograph		1	Anthropomorph	Ceramics	√		Ciboney	
43.	Del Jobo	Pictograph		2	Anthropomorphs	Ceramics	√		Ciboney	
44.	De los Cañones (Seboruco)	Pictograph	Red			Chert	√	9 km	Seboruco	5000 BP
45.	De los Bichos (La Patana)	"Petroglyph, natural sculp-ture"		5	"Anthropomorphs, zoomorphs"	Ceramics		≤1 km	Taíno	600 BP
46.	Del Jaguey (La Patana)	Petroglyph		2	Zoomorphs			≤1 km	Taíno	600 BP

DISTRIBUTION OF ROCK ART SITES

In his 1975 monograph, Núñez Jiménez identifies five primary pictographic regions in the Cuban archipelago. These areas—Isla de Pinos (Isla de la Juventud), Guara, La Habana–Matanzas, Caguanes, and Sierra de Cubitas—are indicated on the geopolitical map in Figure 5.4. Other areas designated on the map contain sites with pictographic or petroglyphic images, or both, featured by Núñez Jiménez in 1985, in his trilingual publication, *Arte Rupestre de Cuba.* In a more recent publication, *Medio siglo explorando a Cuba,* Núñez Jiménez (1990) adds two of these, the Sierra de los Organos in Pinar del Río province and Mayarí in Holguín, along with the original five designated areas as "principal pictographic regions or locations."

In 1991, Escobar Guío and Guarch Rodríguez proposed the designation of a new area of rock art, which they called "Banes-Mayarí." Variations in design and technique of rock art discovered in this area have more recently prompted Guarch Rodríguez and Guarch Rodríguez (1999) to divide this area into two distinct regions which they named "Antilla-Mayarí" and "Báguano-Banes."

Unlike pictographs, petroglyphs are known primarily in sites in the extreme eastern provinces, in the area formerly known as Oriente province (now subdivided into several provinces, including Santiago de Cuba and Guatánamo). However, some examples (now destroyed) had also been recorded for the Cueva de Paredones, in La Habana province (Núñez Jiménez 1990). In addition, a few petroglyphs have been located in the westernmost province, Pinar del Río. In both style and technique these differ from petroglyphs in eastern Cuba. For example, in the Caverna de Santo Tomás in the Sierra de los Organos region, stylized images are incised into soft, claylike rock.

THE SPATIAL VARIABLE

By applying the data provided by Núñez Jiménez (1975) to an analysis of the spatial distribution of pictographic art images throughout Cuba, José Guarch Delmonte (1987) contributed to ongoing efforts by Cuban researchers to refine the spatial distribution of early rock art producers. Based in part on prior research (Guarch Delmonte and Rodríguez Cullel 1980), he distinguished between motifs (elements) and designs (motif combinations), then identified 208 designs for pictographs in 35 of the caves recorded by Núñez Jiménez (1975). These designs he deemed useful for stylistic comparisons with other prehistoric artifacts. He then evaluated their frequency. While eight of the

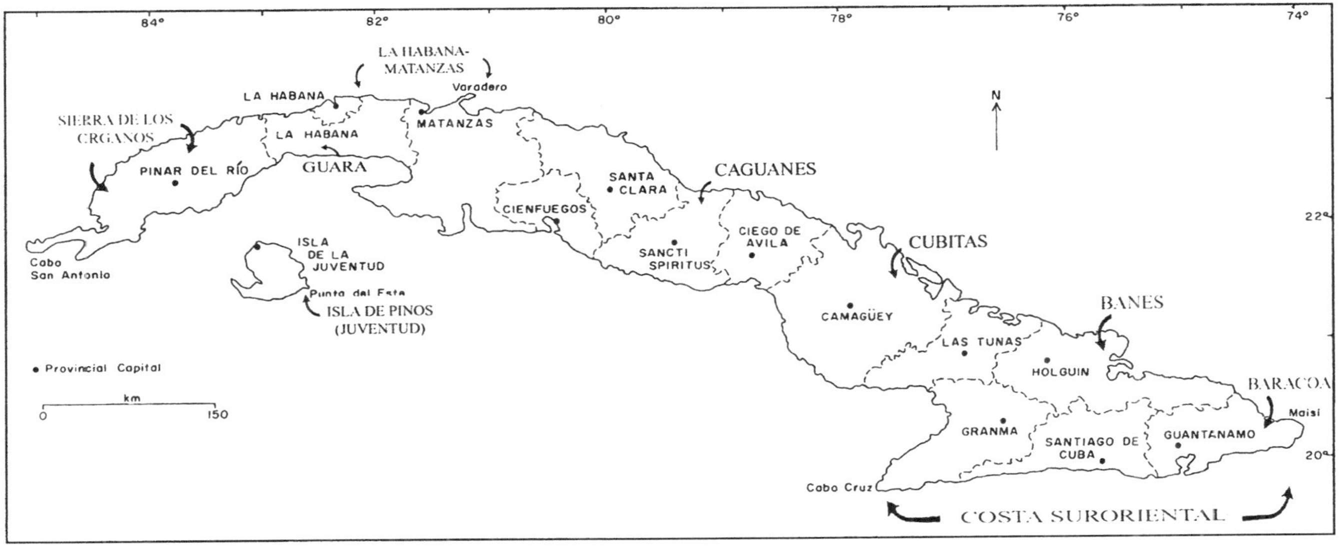

5.4. Geopolitical map of Cuba indicating Rock Art zones. Map modified after Dacal Moure and Rivero de la Calle (1996:2) and Núñez Jiménez (1985:2–3).

caves contained just one design, one cave, the Cueva de García Robiou, contained 22. It is located in La Habana-Matanzas, which Guarch Delmonte identified as the pictograph zone containing the largest number of different design types (84). By contrast, he determined that with just 22 designs, the Guara region contained the fewest (Guarch Delmonte 1987:69).

Guarch Delmonte also produced similarity matrices that revealed parallels between pictograph zones. When these recorded the distribution of individual motifs, rock art regions were related, in order of decreasing similarity, as follows: Habana-Matanzas, Cubitas, Caguanes, Isla de la Juventud, and Guara, such that pictographs in Habana-Matanzas, for example, are most similar to those in Cubitas, and least similar to those in Guara (Guarch Delmonte 1987:87). When images were considered in terms of their designs, the similarities between regions again revealed the closest association between Habana-Matanzas and Cubitas. However, according to these criteria, the relationship between Habana-Matanzas and Guara was closer than that between Guara and Cubitas (Guarch Delmonte 1987:88).

CULTURAL CHRONOLOGY AND ATTRIBUTION

In areas all over the world, rock art challenges archaeological thought on a number of levels, not the least of which are issues of chronology and cultural attribution (Whitley 2001:14). In Cuba, these issues are further complicated by insufficient access to radiocarbon dating (Davis 1996) and by changing approaches to the general prehistoric cultural chronology for the archipelago. While archaeological interpretation is, by its very nature, provisional and therefore subject to continuous revisions, the general lack of Cuban–North American archaeological interchange over the past few decades has been particularly problematic for Cuban researchers attempting to reconcile prerevolutionary models (including those developed by North Americans) with mounting contradictory archaeological data. Table 5.2, which is extracted from the comprehensive Cuadro de los Grupos Culturales Aborigines table by Rivero de la Calle (1966:64–65),[15] reveals one such attempt to reconcile these disparate early models.

Over time, archaeological data, including the time depth provided by radiocarbon dating and evidence from multicomponent sites, have contributed to a complex culture sequence for prehistoric groups in Cuba, one that does not comport well with the dominant, complex area chronology developed outside the archipelago (Rouse 1992). For example, most Cuban archae-

Table 5.2. Table of Early Terminological Equivalents in Indocuban Research. Note: Data from Rivero de la Calle (1966), modified from Pichardo Moya (1956).

CULTURAL GROUP	ARCHAEOLOGICAL IDENTIFICATION	ARCHAEOLOGICAL DISTRIBUTION	HISTORICAL DISTRIBUTION	EQUIVALENT NAMES USED BY ARCHAEOLOGISTS
Guanahatabey (Non-ceramicist)	Habitation sites principally found in Cave and rock shelters. Crude stone objects.	Entire island, but principally on the north coast of Pinar del Río and La Habana. Type site: Guayabo Blanco, Cienaga de Zapata.	Extreme west of Cuba.	Ciboney: Harrington; Ciboney, Guayabo Blanco: Rouse; Aunabey: F. Ortiz; Complex I, Mesa Redonda de Arqueólogos del Caribe.
Ciboney (Non-ceramicist)	Located on the coasts and cays and also in mountainous regions. Symmetrical ceremonial stone objects. Use of lithic flakes and knives and mineral pigments.	Entire island, but principally on the south coast of La Habana, Las Villas and Camagüey, including the Gulf of Guacanayabo in Oriente province. Type site: Cayo Redondo, Pinar del Río	Cays in the south of Camagüey and in other areas of the island.	Ciboney: Harrington; Ciboney Cayo Redondo: Rouse; Guanajatabey: F. Ortiz; Complex II; Mesa Redonda de Arqueólogos del Caribe.
Taíno (Ceramicist)	Located in towns. Bohíos and ceremonial plazas (bateyes). Worked and polished stone. Petaloid hachas, idols and objects of unknown use. Wooden dujos. Knowledge of agriculture. Simple and ornamental ceramics. Griddles.	In the Oriente, Camagüey, part of Las Villas and Matanzas provinces. Classic sites: Pueblo Viejo and the areas of Holguín and Banes.	Cuba and the rest of the Major Antilles and Bahamas	Taínos: Harrington; Taínos and Subtaínos, with distinctive cultural aspects: Rouse; Siboneyes, pre-Taínos and Taínos: F. Ortiz; Complex III: Mesa Redonda de Arqueólogos del Caribe; primitive Ciboneyes: Herrera Fritot.

ologists do not generally recognize the Ciboney as "a local group of Western Taínos in central Cuba" (Alegría 1981:4–9; Rouse 1992). Instead, the data presented by Rivero de la Calle in 1966 provide the historical context that explains the enduring use of the term *Ciboney* to designate Archaic groups that predate Taíno-related peoples in Cuba (Dacal Moure and Rivero de la Calle 1996:10; Núñez Jiménez 1975). This was the definition used by North American archaeologists (Harrington 1921; Osgood 1942; Rouse 1942) whose work continues to be influential in Cuban archaeological research, including efforts to place rock art in its cultural context.

It should be noted that, unlike the 1975 monograph, later publications by Núñez Jiménez (1985, 1990) eschew specific cultural attributions for rock art images in favor of general terms, such as preagriculturalists (*preagroalfarera,* literally "preagroceramist"), agriculturalists (*agroalfarera,* literally "agroceramist"), and others. While this may reflect a general materialist classification of prehistoric cultures in Cuba based on economic stages (Tabío and Rey 1979; Davis 1996), the belated introduction of these terms into Cuban rock art research may also be read as another attempt to reconcile the significant disparities in terminology and cultural sequences developing in Caribbean archaeology (Rouse 1942; Tabío and Rey 1979; Veloz Maggiolo 1976–1977). In 1994, subsequent to publications by other Caribbean archaeologists who incorporate the more specific culture terms, such as *Taíno* (Rouse 1992; Veloz Maggiolo 1991, 1993), Núñez Jiménez (1994) reintroduced these familiar terms into his own work.

It is clear from the research conducted by Núñez Jiménez and others that, to some extent, differences in techniques used in rock art production signal cultural distinctions. For example, petroglyphs are typically associated with Taíno-related agriculturalists (based on artistic style and proximity to cultural remains) and interpreted in terms of Taíno mythology. Historically, such inferences have been supported not only by the distribution of rock art types, with petroglyphs appearing predominantly in the eastern regions associated with prehistoric agriculturalist migrations, but also by ethnohistoric accounts.

Attributions for pictographs are, perhaps, more problematic. The subjects represented in a few of the pictographs clearly support their attribution to the historic period.[16] However, at least 90 percent of all Cuban pictographs have been attributed to preagricultural inhabitants (Dacal Moure and Rivero de la Calle 1996:36).[17] As Dacal Moure and Rivero de la Calle explain, cultural attribution of Cuban pictographs depends either on stylistic similarities between the motifs depicted and other known cultural artifacts or on the proximity of the images to archaeological deposits.

In some cases, multiple lines of evidence may suggest a cultural affiliation. For example, the cultural context for the production of the pictographs of the Cueva No. 1, Punta del Este site, was ultimately established when Ramón Dacal Moure recovered from the cave stone bowls (a type of artifact associated with the early, nonagricultural inhabitants) that retained pigment residues consistent with those used in the production of the pictographs on the cave walls. From this evidence, researchers infer that preceramic, preagricultural people(s) created the images found on the walls of the cave (Dacal Moure and Rivero de la Calle 1996:36). Elements of style and spatial proximity have helped to establish the cultural relationship between this cave and Cueva No. 4 from the same area. In turn, dates provided by radiometric analysis of bone collagen recovered from human burials excavated in Cueva No. 4 suggest that the Punta del Este caves date to 1100 ± 130 B.P. (L-CH-1106) (Tabío and Rey 1979:209). Of the 16 sites in Table 5.1 that are associated with absolute dates, 12 (75 percent) are pictographic sites located on Isla de Pinos (Núñez Jiménez 1975:507). For each of these 12, either the pictographs or associated cultural remains found at the site were deemed consistent with those recovered from the Cueva No. 4 site.

The general dates provided for two petroglyphic sites listed in Table 5.1 are inferred estimates based on historical documents, iconographic and stylistic analyses, and a radiocarbon date obtained in 1964 (Guarch Delmonte 1978:127) for the Laguna de los Limones habitation site, located in Baracoa, Guantánamo, in an area concentrated with sites identified as Taíno (Harrington 1921; Núñez Jiménez 1975:507). A charcoal sample obtained at the site from a hearth closely associated with Taíno cultural remains was analyzed at the Smithsonian Institution (SI-348), providing a radiocarbon date of 640 ± 120 B.P. (Tabío and Rey 1979:211).

Although it has been suggested that neither relative dating nor stylistic seriation have been emphasized in Cuba (Davis 1996:176), according to Guarch Delmonte (1987), elements of style have dominated attempts to identify rock art with distinct culture groups. The fact that many rock art sites in Cuba lack associated archaeological remains has been a contributing factor. Research in the Camagüey province helps to explain this reliance. Of the 300 caves and caverns located in the Sierra de Cubitas area, six have pictographs (El Indio, located in the western zone, Matías, Las Mercedes, María Teresa, and Pichardo in the southeastern zone, and Los Generales in the northeastern area) (Calvera et al. 1991). Researchers attempted to provide cultural associations for the rock art images in these caves through a systematic investigation of the surrounding areas. However, despite extensive survey of the southeastern area of Cubitas, and excavations in the pictograph-bearing caves in Camagüey province, no evidence of permanent settlement that could be firmly associated with these caves was identified (Calvera et al. 1991).

La Rosa Corzo (1994) suggests that analyses such as that completed by Guarch Delmonte (1987) could advance further by including other variables, such as style, technique, color, material, and perhaps aesthetic concepts together with an analysis of motifs and designs. Data on these variables may also inform efforts to analyze complex images in the caves, sites that researchers acknowledge must have been frequented by a variety of peoples, not only throughout the archipelago's prehistory but also during the past five centuries. AMS dating has assisted archaeologists in other areas of the world in their efforts both to establish chronology and to develop a better understanding of the sequences involved in the production of complex images. Without ready access to this technique, rock art researchers in Cuba have, by necessity, relied on more conventional methods. However, as both Guarch Delmonte (1987) and La Rosa Corzo (1994) suggest, the use of such methods, particularly in attempts to identify any diachronic variability, has not generally yielded satisfactory results.

MAKING INFERENCES

What is its purpose? What does it mean? These are basic questions that pervade considerations of prehistoric rock art wherever it is found. In their efforts to understand the meaning in and function of the images, researchers who have interpreted Cuban rock art have considered theories developed in Europe to explain Upper Paleolithic Art. The theories range from the early "art for art's sake" model to Abbé Breuil's "sympathetic hunting magic" theory, so colorfully characterized by Gould as the "if you draw it, it will come" hypothesis (1996:22). For example, despite the paucity of large terrestrial prey, pictographs in the Cueva de los Matojos in Guara, La Havana province, have been interpreted as a hunting scene with a quadruped (Núñez Jiménez 1975).

Although Structuralist theory has not been widely influential within Cuban rock art research, the general idea that caves were systematically decorated to reflect symbolic meaning (rather than painted or engraved at random), advanced in the 1960s by French archaeologist André Leroi-Gourhan, director of the Musée de l'Homme in Paris, has been somewhat more influential in interpretations advanced in Cuba (Nuñez Jiménez 1975; Guarch Delmonte 1978). However, this apparent influence may also be understood as coincidental, since the interpretations of Harrington (1921), Herrera Fritot (1939), Ortiz (1922b, 1935, 1943), and Rouse (1942), advanced decades earlier, are consistent with a symbolic reading of cave art. For these early researchers, the symbolic meaning was religious in nature, related either to petroglyphic "Zemis" (Guarch Delmonte 1973, 1978; Harrington 1921; Rouse 1942) or, in the case of the Cueva No. 1, Punta del Este site, to an "astrological religion" (Ortiz 1922b), the computation of a lunar month by prehistoric artists-priests (Ortiz 1943), or a "solar cult" (Herrera Fritot 1939).

The 1987 study by Guarch Delmonte identified another potential meaning for Cuban pictographs. He found that while three pictographic zones contained motifs unique to the respective region, most motifs were not confined to a single area. This finding led to the conclusion that motifs are generally distributed across the archipelago. From this distribution and correlation of pictographic motifs and designs, Guarch Delmonte (1987:88) inferred that the images could be understood as part of an incipient ideography, one which had not attained sufficient regularity or structure to be considered an ideographic text. Yet he also suggested that both preagricultural and agricultural peoples may have made use of this kind of rock art expression (1987:89). He also acknowledged (1987) that his analysis did not consider a historical origin for some of the pictographic images (La Rosa Corzo 1994). Both of these factors complicate the findings of his study.

While a cave context for most rock art sites in Cuba may provide some support for efforts to advance interpretations to an indexical level (Deacon 1997), higher levels of interpretation are currently more scientifically palatable in Cuba (as elsewhere) when they rest on ethnohistoric evidence. For example, interpretations advanced for a number of rock art images (Fernández Ortega and González Tendero 2000, 2001a; Harrington 1921; Núñez Jiménez 1975) have been supported by the ethnohistorically documented importance of caves in Taíno cosmology. Pané's study (1984) of mythology among the contact peoples of Hispaniola has been particularly influential in these interpretations (Dacal Moure and Rivero de la Calle 1996; Nuñez Jiménez 1975, 1985; Rivero de la Calle 1966).[18] More recent works that incorporate Pané's findings (Arrom 1975) and those of other early chroniclers (e.g., Las Casas 1951, Martyr 1944 [1530]) have also contributed to the analyses of many rock art images and stone "idols" found in caves (Guarch Delmonte 1972, 1973, 1974; Guarch Delmonte and Querejeta Barceló 1992; Núñez Jiménez 1975, 1985).

CURRENT TRENDS IN ROCK ART RESEARCH

In recent years, Cuban archaeologists have begun to reevaluate past approaches to rock art research in the archipelago. La Rosa Corzo (1994) cites, among other shortcomings of early research, the abuse of descriptive analysis and the establishment of parallelisms based on simple aspects of morphology. Yet he notes that after a long period of emphasis on the discovery, registration, and description of rock art sites, Cuban scholars are questioning the conventional style-based methods used to place rock art in the chronology of prehistoric occupation of the Cuban archipelago. Indeed, they have begun to look for other methods with which to evaluate the "enigmatic drawings" that have been so painstakingly recorded throughout the country (La Rosa Corzo 1994).

This does not mean that stylistic analyses no longer play a role in evaluations of rock art in Cuba. On the contrary, considerations of style remain integral to such studies, which increasingly also include technical and stylistic analyses of mobiliary art (Dacal Moure and Rivero de la Calle 1996; Núñez Jiménez 1985, 1990).[19] Cuban researchers are combining these analyses with other factors in their efforts to infer meaning, as well as to identify the cultural context of the production of rock art in Cuba.

Some Cuban researchers have focused on the correlation between an image's style, technique, and content and its physical context (location within the cave or geographical distribution). For example, Izquierdo Díaz and Rives Pantoja suggest that both abstract and geometric images are associated with coastal sites, while figurative images occur predominantly in interior regions. They also associate the color black with closed caverns and the color red with those that are somewhat open (Izquierdo and Rives 1990).

Despite these efforts, some current foci of rock art research have not yet taken root in Cuban scholarship, such as gender-based analyses, ethnographic analogy (including hallucinogenically induced altered states of consciousness), and AMS dating.[20] However, other approaches, identified as "emerging trends" (Ross 2001:543) have long been integral to research efforts of Cuban archaeologists. Among them are the emphasis on the context of rock art images, or "rockscape" (Ross 2001:545), which requires that images be interpreted in the context in which they were produced, and the necessity of understanding the rock images within the context of landscape. In other words, it requires an understanding of "how people 'know their country'" (Ross 2001:546). As the brief overview of the efforts of Nuñez Jiménez and his colleagues in the SEC suggests, Cuban researchers are in the forefront in these areas of research.

HERITAGE AND CONSERVATION

The destruction of archaeological sites is a worldwide problem. For rock art sites, which are typically located in remote areas, the problem is particularly acute. Without the concerted efforts of archaeologists and the cooperation of the general public, "graffiti" and other destructive acts threaten to obliterate any traces of the images that have survived these many years. It should come as no surprise that for many decades it was Núñez Jiménez who spearheaded efforts in Cuba to conserve the nation's rock art heritage. These efforts have been most intense for pictographs located in caves of Punta del Este and for the drawings of the Cueva de Ambrosio. A comparison of early photographs taken at each of these caves with more modern examples clearly reveals the extent of the restoration efforts at each site (cf. Rivero de la Calle 1966 and Núñez Jiménez 1985). José Alonso Lorea (2001) has effectively demonstrated, for example, that restoration efforts in 1969 significantly altered the pictographs of Cueva No. 1, Punta del Este, rendering many of these images inappropriate for many types of scientific analyses, including stylistic, chronometric (either relative or absolute methods), and materials analysis. Yet, considered in both their historical and social contexts, such efforts reveal a sincere desire on the part of Cuban researchers to preserve the artistic legacy of early Cuban peoples for posterity.

In recent years, North American archaeologists have made concerted efforts to present the study of the past to a wider audience. Such public outreach efforts have been an integral part of the SEC from its inception. Reports of cave research that include rock art have routinely been published in the popular press. These have often also been reprinted in publications that celebrate at regular intervals the accomplishments of the organization (Núñez Jiménez 1961, 1980, 1990). The group has also sought to establish interchange, maintain relationships, and celebrate cooperation and friendship with not only similar institutions from other countries but also the Cuban people. For example, during the celebration of the thirtieth anniversary of the SEC, the organization honored the many Cubans who had over the years served as local guides for cave investigations throughout the country (Núñez Jiménez 1990).

It is fortunate that in Cuba the sense of national pride, or *patria,* that has been identified in publications on Cuban archaeology (Davis 1996) extends to the general population. Indeed, the Cuban people broadly support the efforts of the Fundación de la Naturaleza y el Hombre, established by Núñez Jiménez, to continue to achieve the goals defined long ago by the young founders of the SEC. Among them is the conservation and celebration of the nation's cultural patrimony located in caves.

CONCLUSION

For more than half a century, researchers throughout Cuba have participated in interdisciplinary research efforts that have contributed to the steady accumulation of knowledge of Cuba's caves and rock shelters. Among them are archaeologists and physical anthropologists who have meticulously recorded contextual data for the cultural expressions found on rock walls. Together, they continue to update and refine the considerable data that provided the basis for the 1975 publication by Núñez Jiménez, *Cuba: Dibujos rupestres,* which, after more than a quarter of a century, remains the most comprehensive assessment of Cuban rock art sites ever published (La Rosa Corzo 1994). As new theories emerge to guide rock art research, the substantial contributions to our knowledge of Cuban rock art by Núñez Jiménez, Rivero de la Calle, Dacal Moure, and other members of the SEC will continue to provide the foundation for future efforts to understand not only the images painted onto, incised into, or sculpted out of stone but also the cultural context of those who left these enduring transformations on the Cuban landscape.

ACKNOWLEDGMENTS

With fond memories and an enormous sense of gratitude, I dedicate this work to my friend and colleague, the late Dr. Manuel Rivero de la Calle, whose humanity, academic generosity and sense of humor I will never forget. In addition to sharing his extensive knowledge of Cuban archaeology, Dr. Rivero also introduced me to his longtime friend and colleague, the late Ramón Dacal Moure, whose friendship and incalculable efforts on my behalf are deeply appreciated. I also wish to express my gratitude to Dr. Rivero's wonderful family, especially Daniel Rivero and Gisela Ibarra, for providing me a home away from home in Havana, as well as sources used in this work. Among those who facilitated my research in Cuba, I must acknowledge Alejandro Alonso and Marta Arjona, who arranged my visit to the Fundación de la Naturaleza y el Hombre, the faculty of the CUNY Graduate Center, and, especially, Reynold C. Kerr, whose many contributions to my work include the preparation of the figures for this chapter. I also thank my editors, Shannon Dawdy, who invited me to participate in the SAA forum, and her co-organizer, Gabino La Rosa Corzo, who shared his expertise on rock art in Cuba and also provided me with valued resource materials. I am particularly grateful to their coeditor for this volume, L. Antonio Curet, for his insightful comments on early versions of the text and for gently nudging me toward its completion. Thanks are due also to José Oliver for his comprehensive review and helpful suggestions.

AUTHOR'S NOTE

Translations from Spanish are by the author.

NOTES

1. Greer defines the "dark zone" as the area of a cave "where observation [of the rock art] is possible only with artificial light." He defines two other zones, the "entrance zone," where rock art may be viewed in broad daylight, and the "twilight zone," where rock art may be viewed with "limited indirect light" (Greer 2001:677).

2. Guarch Delmonte and Rodríguez Cullel (1980:55) record the use of iron oxides (hematite) to produce a range of colors, from orange to the most intense reds.

3. In 1914 Theodoor de Booy, also of the Museum of the American Indian, Heye Foundation, explored the eastern tip of Cuba. His findings, together with the encouragement of Dr. Luis Montané, of the University of Havana, prompted the museum to sponsor further investigations in the area (Harrington 1921:22).

4. This work may have prompted Ortiz to revisit Lane's discovery at Punta del Este.

5. He also extracted a portion of one of the pictographs for study in the Museo Antropológico Montané (Herrera Fritot 1939:17).

6. The image is reproduced in full color in *The Art and Archaeology of Pre-Columbian Cuba* (Dacal Moure and Rivero de la Calle 1996:58).

7. The term *Ciboney* applies here to preceramic, nonagricultural groups in Cuba.

8. See Dubelaar (1995) for a comprehensive update on the petroglyphs of the Lesser Antilles.

9. This debate was further complicated by ideas issuing from other disciplines. For example, the development of modern art, from figurative to abstract, led some researchers to question the capacity of individuals from simple societies to produce the abstract images found in Cueva No. 1. (Guarch Delmonte 1978; La Rosa Corzo 1994).

10. In the interim, other attributions surfaced. For example, Núñez Jiménez suggested that the producers of the images at Punta del Este were neither Taínos, Ciboneys, nor Guanahatabeyes but others who arrived via a sea route from the northern coast of Venezuela (Núñez Jiménez 1948; La Rosa Corzo 1994:141).

11. The original report is conserved in the Museo Antropológico Montané.

12. Pictographs depicting concentric circles and other abstract motifs from Cueva de Ambrosio are pictured in *The Art and Archaeology of Pre-Columbian Cuba* (Dacal Moure and Rivero de la Calle 1996:75, Figures 10 and 11).

13. Among the sites not included are the Cueva de la Victoria site in Matanzas, discovered in 1968 (Núñez Jiménez 1990:341), and three new pictographs located in the Cueva de los Cañones site, Holguín Province, discovered in 1982.

14. Among the many examples are Guarch Delmonte and Rodríguez Cullel (1980), Guarch Delmonte (1987), Dacal Moure and Rivero de la Calle (1986, 1996), and Greer (2001).

15. Two columns have been omitted: one lists the mainland origin for each group as South America; the other provides group-specific cranial data.

16. Disparate motifs in one of these, the Cueva de Matías, have been identified as "Ciboney" and "postcolumbian," respectively (Núñez Jiménez 1975).

17. In the context of this publication, Dacal Moure and Rivero de la Calle use the term *Ciboney* to designate all preagricultural groups in Cuba (1996:10).

18. As L. Antonio Curet suggests (personal communication, 2002), archaeological evidence increasingly reveals significant cultural distinctions between protohistoric Cuban groups and their Taíno counterparts on Hispaniola, which renders problematic the use of Pané's research in interpretive analyses of Cuban rock art.

19. Not only have researchers recognized that several stone idols in museum collections are cave art taken out of context, they also appreciate the research potential of artifacts produced from other classes of materials, including their utility for relative dating.

20. In some areas of the world, researchers use ethnographic analogy to develop interpretations based on shamanic or other trance behaviors. These suggest that complex thought processes may be involved in the production of rock art (Bahn 1996:593). Although an association between rock art sites and the *cohoba* ritual has long been inferred for Taíno sites in Cuba (Núñez Jiménez 1994), perhaps because few ethno-

graphic sources exist for the archipelago, ethnographic analogy has not been a major theme in studies of Cuban rock art. However, there is evidence that Núñez Jiménez considered a shamanic role in the production of pictographs in Cuba. A late-nineteenth-century article by Hoffmann (1888) on pictographic images produced on bark by Ojibwa shamans is included in the bibliography of Núñez Jiménez's seminal work on Cuban rock art (1975).

Part II
Substantive Archaeological Research

6 / Approaches to Early Ceramics in the Caribbean

Between Diversity and Unilineality

Jorge Ulloa Hung

Several centuries before agricultural ceramic groups from South America arrived in the Greater Antilles, some foraging groups in the islands seemed to have developed ceramic technology independently. This chapter presents and analyzes the different opinions, criteria, and hypotheses regarding the development of these earliest pottery-making communities in Cuba from the perspective of a general Caribbean framework. My intention is to introduce the reader to the theoretical and archaeological treatment that this phenomenon has received in the Caribbean, especially in Cuba (Figure 6.1) and Dominican Republic, moving from general ideas to specific examples.

Interest in this topic in Cuban archaeology is heightened by the fact that this phenomenon has only recently been acknowledged in Caribbean archaeology or the Greater Antilles. Yet, as will be seen from my survey of the field, it has received little attention or has been approached using isolated or unilineal criteria. My goal is to discuss the necessity of new and broader perspectives on the topic. We are in need of new studies that focus on intra- and interisland comparisons that allow us to create a more precise picture of the development of agriculture and ceramics. Such an approach will not only clarify the possible origin of these groups and provide useful descriptions of their assemblages but should help us understand socioeconomic dynamics at the regional level.

Against the backdrop of this critical reassessment, results from new research being conducted in eastern Cuba comprise the remainder of this article. The investigations took place between 1996 and 2000 and were organized in

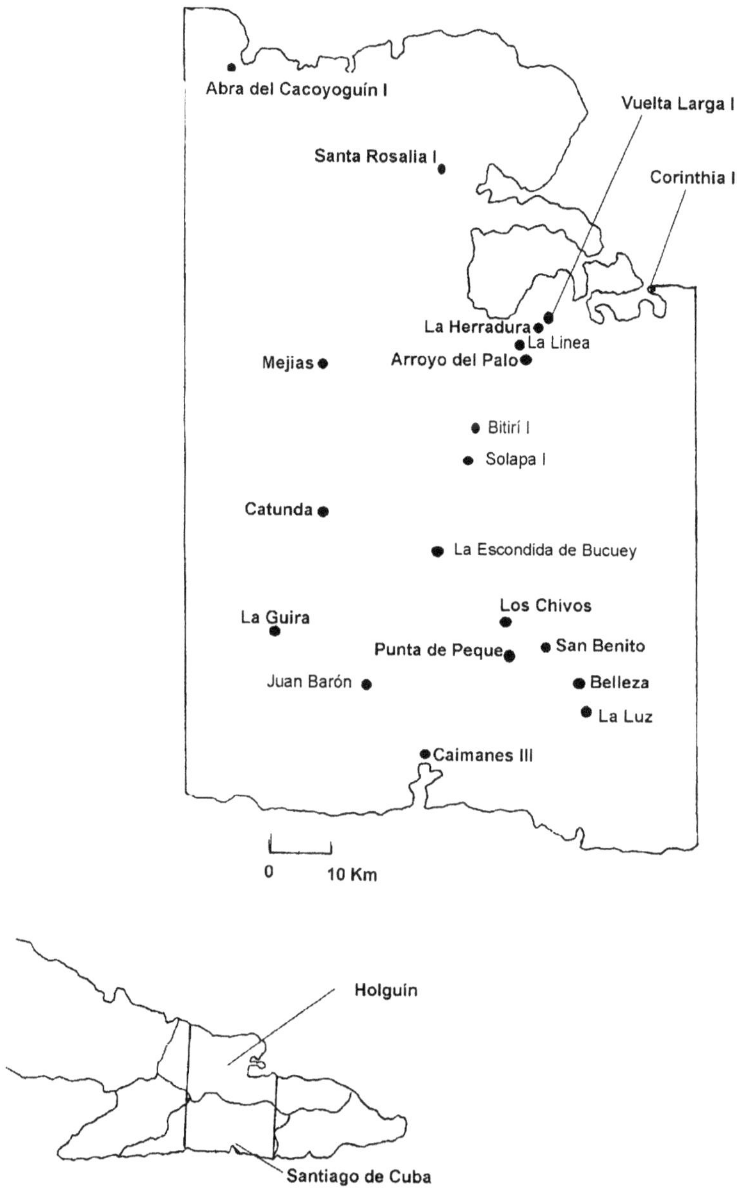

6.1. Map showing the location of many early ceramic sites in eastern Cuba

collaboration with the National Geographic Society in the United States. They were conducted in phases. The first took place between 1996 and 1997 and involved the participation of Cuban and Dominican researchers. The second occurred between 1999 and 2001 and was developed by archaeological research teams from La Casa del Caribe in Santiago de Cuba and the Departamento Centro Oriental de Arqueología del Ministerio de Ciencias, Tecnología y Medioambiente. The first research phase concentrated on the discovery and study of deposits with early ceramics in southeastern Cuba; the second phase intensified studies in this area while also extending the survey to northwestern Cuba. The goal of the second phase was to compose a regional and comparative view of both areas. The final results of these projects are discussed in more detail in a monograph titled *Cerámica temprana en el centro del oriente de Cuba* recently published in Dominican Republic by Jorge Ulloa Hung and Roberto Valcárcel Rojas (2002).

REGIONAL BACKGROUND

Although research on the beginnings of agriculture in the Americas tends to focus on this economic practice as the defining element of the transition into the Neolithic, pottery continues to interest specialists. Ceramics have received a great deal of attention in the archaeology of the hemisphere, justified not only because of the amount of information that this type of evidence provides but also because in many regions climatic conditions affecting preservation mean that scarcely any other type of material is found. Until some decades ago, early ceramics in archaeological contexts in the Americas were interpreted under two alternative views: they could be seen as either intrusive and introduced, or, contrarily, they could become the focus of an analysis that obviated the rest of the contextual information to become a unilineal, defining cultural feature.

Recent evaluations of foraging societies at several sites on the American continent support the possibility that societies with widely variable lifeways utilized pottery. In many cases, it was obtained through exchange. In others, it was manufactured in a systematic manner that expanded the economic and productive possibilities of its makers (Angulo 1992; Hoopes 1994; MacNeish 1992; Politis et al. 2001; Rímoli and Nadal 1983; Scott et al. 1991; Smith 1995; Veloz Maggiolo 1991; Williams 1992). In Caribbean environments rich in fauna, foraging societies in several regions developed a high population density that created conditions for a sedentary or semisedentary life. Fixed or seasonal villages arose, and some cultivated plants were added to the subsistence repertoire. The development of a pottery tradition soon followed.

The Caribbean coast of Colombia is one of those areas where expressions of early pottery have been reported. Shell middens such as Puerto Hormiga (5100–4500 B.P. or 3150–2550 B.C.) and San Jacinto (5900–5200 B.P. or 4000 B.C.) (Angulo 1992; Ford 1969; Scott et al. 1991; Veloz Maggiolo 1991), with dates that go back to 4000 B.C. and the contemporaneous Monsú, seem to demonstrate the first attempts of village life in the region. Their general characteristics suggest a transition from incipient agricultural practices and intensive gathering to a reliance on cultivated tubers such as manioc. This seems to be the case at other Colombian sites, such as Rotinet and Malambo, where the consumption of manioc in the form of cassava became habitual toward 2000 and 1200 B.C., respectively (Angulo 1992). In Guyana, on the other hand, studies on late phases of the archaic groups associated with shell middens (such as Hosororo Creek with a date of 3975 ± 45 B.P. or 2025 B.C.) document how communities with a basic gathering economy developed an undecorated pottery with very simple forms (Williams 1992).

Sites studied in the region of Carúpano in Venezuela (Sanoja 1988; Vargas 1987) provide significant examples of the development reached by the foraging groups from this region of South America. These sites consist of large shell middens with surface ceramics and a mixed economy. The foragers of this area of Venezuela settled coastal areas along the Atlantic and Caribbean coasts, predominantly in areas near mangroves and lagoons in the Gulfs of Paria and Cariaco. Not less important were the settlements around valleys and fluvial basins in inland areas. According to Mario Sanoja and Iraida Vargas, who have classified these populations into three groups according to their historical developments (Sanoja and Vargas 1995), the chronological evidence for these sites from Venezuela ranges from 8000 to 7000 B.P. (6050–5050 B.C.). These assemblages represent contemporaneous and culturally related groups that inhabited similar regions but developed different socioeconomic dynamics. However, any pottery present at these sites has been considered intrusive. The Barrancoid ceramics are assumed to be the earliest ceramics in the Orinoco delta, dating to 2900 B.P. (950 B.C.).

In Venezuela, the pottery of the Camay area has been reevaluated recently (Sanoja 2001). This archaeological area is located at the junction of the Cordillera de los Andes and the Sierra of Baragua, the latter approximately 1,200 km along the Caribbean coast to the Peninsula of Paria. Recent analysis of the collections of decorated ceramics made in 1953 suggests some stylistic similarities with some of the early pottery of the Valdivia phase of Ecuador (Meggers et al. 1965), as well as with the well-known styles of northeastern Venezuela known as Santa Ana and Tocuyano (Sanoja 2001:4). According to Sanoja, the material of Camay exhibits characteristics that correspond to so-called Periods B (4300–4000 B.P. or 2350–2050 B.C.) and C (4000–3400 B.P. or 2050–1450 B.C.) of Valdivia. This suggests a chronological correlation that, if confirmed, would substantially revise the theories of the peopling of the Venezuelan northeast, the Andean region, and Lake Maracaibo, besides shedding light on some of the particularities that characterize the later ceramic styles of the region. This new perspective makes the Venezuelan northeast a nuclear center whose cultural influences would have contributed to shaping the aboriginal societies of much of northeastern South America. The groups of the Camay and Quibor valleys may have begun to develop tribal or neolithic social characteristics in the second millennium B.C. and initiated the transition toward complex hierarchical social forms around the first millennium (Sanoja 2001:17–18; see Arvelo 1995 for a different position on the social developments in this sequence).

In Central America, some shell middens like Monagrillo (4500–3200 B.P. or 2550–1250 B.C.), located in the Gulf of Panama, have evidence of a ceramic industry related to the use and exploitation of nearby resources in the mangrove swamp. The pottery at this site supports the impression that this location was home to an important phase in the dispersion and exchange of ceramic traditions in the Americas. A marked similarity between this first Panamanian pottery and that from sites in Colombia, such as Puerto Hormiga, supports this view (Veloz Maggiolo 1991).[1] To this we have to add the benefits of the marine resources that in some general ways may have influenced the shifts of the first foraging/ceramic groups under similar conditions.

In general, the shell middens with ceramics from Colombia, the coast of Venezuela, Guyana, and Panama may reflect a phase of growth and intensification of foraging lifeways in the continental or riverine Caribbean, characterized by experimentation with some horticultural practices and the manufacturing of wood-working instruments and tools. Assemblages of simple pottery appear to be correlated with an increase in site size and the production of grinding tools. All this seems to be in agreement with the transformations that took place in the economy of foraging societies, in which the consumption of vegetable foods shifted from marginal importance to become a central production process. It is important to keep in mind that in spite of the peculiarities of each site, pottery is an element present at each one. While this does not mean that each group underwent an identical development, the emergence of a ceramic tradition does highlight a significant and complex process that should not be explained using merely diffusionist or chronological approaches.

THE ANTILLES: THE CASES OF CUBA AND DOMINICAN REPUBLIC

The Island of Cuba

Until the 1970s, Caribbean archaeology had focused almost exclusively on the ceramics of farming communities that arrived in the Lesser Antilles around the third century B.C. from northeastern Venezuela. The chronological and spatial outline created by North American archaeologist Irving Rouse and Spanish archaeologist José M. Cruxent (1961) was one of the most comprehensive attempts to consider variations in this type of industry. Their definition of styles and series arising from technical, stylistic, and chronological studies created a model that attempted to explain ceramic transformations through the construction of a phylogenetic tree for the Caribbean Basin based on historic/evolutionary development. However, when this "tree" is studied at a more localized level, local sequences tended to be unilineal. Type sites in the model provided examples from which the rest of the cultural characteristics could be inferred. On occasions, assemblages were forced into a certain style or series without considering other reasons for variation, such as migration by the ceramists or the local development of new pottery traditions.

This schematic research approach affected investigations of foraging communities. The meaning of the term *Ciboney,* coined by the early Spanish chronicles for hunter and gatherer groups and later developed as an archaeological cultural term by the North American investigator Mark R. Harrington (1935), was expanded and divided into two cultural traditions based on the Cuban sites of Cayo Redondo and Guayabo Blanco. Through the anthropological prism of North American historical particularism, the general designation *Ciboney,* combined with the considerations of so-called diagnostic objects, established a supposed and necessary evolution from one aspect to another that spanned several chronological periods that did not include the development of a ceramic tradition. Further, the classification created for Cuban foraging groups was considered a valid model for the rest of the Antilles, and the differences and variations between settlements within the same category were obscured. The few ceramics found in contexts classified as Ciboney were considered atypical, intrusive, unimportant, or, at best, an expression of cultural superimposition by agricultural groups in multicomponent sites. This lineal and obligatory typology that only valued certain types of artifacts and cultural characteristics ignored the possible interactions between different technological and economic traditions or expressions of variability within the foraging lifeway. In this way, the process of transculturation and influential ecological elements that could have either delayed or accelerated many evolutionary processes were not fully evaluated.

The 1960s and 1970s were marked by important trends in the conception of cultural evolution in the Caribbean. Studies carried out at the sites of Arroyo del Palo and Mejías in eastern Cuba began a new stage and a new way of approaching the emergence of pottery in Cuban archaeology. The consideration of these locations—mainly Arroyo del Palo—as expressions of a new culture (Tabío and Guarch 1966) that coexisted with the last expressions of the so-called Ciboney Cayo Redondo and the first of the Subtaíno agricultural groups was driven by an interest in locating a context in which elements characteristic of the foraging lifeway converged with the presence of ceramics. Up to that moment, except for the studies by Felipe Pichardo Moya (1990) and a few others, pottery had been considered one of the fundamental indicators of a culturally advanced Neolithic stage among Cuba's aboriginal communities, without leaving room for *sui generis* expressions of the transitional process.

The consideration of pottery from Mayarí as a marginal expression of the so-called Ostionoid series (Tabío and Guarch 1966:75), with chronology between the ninth and eleventh centuries A.D. (Tabío and Rey 1979), added to doubts about the classification of early ceramicists. The identification of Mayarí as a new culture (Córdova n.d.) spurred examinations of similar archaeological assemblages as expressions of differentiated groups, independent of their archaic associations. The discovery and study of other sites with very simple ceramics and foraging technologies, among them the Aguas Verdes (Febles 1991; Kozlowski 1972), Canímar (Febles 1982), and Playitas (Dacal Moure 1986) sites, added another perspective to the criteria developed from considerations of the so-called Mayarí culture. In this case, the center of attention shifted to the lithic industry whose particularities became the signature used to follow these communities in their treks through the different regions of the island (Figure 6.2). Classifications resulting from the lithic studies served as the basis to support supposed cultural differentiations but also reproduced a unilineal development scheme that had so long been used to describe foraging groups. Approaches to the lithic industry show the direct

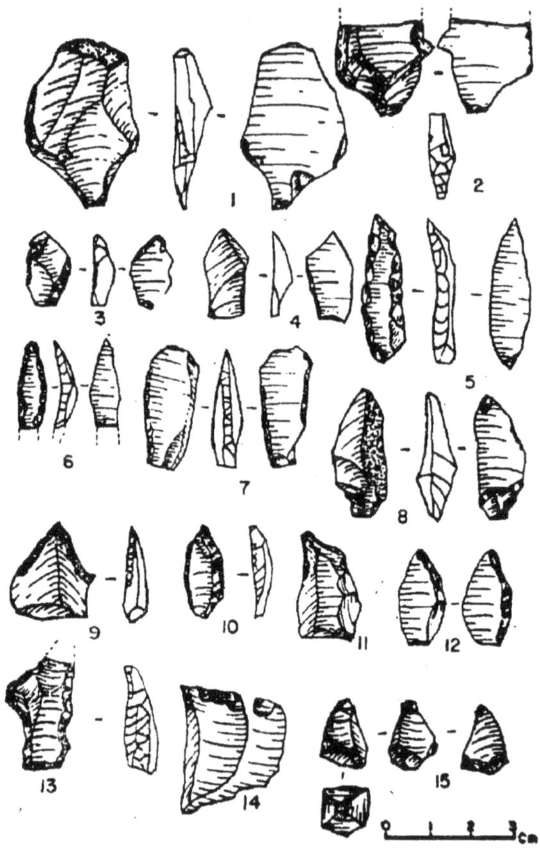

6.2. Flaked stone tools from Canímar I. After Febles 1982.

influence of the Polish archaeologist Januz Kozlowski who, based on a correlation of technological features and the typological compositions of lithic tool assemblages, proposed different industries or industrial cycles including the Canímar–Aguas Verdes complex. This complex had as an essential characteristic a laminated microlithic technique, based on conical or subconical nuclei, with some differences between the type sites of Canímar and Playitas that were attributed to different settlements within the same cultural tradition (Kozlowski 1975).[2] Geographically, this complex was located on the north coast of Cuba, near Matanzas and Havana, as well as in Baracoa in the east. The possible origins of the source material, according to the microliths and their characteristics, were located in two regions of the Americas, the region covered by the Jaketown ceramics in the Mississippi Valley and the area of the Momil I culture, this last an expression of the Formative Period in Colombia.

Kozlowski's interpretations were revised and enlarged later by Cuban archaeologists (Febles 1991) who focused on the observable differences between the Canímar and Aguas Verdes sites and on similarities with lithic production sites in the southeastern United States. Some of these coincidences, with chronological evidence, caused them to suggest a direct migration from the Mississippi Valley to Cuba, mainly to the area of Canímar. The theories of Kozlowski (1975) were used to develop a hypothesis for approaching the phenomenon of the early pottery in Cuba. The lithic evidence helped develop the argument that pottery examples at and similar to those of Canímar were the predecessors of the Mayarí type, in this way establishing a chronological relationship between the two traditions. At the core of this argument lay the higher variability in some archaeological assemblages, the particularities of some lithic components, and other contrasting factors of their settlement patterns (Tabío 1984).

The *sui generis* microlith industry isolated by Kozlowski at only two sites was elevated by archaeologist Dr. Ernesto Tabío (1984) to the concept of *protoagrícola* (protoagriculturalist) and later used to define both a culture and a transitional stage. In addition to the lithic evidence, the author considered other archaeological elements, among them the presence of pottery: "In this transitional phase between the preagricultural and agricultural stages, in addition to having an assemblage similar to that of the preagriculturalists, some Cuban aboriginal communities are distinguished by having evidence of ceramic vessel use, almost always simple and scarce in number, but without the presence of the 'burén' [cassava griddle], indirect evidence of manioc agriculture" (Tabío 1984:38).

Within the definition of the protoagriculturalist stage, Tabío established two periods based on the site of Arroyo del Palo, which in addition to possessing the basic characteristics also produced an abundant and well-developed decorated ceramic assemblage. Since Tabío, this archaeological expression (and other similar ones) has been considered a late manifestation of the protoagriculturalists. A similar result was obtained when he used studies on the sites of Canímar, Playas, and Aguas Verdes to define an early manifestation of the stage. Within this approach, the regular presence of pottery was assumed to be a characteristic of the late period and vice versa, at the same time that the defined periods were indirectly and automatically identified with particular phases of socioeconomic development.

This rule set down the bases for new approaches which, far from shedding light on the diversity of forms and contexts, contributed to a situation in which one assemblage could be assigned to several classifications according to the criteria used to evaluate it. Pedro Pablo Godo (1997) observes that the term *protoagriculturalists* and its concept have undergone some significant changes. First, simple ceramics functioned as a central element in the definition of the term, creating a situation in which the term *protoagrícola* included all the sites of Cayo Redondo with ceramic evidence. Later, interpretations changed as the emphasis shifted to lithics. The scheme became an early phase defined by the presence of microliths and the absence of ceramics, followed by a Cayo Redondo expression or, if microliths and ceramics were both present, a protoagricultural expression (Godo 1997:24). In other cases and regions, the presence of microliths, laminar fragmentation, and retouched flakes, even in the absence of ceramics, have been assumed to be indicators of a protoagricultural occupation.

The site of Arroyo del Palo provides an example of this multiplicity of classifications. In some classifications, it has been framed within the agricultural/ceramic stage (Dacal Moure and Rivero de La Calle 1986) based on the variability of its ceramic industry as well as some elements of the ground stone assemblage. The conclusions have been that preagricultural people coexisted with Arawak groups or borrowed their early ceramic technology and assimilated it within their means of production. That is to say, the inclusion of this site in the protoagricultural stage was due to technological reasons; it is considered part of a transculturation process between foragers and *arauacos* (Arawak horticulturalists). Although this last possibility cannot be discarded completely, with the evidence now at hand this possible process of transculturation or exchange does not show the adoption of agriculture, at least in the traditional way. If it occurred, the assimilation must have been more on the order of stylistic and formal elements on the part of a community that already knew this technique before contact with the Arawak. On the other hand, if agricultural practices existed, they could have been present at an incipient level without displacing foraging activities in importance.

In other classifications, assemblages with simple pottery have been considered late expressions of the so-called Mesolithic societies, placed within a protoagricultural process that has its origins around 500 B.C. (Dominguez et al. 1994). In this case, the evolutionary chronology in which these expressions are situated has compartmental aspects, in which new discoveries can be integrated within the scheme by the presence or absence of certain archaeo-

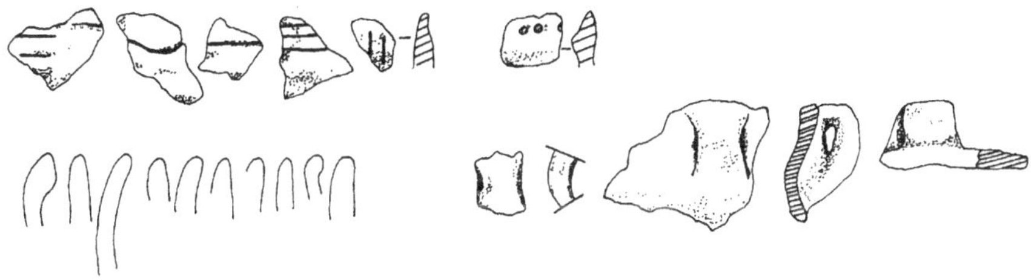

6.3. Examples of ceramic decorations from the Belleza site, Santiago de Cuba

logical components. Sites with simple ceramics, certain lithic particularities, shell assemblages, and coastal settlement patterns can be considered an early protoagriculturalist phase, while assemblages with more complex ceramics, including some with decorations (Figures 6.3 and 6.4), a significant lithic industry, and inland settlement patterns can be defined as late. This scheme is similar to the approaches of Tabío. A circular logic inherent in the definitions means that variations can be overridden by environmental factors or different modalities of the same archaeological culture.

Perhaps the most comprehensive and open attempt to evaluate these expressions can be found in the work of José M. Guarch *Estructura para las comunidades aborígenes de Cuba* (1990), in which the complexity of the phenomena is sketched beyond mere classification. His generalizing approach to the protoagricultural term attempts to establish differences in the organization of the economic activities and technical complexes of early ceramic communities. It also leaves open the possibility that this economic organization, as well as the selection of the location of their settlements in the landscape, may relate to different cultural traditions and not to different chronological periods. In a general way, this phenomenon is evaluated as a phase within a period of change in which the importance of the evolution and the influence of the processes of transculturation are not discarded. To emphasize the observable differences within these archaeological contexts as results of these processes, the term *variety* was used, in which environmental factors played a significant role.

A more recent line of thought (Godo 1997) has evaluated the problem through a different optic. Considering protoagriculturalism as a differentiated event seems to have been one of the main problems in studying its variability. The direct relationship between the contexts of Canímar and Mayarí (where one is deemed to be the antecedent of the other) repeated earlier assumptions used to evaluate the foraging communities where the supposedly simple as-

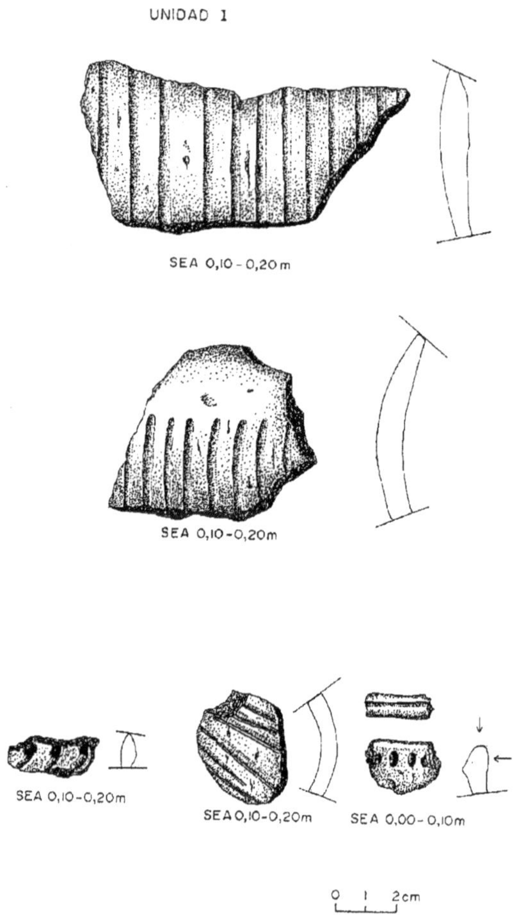

6.4. Examples of ceramic decorations from the Abra del Cacoygüín site, Holguín, Cuba

semblage was considered early and the supposedly complex assemblage as late and already evolved. In this way, foraging lifeways, their consolidation in particular regions, and their variability ceased to be important variables in evaluating protoagriculturalism (Godo 1997). In spite of the poverty of the ceramic industry, the contexts where it is present indicate an association with foraging communities, whose cultural variability correlates with the variability of the different environments they exploited. If, in fact, we are dealing with a transformation to Neolithic culture, ceramic-producing societies should always be marked by the development of a previous Archaic community that accelerated the processes of pottery production either because of external influences or through its own internal development.

In the past few years, interest in early pottery has also been directed toward the analysis of its technological aspects (Jouravleva n.d.; Jouravleva and Gonzáles 2000) as a way of generating new interpretations, especially in relation to the origins of ceramics at key sites such as Arroyo del Palo and other regions of the island. These studies, carried out with precise archaeometric methods, have been designed to establish parameters that capture the evolution of ceramic technology in different contexts and to isolate phases within its development. The phases, defined stratigraphically and chronologically, are intended to identify cultural contexts. This approach attempts to define the informational importance that each chosen parameter has, as well as its range of variability, in order to use it as a diagnostic within the classification. The result is a stable and independent classificatory scheme based on manufacturing methods that can be used to interpret field data. A profile of the technological particularities inherent in the different phases of ceramic development (either early, middle, or late) involves observations on local invention, the borrowing of practices, or a migratory process. This system establishes a strict relationship between technological parameters and cultural identifications, leading to much richer interpretations that grant importance to multiple elements of the context. This approach represents an interpretative logic where if A is present then B, or if A is absent then C. This line of investigation is unique within the analysis of Cuban ceramics and exemplifies steps that should be considered in any process of interpretation. It has the advantage of making it impossible to reduce explanation of any cultural or social phenomenon to the absence or presence of technological features. On the other hand, it is misleading to establish an abrupt break between one period of ceramic development and another. More than anything, the approach identifies different forms and trends independent of models that predetermine the rest of the culture. The archaeometric approach has achieved important results in locating sources of raw materials used in the manufacture of pottery and the presence of the deposits in a particular region, as well as traces of fatty acids that provide information about the alimentary habits of these communities. These results have then been compared to the sites of traditional agriculturalist/ceramic groups (Jouravleva and Gonzáles 2000). To summarize, we can classify studies on early ceramic communities in Cuba as follows:

(1) Morpho-typological, evolutionary-chronological, and in some ways,

ecological points of view, characterized by restrictive typological concepts and individual sequences that have been used to generalize the rest of the island. Under this approach, the beginning of the Neolithic transition in Cuba has generally been defined by the presence of ceramics and of certain traits in flintknapping techniques and the typology of lithic manufacture. The lack of analysis of early plant domestication has contributed to an uncritical acceptance of these other two elements as valid and diagnostic indicators of this stage.

(2) The position that lithic technology is an absolute, indicative trait of homotaxonomy. Instances of contemporaneity of sites have caused some local sequences to be assigned to cultural traditions defined by points of reference similar to site types. When the protoagriculturalists of Cuba are analyzed with reference to certain lithic typologies, the areas where diagnostic types are not manifested appear as a kind of black hole. Long-distance migrations have been proposed to explain these gaps. This approach to the problem does not take into account the geographical conditions of those supposedly empty spaces and the characteristics of the foraging populations that occupied them. In addition, communities that do not fit into the lithic sequence will be classified as something different.

(3) As part of the process of the Neolithic transition in Cuba, variations in aspects of the archaeological record have been isolated, particularly some features of ceramic and lithic technology and of settlement patterns. This has led to an elaboration of successive variants or phases. However, the technical parameters of the Archaic traditions were not abandoned. What actually changed was the relative importance of some technologies. In considering the archaeological record of communities with these characteristics, it seems reasonable to contemplate their settlement and subsistence patterns as closely related, specifically the former as deriving from the latter. In that case, some of the contextual differences may result from alternative solutions applied to concrete problems that demanded either a gathering or a predation strategy. Some of these strategies could have become consolidated with transformative consequences, leading to stable and discernible patterns.

(4) Some of the cultural groupings that form the Cuban protoagriculturalist stage are defined by relationships of homotaxonomy between different archaeological contexts. For the purpose of interpretation, these cultural groupings are almost always treated as equivalents. Their significance has been deduced according to a lineal focus, where homotaxonomy corresponds to a supposed synchronism.

According to the studies carried out to date, one of the main characteristics of the transitional process toward the Neolithic in other parts of the Caribbean is an economic specialization of sites. The problem for Cuba is that a comparative analysis of several regional contexts still needs to be done in order to understand the local processes of this transition.

The Dominican Republic

As an expression of the scientific interest in studying the phenomenon of protoagriculturalism and early ceramic cultures, Caribbean archaeologists have undertaken a number of important studies in the Dominican Republic. Analyses of the well-known site of El Caimito (Veloz et al. 1974) resulted in one of the first acknowledgments that not all early Caribbean ceramic assemblages conformed to the styles and series defined by the North American archaeologist Irving Rouse (Rouse and Cruxent 1961). This recognition derived from considering the features and chronology of these assemblages as evidence for a diffusionary model for the early pottery toward the Greater Antilles. The site of El Caimito, interpreted as a food preparation area, is located on the roof of a rock shelter and is characterized by the presence of highly fragmented ceramics in small quantities. The midden is relatively small and formed by a single stratum of shallow topsoil (a maximum of 40 cm) and compact ash. Pollen analyses conducted in samples from El Caimito produced no evidence of cultivation of plants known to be used by precolumbian groups, such as manioc or corn. Instead, analysis showed intense gathering activities that included the exploitation of products such as *guáyiga* (*Zamia* sp.), palm seeds (*Roystonea* sp.), and *corozo* (*Acrocomia* sp.).

In terms of pottery, the study of El Caimito opened two new possibilities. On the one hand, it was possible to argue for the existence of Caribbean foraging groups who developed the knowledge to manufacture pottery as the result of local evolution. On the other, it was possible to contend that from an early period foraging groups developed close relationships with settled ceramic populations, whose modes of making pottery were not part of the traditional styles defined for the region.

Similar archaeological contexts have been discovered and studied, such as Honduras del Oeste (Rímoli and Nadal 1980) and Musiepedro (Veloz et al. 1976), among others. These sites and a revised interpretation of foraging group sites with pottery in Dominican Republic have caused Rímoli and Nadal (1983) to suggest the existence of an early ceramic horizon which many call *Caimitoide.* An important element stressed by these authors in most of the analyzed sites is that its assemblage seems to correspond to a wide range and variety of expressions indicative of a possible hybridization of preagricultural traditions. This situation seems also to coincide with a movement from the coast to the exploitation of forested areas or exploitation of both.[3]

The isolated ceramic typology from El Caimito considered with these new elements seems to fall in line with the diffusionary explanation for this early pottery. The model proposed by Venezuelan researcher Alberta Zucchi (1984) considers the ceramic typology unique to the site of El Caimito as related to the *Cedeñoide* series of some sites of the area of the Middle Orinoco, especially the well-known site of Aguerito. This relationship, according to Zucchi, can be perceived in the following two aspects.

(1) El Caimito and the existence of a ceramic tradition recognized as Cedeñoide in the Middle Orinoco are manifestations of a pre-Saladoid ceramic horizon in both areas, with dates corresponding to the first millennium B.C.

(2) The chronological correspondence between El Caimito and the early Cedeñoide material, together with the similarities in subsistence systems and ceramic styles, allows us to conclude that the Dominican site represents a group that migrated to the Greater Antilles at the end of the first millennium B.C. The technical and decorative similarities of the Cedeñoide ceramic and that of El Caimito, combined with similarities in vessel types, are the main elements that are used to define an Antillean Cedeñoide horizon. Although the early pottery of the Antilles is not interpreted as a replica of the Cedeñoide material, it presents enough elements of similarity to suggest that they were produced by the same community, to which we can add the significant fact of the lack of *burenes* (cassava griddles) at both sites. These theories imply the possibility of a new migratory route for the first ceramists of the Greater Antilles, suggesting a direct movement from the Middle Orinoco. At this time, there is no evidence of Cedeñoide or Caimitoide expressions in the Lesser Antilles.

Although this thesis cannot be completely discarded, it tends to overestimate some features of the pottery and ignores other representative and substantial features of Antillean Archaic components. In addition, analysis of the shared ceramic features are confined to a single ceramic group—that of the site of El Caimito—without considering either the chronological or the ceramic particularities of other areas in the Caribbean islands, where perhaps the coincidences in these aspects are minimal or nonexistent. It is therefore premature to speak of an Antillean Cedeñoide ceramic horizon.

In a similar vein, authors such as Venezuelan archaeologist Mario Sanoja have pointed out similarities to the early Barrancas style and a possible influence in the Antilles, while North Americans Betty Meggers and Clifford Evans (n.d.) relate the pottery of El Caimito to other South American sites and consider possible cultural transformations and diffusion processes. According to Meggers and Evans, the ceramics of the El Caimito site exhibit several of the diagnostic characteristics of early ceramics from South America, especially the coastal complexes of Colombia, suggesting the possibility of trans-Caribbean dispersion. This route seems to be related to climatic changes that helped accelerate migration toward the Antilles.

Meggers (1987) documents the correspondence between the evidence for migration and a long arid episode identified in palynological and geological sequences that affected much of South America between 2700 and 2000 years B.P. She suggests that the appearance of pottery at El Caimito might be the result of a population movement toward the Antilles during the final phase of this event. Understanding the interplay of climatic influences on migrations through the Antillean arch with a phenomenon of cultural transcendency constitutes an important observation in understanding the peopling of this portion of the Caribbean. Nevertheless, a larger data set is still needed to affirm the migration of the first ceramicist groups from the Colombian regions to the Greater Antilles, and particularly to the island of Hispaniola.

The North American investigator Irving Rouse (1992) has also reevaluated the presence of pottery in contexts characteristic of foraging communities. His new theories have tried to reform the older schema to account for the results of recent archaeological investigations in the Caribbean. The concepts of "age" and "subseries" are the mechanisms he uses to assimilate new information in order to adapt it to a persistent unilineal conception of technological development and to demonstrate, through some changes in the assemblages, shifts from one subseries or age to another are now conceived with a greater chronological flexibility. Under this view, the antecedents of Taíno culture are divided into two ages, the Lithic or Paleoindian Age and the Archaic or Mesoindian Age, each possessing a chronological range and defined by the appearance of a technological innovation—flintknapped stone for the Lithic Age and ground stones, shell artifacts, and worked bone in the Archaic Age. In this case, as in his earlier models, Rouse assumes that the archaeological cultures diverged historically from an original common ancestral complex, similar to the phylogenetic trees used in linguistics. From this point of view, the changes in this model, produced by the divergent process, are explained using historic arguments such as acculturation, migration, and other forms of interaction (José Oliver, personal communication). This is done even when the general sense of the argument is evolutionary or developmental. In general, this interpretation of the precolumbian world of the Caribbean focuses on locating archaeological cultures (designated subseries) within certain spaces as isolated and circumscribed boxes, where the relationships between communities are obscured to the point of establishing cultural frontiers that are demonstrable from neither archaeological nor historical sources.

This approach is especially apparent in interpreting pottery from foraging contexts, where Rouse uses only the data generated by the archaeology of the Dominican Republic and limits it to the existence of a frontier between Archaic populations and farming populations belonging to the Saladoid ceramic series dating to between 200 B.C. and A.D. 600. The reference point in this case is the presence of Saladoid pottery in the well-known region of La Caleta, near the area of La Romana in the Dominican Republic, that, together with a date of 240 B.C. for a pottery similar to that of the Puerto Rican site of Hacienda Grande, justifies a relationship between the points. The movement of groups from Hacienda Grande to the island of Hispaniola would have displaced Archaic residents upon whom a rudimentary pottery was imposed, as in El Caimito (Rouse 1992). With this hypothesis, the author solves the presence of early pottery in the Antilles and in synthesis proposes its origins from Saladoid pottery. Rouse's thesis also depends on the assumption of chronological contemporaneity between the first ceramic sites in the Dominican Republic and the site of Hacienda Grande. According to him, the Archaic component of the Dominican sites reflects the possibility that a process of transculturation occurred between the ceramists from Puerto Rico and the foragers from Hispaniola, where the latter copied the Hacienda Grande pottery style.

Perhaps the most intensive analyses of this process in the island of Hispaniola have been carried out by specialists from the region (Rímoli and Nadal 1983; Veloz 1991, 1992; Veloz et al. 1974). Their investigations recognize that there is little evidence for a relationship between the first pottery of the Dominican Republic and the Saladoid ceramics. Their evaluations have focused on more complex and important questions, such as settlement patterns and economic activities. This focus has led to the conclusion that an early ceramic horizon existed before 240 B.C., in addition to reaffirming the essentially foraging character of these communities.

The question of origins has also been of interest. In this case, authors like

Rímoli and Nadal (1983) have rejected the high diagnostic value attributed to the lithic industry by some investigators of early ceramic sites in Cuba, mainly the sites of Canímar and Aguas Verdes (Kozlowski 1975). This approach emphasizes consideration of the variety of technologies present in Antillean foraging cultures and the lack of evidence corroborating a single, unique origin of cultural practices in early ceramic communities. In fact, the idea of an early ceramic horizon seems to be correct for the island of Hispaniola. In the case of Cuba, it is necessary to clarify that the foraging contexts with pottery seem to appear across a much wider chronological range after A.D. 830, having a confirmed relationship in some regions of the island to the earliest nuclei of Arawak populations. This situation opens up the possibility of cultural relationship between these groups, causing the transformations among the first ceramists as well as the late acquisition of the pottery or of certain ceramic features. As part of this process, the assimilation of elements of an incipient agricultural Archaic population cannot be discarded. In Cuba, the presence of foraging communities is documented in historical chronicles up through the sixteenth century.

Marcio Veloz Maggiolo (1980, 1991) has also approached important aspects of the first ceramic societies of the island of Hispaniola, especially in dealing with the particularities of the contexts and their socioeconomic characteristics. In his opinion, this phenomenon reflects ceramic communities without agriculture, at least as traditionally defined. He therefore interprets the arrival in the Antilles of a pottery without manioc cultivation as part of a cultural process in which seafaring groups introduced this technology to Antillean foraging communities. Veloz's research questions underscore the important problems: (1) Were these Archaic, preagricultural communities who were interacting or trading with ceramic populations present on the island from an early period? and (2) Did these Archaic groups also begin producing ceramics as a result of a local evolution? In fact, it is possible to grant a certain margin of possibility to both alternatives as key factors that influenced the development of early ceramics. It would also be appropriate to think of several processes coexisting at the same time, or at least not to disregard that the development of the pottery, either through assimilation or reproduction, needs a cultural base that allows its adoption by the core of a community.

For his analyses of this problem in areas of the Dominican Republic, Veloz Maggiolo (1992) has used the concept of *productive symbiosis* by arguing that the exploitation of ecological niches in the mangrove areas, one of the main sources of subsistence among Antillean foraging groups, was losing its importance among the early ceramists at the same time that tropical forest environments were gradually becoming quite important in the economy of these groups. That is to say, the foraging mode of life was undergoing change, and the forest began to be alternatively exploited so that the use of wild plants such as the *guáyiga* or *zamia* in some contexts took on an important role in subsistence of the group. According to Veloz, this transition from the exploitation of mangroves toward a new productive model reformed millennia-old traditions of the preceramic groups. Archaeological evidence shows an Archaic people deliberately reorienting their economic patterns toward terrestrial gathering, in which they more intensively exploited faunal resources.

It is helpful to consider some differences with regard to the Cuban context. While in the island of Hispaniola early ceramic sites usually fit a well-defined pattern (especially those linked to the karst areas), in Cuba they tend to demonstrate a greater variety of patterns, many consistent with those observed for the traditional foraging communities. Also, analysis of the early pottery from Santo Domingo exhibits a variety of types, suggesting that when these groups received or began making ceramics, they had the appropriate socioeconomic conditions for using them.

In the past few years, questions related to the earliest Dominican pottery have expanded further as a result of new investigations. The study of Punta Cana, located in the southeast corner of the island, produced very early dates for an agricultural-ceramic population from the Greater Antilles, 340 and 240 B.C., providing evidence of an early occupation by these groups in Santo Domingo. The Punta Cana investigations have been able to isolate three habitational phases, extending its chronology into the ninth century A.D., demonstrating that the locations had been used by farmers for centuries and supporting the argument that they arrived in the Greater Antilles at the same time or even earlier than in other islands of the Caribbean. Traditional manioc cultivation is evidenced by the presence of the remains of *burén* dated to at least 340 B.C. For this reason, this settlement is not only one of the earliest agricultural occupations in the Antillean arch but has also become a key site in the explanation of the diffusion of the first ceramic types in Santo Domingo, since its chronology coincides with most of the forager-ceramicist contexts in the area.

However, the pottery patterns from the Punta Cana midden differ from those traditionally assumed for the Saladoid ceramic series and share features with the pottery of El Caimito, especially the incised types. This may suggest a possible transmission of the ceramic technology from the first farmers of Punta Cana to the foraging groups, who perhaps incorporated some elements while excluding the burén, since this pottery type would not have had an important role within a basic foraging mode of life.

The early dates from Punta Cana contribute a new and interesting fact to the archaeology of the Caribbean by demonstrating that groups with Saladoid ceramics were neither the first nor the only farming occupants of the Greater Antilles (Veloz and Ortega 1995). Societies with other ceramic expressions arrived there at the same time, or perhaps earlier. This intriguing hypothesis, which needs additional data and validation, may explain the appearance of pottery at such an early date in Santo Domingo.

CONCLUSIONS

Five general conclusions can be drawn from a synthesis of these findings.

(1) Recent evaluations of foraging societies from various regions of the Americas have demonstrated that societies practicing various hunting and gathering lifeways also used pottery. This situation is common in the Caribbean, where the richness of the surroundings promoted a sedentary or semi-sedentary lifeway and the initial development of settled communities with incipient agriculture and ceramics.

(2) Analysis of shell middens in Colombia, Venezuela, Guyana, and Panama, among others, indicate that the presence of ceramics is associated with changes in the productive assemblages and, therefore, with a transformation of the economy in which the consumption of plant resources shifted from playing a peripheral to a more centralized role in the daily life of the community.

(3) The general designation developed for foraging groups in Cuba using the North American historical particularist framework made it difficult to recognize the Neolithic transition in the Caribbean. This classification obviated the differences and variability among foraging sites located within the same cultural formation. Pottery, when present, was considered atypical.

(4) The ceramics present in foraging contexts in the Caribbean have undergone a reevaluation since the 1960s and 1970s, especially in Cuba and Dominican Republic. Studies on this topic in both countries have gone through several phases and developed from different perspectives that could be summarized or grouped as follows:

- Diffusionist perspectives, in some instances extremist, based on two technological criteria, a lithic typology and ceramic traits.
- Evolutionist perspectives, in almost all cases unilineal in principle. The variability of the phenomenon is not considered, and they focus on the totality of socioeconomic reality before and after the appearance of pottery. In

the case of Cuba, this tendency inferred socioeconomic changes from indirect indexes such as productive tools or settlement patterns, owing to a lack of analysis that could provide more concrete evidence.

- Close analytical perspectives that assumed a certain dependency between technological analysis and cultural interpretations, where other elements of the archaeological context are ignored.
- Descriptive, chronological perspectives based on simple classification of the contexts according to a traditional taxonomy and predetermined characteristics.
- Multilineal positions where the previous perspectives are combined, but where one of them is emphasized, especially the analytical perspective.
- Recent multilineal views, where the previous criteria are used as ways of describing, analyzing, and evaluating the phenomenon in its variability and spatial relations but disentangling it from regional manifestations and looking at broader patterns.

(5) The unilineal approach that up to this date has dominated the classification, study, and conceptualization of phenomena related to the Neolithic transition in the Caribbean is related to the powerful sway that the traditional classifications of archaeological materials hold in this region. This approach emphasizes aspects of a chronological and stylistic nature more than an analysis of socioeconomic changes.

NOTES

1. Along the Caribbean coast of Central America, incipient ceramics are also manifested in assemblages such as that from the Monkey Point site on the Atlantic coast of Nicaragua and south of the Laguna de las Perlas (Veloz Maggiolo 1991).

2. Although Kozlowski did not discard the intercultural relationships between the foraging communities in the Caribbean, they were evaluated in a technological, stylistic, or formal sense, more than from an integral perspective or with a consideration of changes in the core sociocultural structures.

3. An interesting example of this process is the site of Cueva de Berna where a wide variety of tools is evident, suggesting a dense preceramic occupation that contained characteristics from diverse cultural traditions. This site provides an example of one of the earliest processes of hybridization in the Antilles—1890 B.C. At the end of the occupation, ceramic fragments in the upper layers seem to indicate what pottery was adopted.

7 / El Chorro de Maíta

Social Inequality and Mortuary Space

Roberto Valcárcel Rojas and César A. Rodríguez Arce

Understanding of the social and political organization of the Arawak aboriginal communities of Cuba, better known as the Taínos, Subtaínos, or groups of the *etapa agroalfarera* (agricultural-ceramist stage), has been limited by a shortage of historical and archaeological data. With respect to chiefdoms on the island, the prevailing view is that the power of *caciques* was limited to their local community (Domínguez et al. 1994:46; Guarch Delmonte et al. 1995; Tabío and Rey 1985:164), although historical evidence suggests that leadership in some areas may have been more complex and stratified. In 1514, Diego Velázquez mentioned that the native province of Cabaneque was subordinate to that of Camagüey (Pichardo Moya 1971:66). The letter also mentions Yaguacayex, "the main *cacique* of the province (Havana)" (Pichardo Moya 1971:68). Pichardo Moya's document collection (1971:50) also includes a comment from Las Casas on the existence of "kings and gentlemen," suggesting multiple levels among the elite.

Torre (1841) used historical references to Indian provinces to create a map of *cacicazgos* in Cuba. These have been interpreted by some researchers as evidence of a widespread structure of chiefdoms with incipient tributary relationships (Moscoso 1986:374). However, as noted by several scholars (Domínguez et al. 1994:48; Guarch Delmonte et al. 1995), we lack the data necessary to define the structure of these supposed political units. Furthermore, it is not clear what form of dependent relationship existed between the provinces of Cabaneque and Camagüey, nor is there evidence that we can generalize this case as common to the whole island.

The presence of archaeological sites distinguished by their larger size, higher artifact density, and associations with settlement clusters has also generated some debate. In Banes, located in the northwestern part of the island, Rouse (1942:155, 157) linked the size differences among the archaeological sites to the existence of central and subordinate villages, organized in a political structure that could correspond to that of the historically described chiefdoms. However, according to some authors (Domínguez et al. 1994; Guarch Delmonte et al. 1995), there is no evidence for a process of social differentiation between the sites or for the presence of an elite with regional power, such as would be expected in a confederation. An alternative interpretation is suggested by evidence from another important concentration of settlements in south-central Cuba. Archaeologists believe that the relationships between sites possibly indicate a level of centralization within a framework of economic specialization, designed to take advantage of diverse ecological areas (Domínguez 1991:69). Guarch Delmonte et al. (1995) summarized the nature of this last perspective in the following terms: "We think it is possible that the *cacique,* the *behique* [shaman], and some other administrators practiced some form of 'interior exploitation' of their own tribe. It also seems probable that a certain dependency and exploitation between subordinate and nuclear settlements existed in areas where we find a large concentration of archaeological sites a short distance from each other. This dependency would have simply resulted from tribal fissioning from the parental group due to demographic reasons or other factors."

When comparisons with the abundant data from Hispaniola and Puerto Rico were made in an attempt to refine the historical and archaeological views, Cuba's sites appeared to represent a simpler level of complexity (Domínguez et al. 1994:46; Tabío and Rey 1985:163; Trincado 1984:40). Despite the shortage of detailed data, this conclusion tended to be generalized, imposing an idea of egalitarianism on groups belonging to the indigenous community and characterizing them at the stage of a developed tribal community (Domínguez et al. 1994:51; Guarch Delmonte 1990:16; Guarch Delmonte et al. 1995). A level of higher social complexity and of an incipient disintegration of the tribal relationships was acknowledged to exist only among the late communities of the eastern tip, perhaps linked to influences from Hispaniola (Domínguez et al. 1994:46; Trincado 1984:41).

Recent considerations, however, suggest other possibilities. Moreira (1999: 166–182) uses the discovery of a large amount of sumptuary material at the site of Los Buchillones (Calvera et al. 1996; Jardines and Calvera 1999), the evidence for centralization in the south-central part of the island (Domínguez 1991), and the concentrations of sites already mentioned to suggest the formation of possible chiefdoms and a more extended process of disintegration of communal, egalitarian relationships.

The information from Los Buchillones is important because, among other reasons, it allows us to overcome the existing idea of simplicity and provides evidence from wooden objects rarely found on Cuban sites. The quality of the craftsmanship and especially the abundance of sumptuary and symbolic objects (idols, *duhos* or ceremonial stools, trays, vessels, etc.) indicate a certain level of specialization and the existence of social demand. This pattern could be true for other parts of Cuba. If we correlate the general characteristics of this settlement with those of other large sites and clusters of sites in eastern Cuba, we could expect a much more complex view than the one that has generally prevailed.

One of these sites, El Chorro de Maíta, has produced burials with a significant number of body ornaments. Their distribution was restricted, and they were produced of materials of limited circulation. It has been suggested that these artifacts express the high social position of their users in a well-defined hierarchy (Rodríguez 1989:5; Valcárcel 1999:92). El Chorro de Maíta is a large settlement surrounded by smaller sites. It possesses the largest number of ceremonial objects and corporal ornaments reported for its zone, as well as the only cemetery dating to Cuba's prehistoric agricultural stage. This evidence suggests that the site may have had a preeminent position in its relationship with nearby sites, being the residential settlement of high-ranking individuals who themselves may have been linked to a well-differentiated hierarchy (Valcárcel 1999:93).

For the time being, it is difficult to evaluate how widespread this situation was or how it fits with the political organization described in historical accounts. Even so, the information from El Chorro de Maíta presented in this chapter opens the door to a better understanding of the processes related to the development of social complexity and perhaps to an emerging revision of Cuban archaeology itself.

SOCIAL INEQUALITY, INHERITANCE, AND ANCESTORS

Social inequality is defined as an asymmetric or unequal relationship of power between members or groups of a society (Siegel 1999:210). The transition from an egalitarian to a stratified society is marked by the institutionalization of the forms of social inequality present in egalitarian communities. According to Price and Feinman (1995), this institutionalization becomes hereditary, socially reproducing the inequalities and forms of hierarchies that were previously established by personal prestige or prerogatives related to sex or age (see also Andrade de Lima and López Mazz 2000:132; Curet and Oliver 1998:218; Siegel 1999:210). Social inequality, and especially inequality reproduced by means of inheritance, is incorporated in mortuary contexts through mechanisms that identify the person's identity and his/her parental link with the elite. This action represents a symbolic act of respect toward the dead, but it also expresses and reinforces continuing social relationships (Gamble et al. 2001:198; Renfrew and Bahn 1993:184).

The presence of important funerary offerings is often considered evidence of social inequality. In nonegalitarian societies, funerary distinctions become more necessary because they symbolically underscore the hereditary character of status, as well as the social limits that the status establishes (Gamble et al. 2001:198). When these objects are associated with small children, it suggests a differential reproduction by means of hereditary formulas, since it is very difficult for a child to acquire the status that allows him/her access to these goods based on meritorious deeds (Renfrew and Bahn 1993:184). This context indicates the child's importance as a member of the elite based on his/her descent.

Within the context of death, this manipulation of the symbols of wealth and power by the elite extends also to the manipulation of the cult of the ancestors as well as to the control of the funeral space as the residential and ceremonial space of the ancestors. According to Curet and Oliver (1998), these elements were originally used by the Saladoid (egalitarian groups of the ceramic phase in precolumbian Puerto Rico) as means of fomenting social cohesion, but later on they were redirected by the emergent elite to legitimate their control of power. The burials in the Saladoid period do not show a differential mortuary treatment (Curet and Oliver 1998:222). These burials, which lack any visible individual markers, are concentrated in the central plazas of the settlements. According to the cosmological principles that define the structure of the village, the ancestors kept in this plaza represent the physical point where the natural and supernatural worlds come into contact. Locating the burials in this place facilitates the passage of the dead to the world of the ancestors and facilitates communication between the dead and the living. In this way, the plaza marks an egalitarian access to the ancestors and legitimizes the right of the community over the resources and the territory, as well as the ideology that perpetuates such rights (Curet and Oliver 1998:230).

During post-Saladoid times, the central plaza ceased to be used for the disposal of the dead, and burials were more often located in domestic contexts. The community, as an effective social and political unit, was displaced by nuclear households (Curet and Oliver 1998:231) and the cult of the ancestors reoriented toward the maintenance of domestic unit (Curet and Oliver 1998:231). The world of the ancestors assumed a hierarchical structure while the natural world became a replica of the supernatural world. In this new cosmology, the ancestors of the elite group came to be considered as more powerful than the rest. The chiefs developed a role for themselves as mediators between the natural and the supernatural worlds through a greater control over ceremonies and iconography and a process giving them preferential access to the ancestors. Their hierarchical position in society was elevated and legitimated by this process because they possessed the most important ancestors.

New, specialized ceremonial spaces with greater segregation were created in this period, suggesting a more restricted participation and specialized access to the ceremonial activities and rituals (Curet and Oliver 1998:234). Siegel (1999) also recognizes the process of formalization of ceremonial space in Puerto Rico as a strategy of institutionalization of social inequality. He emphasizes its transitional character, which he extends to burial practices (Siegel 1999:217–220). Contrary to Curet and Oliver (1998), he estimates that in the first part of the post-Saladoid period the use of the cemetery in the central plaza was maintained in some, but not all, sites concurrently with the burials in household areas. This interpretation suggests that at this time the communal and domestic/private spheres were not exclusionary (Siegel 1999:219). Siegel's idea is important because it makes evident the fact that, in certain circumstances, elements of the communal structure coexist with elements characteristic of the hierarchical structure. This helps us understand the diversity of forms possible in the process toward institutionalized social inequality.

In this chapter we assess the presence of objects of limited circulation and of high symbolic value associated with burials of El Chorro de Maíta's cemetery as an expression of the process of social differentiation. The important presence of these objects in children's burials is assumed to be indicative of the existence of a hereditary elite and of the institutionalization of social inequality.

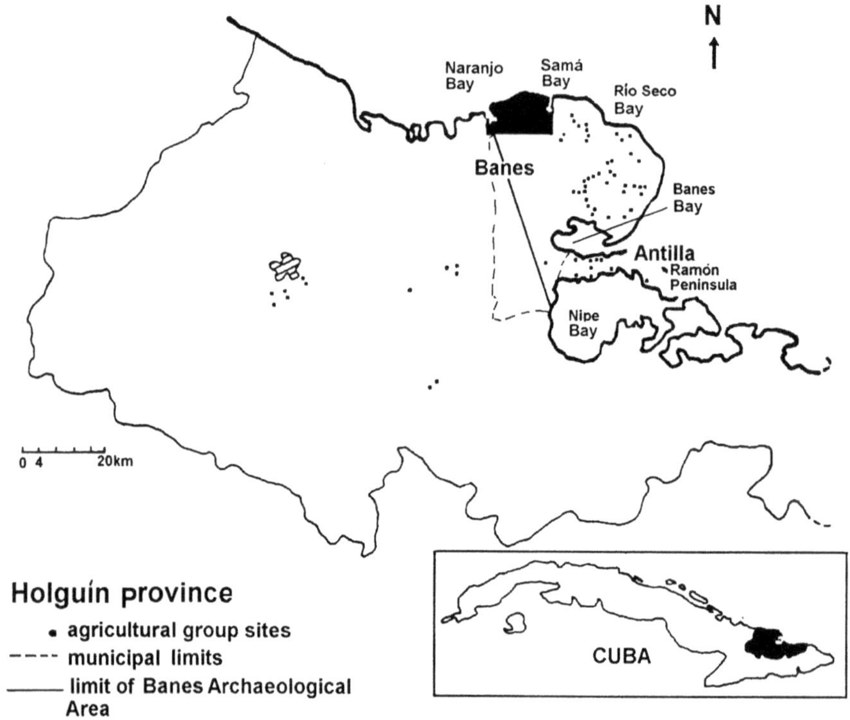

7.1. Map of the Province of Holguín showing the location of the Área Arqueológica de Banes and the Yaguajay zone

EL CHORRO DE MAÍTA

The archaeological site of El Chorro de Maíta is located at the northeastern end of Cuba within the municipality of Banes, Province of Holguín. Part of this municipality and part of neighboring Antilla possess large concentrations of archaeological settlements belonging to agricultural groups within a space that has been denominated the Banes Archaeological Area (Area Arqueológica de Banes) (Valcárcel 2002a:26–28). The concentration of sites is organized in clusters that are distributed in well-defined zones. El Chorro de Maíta is situated in the Yaguajay zone, a territory of approximately 55 km^2 bordered on the north by the Atlantic Ocean, to the east by the Bay of Samá, to the west by the Bay of Naranjo, and to the south by the border of Yaguajay Hill (see Figure 7.1). This zone possesses the highest density of archaeological sites per km^2 in Banes and an environment characterized by a variety of physical-geographical landscapes, rich soil, and a diversity of coastal fauna.

El Chorro de Maíta is situated on the eastern hillside of the Yaguajay Hill, at 160 m above sea level and 4 km from the coast. The wind patterns and elevation in this location create a comfortable climate with a permanent stream, fertile soils, and easy access to the interior forests and the coast. According to Rouse (1942:103), in 1927 the area was already frequented by collectors and known for its abundance of beads and stone objects. He visited the locality in 1941 and prepared a description of the site (Rouse 1942:103–106) that he considered to be one of the most important in Yaguajay or Banes. At that time, the site was known simply as "Yaguajay."

In 1979, a research team of the Sección de Arqueología de la Academia de Ciencias de Cuba en Holguín evaluated the archaeological potential of the site and carried out a topographical study. From that point on, the site began to be known in the scientific literature by its current denomination, "El Chorro de Maíta." Between 1986 and 1987, the Departamento Centro Oriental de Arqueología de Holguín, under the direction of archaeologist J. M. Guarch Delmonte, excavated the site and located 110 human remains buried in a space surrounded by domestic middens. Considering the abundance of burials, their high density, and that the area was not used for other domestic activities, this location was interpreted as a cemetery associated with the habitation site. The burial area covered 2,000 m^2, and it was related to an area of deposits that spanned 22,000 m^2 (Guarch Delmonte 1994:7, 1996:6).

El Chorro de Maíta is one of two locations with the largest quantity of body ornaments and ceremonial artifacts in the whole Banes Archaeological Area and which has the largest amount in Yaguajay (Valcárcel 1999:88). According to Guarch Delmonte (1996:17), the site has produced the largest quantity of quartzite beads in Cuba—not an incidental detail because such beads were highly valued by the indigenous populations (Alegría 1980:26; Guarch Delmonte 1994:8). Many caciques sent them to the Spaniards as important presents and tokens of their friendship (Alegría 1980:26), and they are mentioned in religious myths as valuable symbolic objects (Arrom 1975:154). Many of the beads at the site appear in early stages of production, indicating that they were being manufactured at the site. The notable presence of these beads, other types of body ornaments, and ceremonial objects with complex designs and of diverse materials suggests processes of craft production with a certain degree of intensity, as well as strongly developed ceremonial rituals and the presence of an elite that consumed these products (Valcárcel 1999:93). It also suggests an economic productivity high enough to sustain a group of people (i.e., the elite) not associated with the productive process.

The settling of agricultural groups in Banes seems to have begun in the early A.D. 900s with occupation continuing until the 1400s or 1500s (Valcárcel 2002a:74). El Chorro de Maíta fits within this scheme. Two of the radiocarbon samples obtained from the cemetery set beginning and ending dates similar to these: 870 ± 70 B.P. (Beta—148956; human bone; d 13c/12c = −19 percent) and 360 ± 80 B.P. (Beta—148955; human bone; d 13c/12c = −19 percent) (Valcárcel 2002a:142). The late date is also supported by the abundance of European material mixed with indigenous objects in residential areas. A third date of 730 ± 60 B.P. (Beta—148957; charred wood; d 13c/12c = −25 percent) was obtained in a domestic context located next to the burial area (Valcárcel 2002a:142).

While difficult to prove with the information at hand, use of the cemetery could date to the beginning of residential settlement. In fact, this conclusion is consistent with the chronological trends of the region. It suggests a logical action by indigenous groups to assure the possession of a territory of exceptional environmental quality. If this is the case, we are dealing with a space utilized across five centuries. Although habitations may not have been continuously occupied in the same location, they were within a very rich environment that allowed the concentration of a large population for at least some of the time, as suggested by the large size of the site.

A date of 670 ± 70 B.P. (Beta—148958; charred wood; d 13c/12c = −25 percent) marks the beginning of occupation of the El Boniato site (Valcárcel 2002a:142), located 500 m from El Chorro de Maíta (see Figure 7.2). The sigma of the date of 730 ± 60 B.P. of El Chorro de Maíta and its calibrated dates (2 sigma calibration: Cal A.D. 1200 to 1320 [Cal 750 to 630 B.P.] and Cal A.D. 1350 to 1390 [Cal B.P. 600 to 560]) indicate some degree of contemporaneity and, given their proximity, some level of relationship between these settlements. El Boniato is a small location with fewer human remains and scarce objects associated with body ornamentation. Its presence affects the areas of economic exploitation of El Chorro de Maíta and the limits of the space where the work of the community should have been invested in crop cultivation. It is improbable that the population of El Chorro de Maíta would have allowed strange or unfriendly people to settle so close to the site. The similarity of the material culture suggests the possibility that El Boniato represents a community that either splintered from El Chorro de Maíta or was linked to it through kinship nexuses or alliances.

In addition to El Boniato, three other village sites are located less than 2 km from El Chorro de Maíta, as well as a ceremonial cave site, a funerary

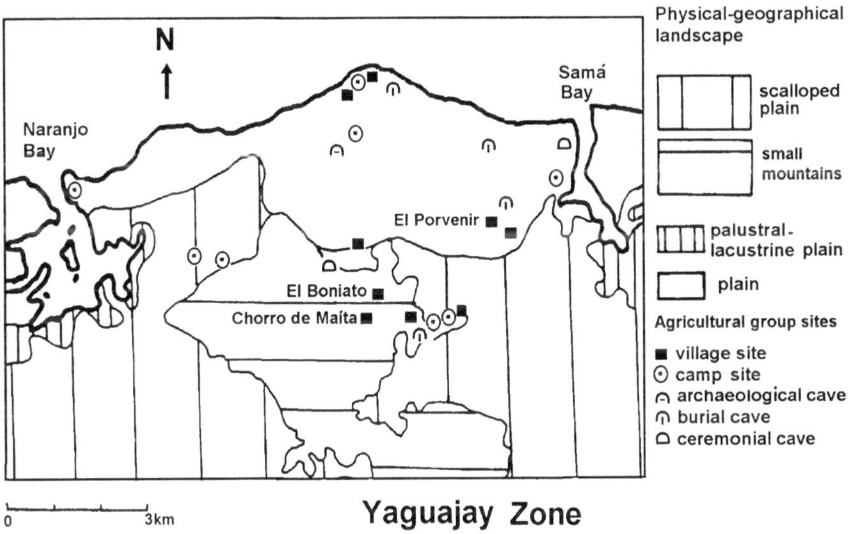

7.2. Map of the Yaguajay Zone showing the location of archaeological sites

cave site, and two campsites (see Figure 7.2). Pairs of sites are common in the area of Banes but not clusters such as this one. Considering the long sequence of El Chorro de Maíta, it is possible that at one time many of these sites were occupied synchronically. As does El Boniato, they share with El Chorro de Maíta cultural features that go beyond the general similarities of the archaeological area. They even possess common characteristics in terms of certain objects of body ornamentation and ceremonial use (Valcárcel 1999:91) not observed in other groupings, which define a unique identity for Yaguajay. These archaeological elements reflect an important link, perhaps of kinship relationships.

According to Cassá (1992:90), the pattern of large villages surrounded by smaller villages is described in the historical data of Hispaniola, where it corresponded to tribal relationships in which the largest settlements assumed the leadership of the group. For some investigators (Guarch Delmonte et al. 1995) this settlement pattern in Cuba suggests "a tribal dependence, produced by fissioning of the parent group due to demographic or other causes." Given its higher demographic and economic potential and its strong development of ceremonial elements and hierarchical structures, El Chorro de Maíta could have operated as the head settlement of this group of sites in Banes. However, it is still difficult to define the particular characteristics of its leadership.

THE CEMETERY

The presence of a cemetery is another element that distinguishes El Chorro de Maíta because, in other contexts in Banes, caves constitute the typical funerary space (Guarch Delmonte 1996:15; Rodríguez 1989:2; Rouse 1942:149). In addition, burials in open-air sites such as those at El Chorro de Maíta are known at only two other places. However, in these cases, the burials are located in mounds formed and used for the disposal of domestic waste and not with the exclusive purpose of containing burials (Miguel 1949:176; Rouse 1942:137).

The Departamento Centro Oriental de Arqueología excavated the main part of the cemetery. While other areas remain to be studied, test excavations suggest that they contain low concentrations of burials. In one of the most important excavation units (denominated Unit 3), 93 indigenous skeletons were unearthed as well as one European skull from the Indo-Hispanic contact period and an intrusive contemporary skeleton (see Figure 7.3). In areas adjoining this unit, 17 additional aboriginal skeletons were found, for a total of 110 skeletons associated with indigenous groups. In addition, two years before this excavation, 17 aboriginal skeletons of the burial area were excavated by local people (Guarch Delmonte et al. 1987:25); Rouse (1942:104) reported the discovery of another burial. Altogether, no fewer than 128 indigenous skeletons have been extracted from the site.

The collections excavated by the Departamento Centro Oriental de Arqueología have been partially analyzed. Using the age groups recommended by Ubelaker (1991), the investigation conducted by César Rodríguez Arce of 106 of the indigenous skeletons established the presence of 20 infants, 6 adolescents, 35 adult males, 43 adult females, and 2 adults of undetermined sex. Part of Rodríguez Arce's results, published in various articles (Guarch Delmonte 1996:17–20; Guarch Delmonte et al. 1987:31–36), indicates the presence of cranial deformation of the occipital-frontal tabular oblique type, a characteristic common among the groups of Arawak origin. Analysis also indicated a great variability in the orientation of the skeletons and burial positions.

A preliminary analysis of health indicators distinguishes several dental afflictions but few other osteological pathologies. The only pathologies detected were bony calluses and two fractured ribs in burial no. 47 and a chronic dental abscess that left a round opening in the exterior of the left side of the maxilla of burial no. 25. Despite the large quantity of burials localized in the Area Arquelógica de Banes, few of them have been studied in this way. Ac-

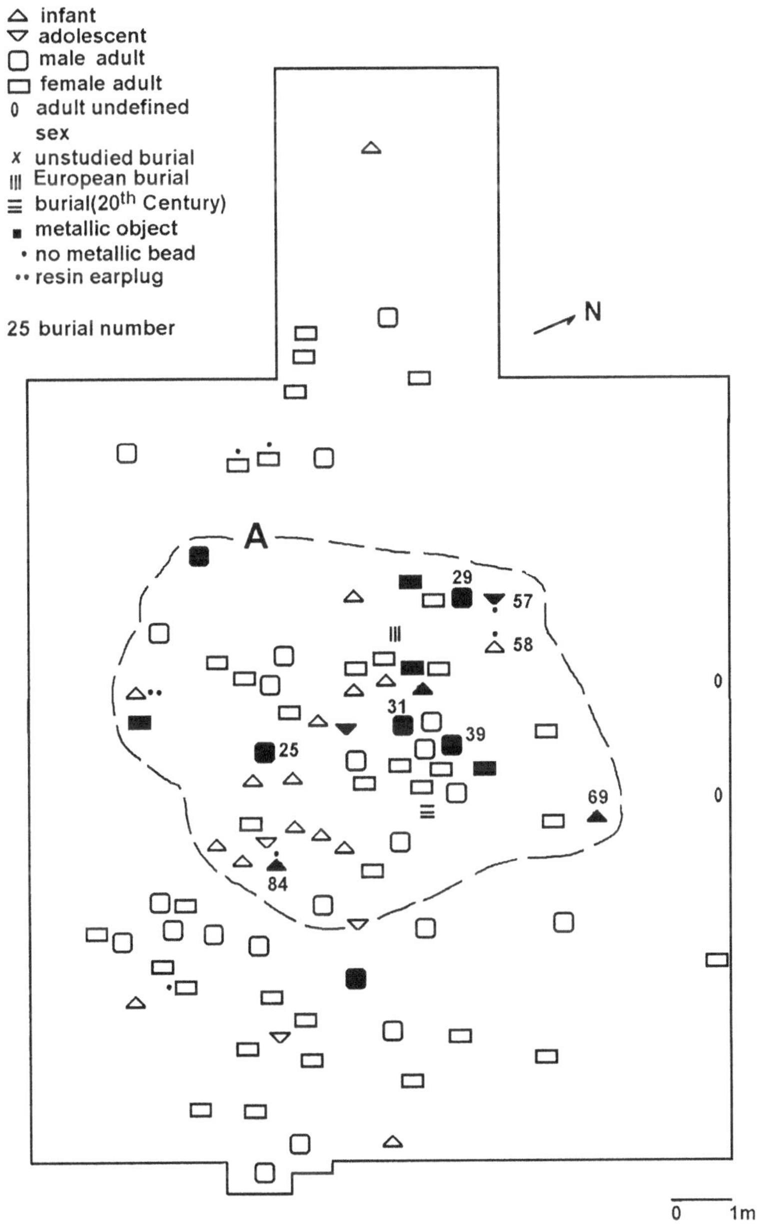

7.3. Sketch of Excavation Unit 3 with the distribution of burials and associated objects from El Chorro de Maíta cemetery

cording to Torres and Rivero de la Calle (1972) there is only one case of porotic *hiperostosis* or *criba orbitalia* and one *osteomalacia* in the femurs of an adult female reported from the site of El Porvenir, located 3.5 km from El Chorro de Maíta. These authors also mention one case of *osteitis* produced by reaction to an inflammation, which is suspected to be related to syphilis, found in the cranium of an unprovenienced infant, and a bone tumor (primary *osteoma*) found in the left humerus of a burial in the zone of Cañada Honda. It is significant that despite the large size of the sample, none of these pathologies was found in the sample of human remains from El Chorro de Maíta, suggesting some differences in health conditions between sites.

The absence of osteological pathologies related to subsistence stress and the relatively small number of infant deaths suggest a stable access to necessary nutrients. A paleonutrition study where strontium is used as a tracing element indicates the presence in Chorro de Maíta of a diverse diet that highlights the population's omnivorous character (Taylor 1990:51–52). This profile agrees with the analysis of subsistence activities based on the faunal remains (Rodríguez 1987), which concluded that inhabitants depended about equally on marine and terrestrial species. However, the paleonutrition analysis (Taylor 1990: 51–52) assumes similar dietary practices in the population at large and did not consider differential access to subsistence products according to sex or possibly to status differentiation.

OBJECTS ASSOCIATED WITH BURIALS

Burials with ceramic vessels are reported frequently in the archaeological area of Banes (Miguel 1949:177; Rouse 1942:149; Valcárcel et al. 2002:5), some of them containing food remains (Miguel 1949:176; Valcárcel et al. 2002:9). The presence of stone celts and necklaces of stone beads have also been reported (Miguel 1949:176; Rouse 1942: 8, 88, 95), but they tend to be uncommon. In El Chorro de Maíta, none of the burials included ceramic vessels and few had stone beads. Small and isolated fragments of indigenous or European ceramics were found near some of the burials, on occasion accompanied with pig, boar, or seashell remains. In the extensive excavations of 1986 and 1987, only seven burials included stone beads, most of them of quartzite generally used in necklaces.

The type of object found in the largest number of the burials from Chorro de Maíta is a small, metallic tube with an average length of 29 mm and a diameter of 2 mm, produced by the rolling of a fine metal sheet (Guarch

Delmonte 1996:20). The tubular form allows the metal to be strung on thread for use in necklaces, pendants, or other body ornaments. These metal tubes appear located mostly near the neck, thorax, pelvis, and wrist of the skeletons. In burial number 25, five of these tubular pieces were found together with a metallic disk covered with a cotton textile (see Figure 7.4) placed under the left knee (Guarch Delmonte 1996:20).

Until recently, it was assumed that these tubes were made of copper (Guarch Delmonte 1996:20), but recent analysis of X-ray fluorescence has determined that one of the tubes from burial no. 60 and the one from burial no. 84 were made of an alloy known as *latón* or brass (a copper-zinc alloy). One of the tubes found with the medallion of burial no. 25 was produced from an alloy with a high concentration of copper (Valcárcel 2002b).

Besides stone beads and metallic tubular pieces, three skeletons are accompanied by several beads made of a material that could be coral (Guarch Delmonte 1996:22), another one by beads of vegetable resin, and two others with ear spools (in one case made of vegetable resin and in the other of quartzite). Another skeleton had a half-finished bead made of fish vertebra, and two others had three pearl beads. Some of the burials contained pieces made of yet different materials. Burial 57 can be considered an exceptional case since it included possible coral and quartzite beads, one metallic tubular pendant and, unique in the cemetery, an ornitomorphic pendant elaborated from an alloy of gold, copper, and silver, as well as four laminar pendants and a bell made of the same alloy (see Figure 7.4), three pearl beads, two beads seemingly manufactured from gold wire, and a hollow spherical bead that seems to be made of an alloy of gold, copper, and silver (Guarch Delmonte 1996:21–22).

In addition to these objects, burials 47, 57, and 72 have small cloth remnants, and next to burial 31 part of a human bone marked with incisions (Guarch Delmonte 1996:21) was found. It is interesting that both burials 31 and 57 include metallic tubular pieces or other ornaments, suggesting a strong concentration of metallic materials among a restricted number of individuals. Excluding burials 72 and 47 that had only textile remains, all the objects mentioned are concentrated on only 25 skeletons of the 110 extracted by the Departamento Centro Oriental de Arqueología, that is to say 22.7 percent of the total sample. A metal disc accompanied burial no. 25, the metallic tubular pieces appear in 17 burials, and ornaments of gold, copper, and silver, as well as the pearls, are all represented in single burials; the nonmetallic body ornaments are located in 10 burials.

As with the stone beads, all these artifacts seem to be highly valued and

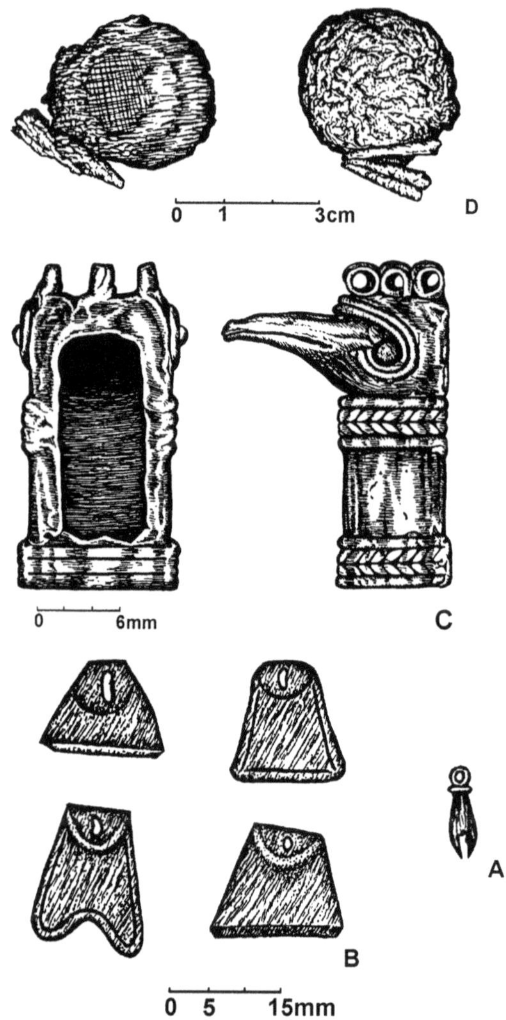

7.4. Objects associated with burials from the Chorro de Maíta cemetery: (a) bells made of guanín, Burial no. 57; (b) laminar pendant made of guanín, Burial no. 57; (c) ornitomorphic pendant made of a gold, copper, and silver alloy, Burial no. 57; (d) metallic disk covered with a piece of textile and attached with metallic tubes (both sides), Burial no. 25. Drawings by Antonio Cruz Bermúdez.

symbolic objects. Vega (1979), in an extensive revision of historic Antillean metal use, stresses the especially valuable character of the objects elaborated from the alloy of gold, copper, and silver called *guanín.* The guaníns constituted rare high-status objects that had to be imported from South America (Vega 1979:54). According to Oliver (2000:213–215), they represented a metaphor of the divine and celestial that was supported by diverse myths and gave the cacique his/her sacred nature. Because of its similarity to guanín, the latón or brass (copper-zinc alloy) brought by Europeans acquired the same sociocultural value and symbolic connotation. The gold was used in body ornaments and in the decorations of ceremonial objects to give them special powers (Oliver 2000:215). Some symbols of command were also detailed with this metal (Alegría 1980:11), and the names of several important caciques or chiefs from Hispaniola include a version of this term (Vega 1979:52, 55).

The four laminar pendants and the bell found with burial 57 (see Figure 7.4) present a proportion of gold, copper, silver, and silicon (Guarch Delmonte 1996:24) in agreement with the ranges identified by Siegel and Severin (1993:76) to estimate the presence of guanín. The possibility that other pieces containing gold, copper, and silver, but not analyzed quantitatively, could represent guaníns should not be ruled out.

In addition to the metals, the probable coral, pearl, and resin beads and the earspool made of resin must have been highly esteemed. Their forms, materials, and dimensions required a complex manufacturing process and a careful process of extraction. As evidence, we can point to microbeads found in burial no. 57 that originally were thought to be made of shell (Guarch Delmonte 1996:22). It has since been determined that they are made of quartzite. These pieces are exceptionally small, with a diameter of 1.5 mm and a thickness of 1 mm, and they were produced from a very hard material. These beads exemplify the degree of complexity that the producers had to face and their level of technical skills.

The objects associated with burials are also significant for their rarity. The resin beads and ear spools, the pearl beads, and the possible coral beads have not been discovered on any other site in Cuba, nor have quartzite beads of such small size been found. The metal pieces have appeared only in four places in Banes, and they always consist of a single object (Valcárcel 1999:89). This dearth of ornaments holds true for the rest of Cuba (Guarch Delmonte 1996:24). In El Chorro de Maíta, however, there are 9 objects of gold or gold alloyed with copper and silver, a metallic disk in burial no. 25, and 28 metallic tubular objects between the complete and broken pieces (Valcárcel 2002b).

The significant presence of these materials in the cemetery of El Chorro de Maíta does not seem attributable to any differential conservation due to soil characteristics since the matrix is similar to that found elsewhere in Cuba. It appears instead that we are seeing a situation of differential access to goods of limited circulation and high sumptuary and symbolic value owing to the special peculiarities of the settlement itself.

Bearing in mind the exclusive character of the objects associated with the burials and their limited use, it is difficult to think that their distribution was arbitrary or random. Considering further the attributes of the settlement and its significance in relationship to the neighboring sites, the site seems to express social distinctions related to leadership positions. The typology of the objects reinforces this idea. Rather than ceramic vessels carrying food for the afterlife, they are body ornaments, symbols of their user's special status.

Elite distinctions are not seen in evidence of better health and diet of the persons buried with the objects. However, the interpretation of a hereditary elite is reinforced by access to the objects by children and by the spatial distribution of the burials with such goods.

The distribution of metallic objects by sex is even between adult males (n=6) and females (n=6). They are also present in the burials of three of the children and two adolescents. Nonmetallic objects are distributed mostly among mature women (n=5), children (n=3), and adolescents (n=2). Children and adolescents comprise 29.4 percent of the burials with metallic objects and 50 percent of the burials with nonmetallic objects.

In a striking way, the most complex groups of objects are associated with a female adolescent approximately nineteen years of age (burial 57) and with a boy 0–6 months (burial 58) (Guarch Delmonte 1996:22). While it is still possible that a person in a society of this type could accumulate personal merits that made him/her deserve a differential treatment before the age of twenty (limit for the adolescent age group), it is impossible to assume this for small children.

An adult male (burial 29) is located near burial 57. Both burials have the same position, are buried to a similar depth, and do not overlap or impact each other. Burial 58 is located toward the feet of burial 57 (see Figure 7.3). It also shows marked similarities to burial 57 regarding the depth of interment and the lack of interference. In a cemetery where it is common to bury a body by removing parts of previous burials, these three individuals (57, 29, and 58) seem to have been buried at the same time. It is noteworthy that burial 29 possesses a metal tubular piece and burial 57 and 58 hold the highest variability and the most important objects. It is possible that these features represent either a family burial—a cacique with his wife and son—or a burial of mother and child (Rodríguez Arce 1989:8). References to both situations occur in the historic documents for Hispaniola, but archaeologically it is difficult to define the relationship in a more precise manner.

The presence of several children with objects suggests that the hereditary transmission of status was not unusual but rather that it was a socially accepted and institutionalized practice. The parity between men and women in the use of metallic objects and the concentration of nonmetallic objects for women, children, and adolescents seem to support this conjecture. Even when it is admitted that some women achieved status through marriage (not ascribed), these burials still include individuals from sex and age groups with few possibilities of raising their status through personal deeds.

While most of the indigenous burials (n=93) and objects are located in Unit 3, the rest of the excavations report only two burials with metallic objects and three with nonmetallic objects. In Unit 3, the largest quantity of objects and burials is clustered in its central part, designated Zone A (see Figure 7.3). This zone includes 53 burials representing 56.9 percent of all human remains recovered from Unit 3 and 48.1 percent for the whole sample unearthed during excavations by the Departamento Centro Oriental de Arqueología. Zone A also includes 93.3 percent of the burials from Unit 3 with metallic objects and 57.1 percent of the burials with nonmetallic objects. Regarding the total number of burials with objects in the cemetery, Zone A represents 82.3 percent of the burials with metallic ornaments and 40 percent of the burials with nonmetallic ornaments. Undoubtedly the differentiated treatment received by certain people in their burials goes well beyond the attribution of special objects. It also includes their location in a particular area within the cemetery, which seems to have been considered very important since it contains the largest number of burials.

The chronology of the burials has not been established properly, and therefore it is difficult to understand the presence of the objects in a temporal sense. Burial 25, which possesses a metal medallion and cloth, has been dated to 870 ± 70 B.P. (Beta—148956; human bone; d 13c/12c = −19 percent). Burial 39, with a metal tubular piece, is dated to 360 ± 80 B.P. (Beta—148955; human bone; d 13c/12c = −19 percent), and burials 69 and 84 have tubes of latón that date their interment to after 1492. These findings suggest a consistent tradition in the employment of metals, a tradition that survived contact with Europeans by adapting new raw materials. The ornitomorphic pendant of gold, copper, and silver and the guanín bell belong to a non-Antillean typology. J. R. Oliver (2000:201, 216n.37) considers that the bird piece could have originated from the Caribbean coast of Colombia, perhaps related to the Tairona culture. It is unknown how and when it was introduced to the island, but in any case the distinctive character that these objects lent their users is notable during both the pre-Hispanic period and after the European invasion. It is important to mention that while the specific relations between this community and the Europeans are not clear, the presence of three skeletons (nos. 39, 69, 84) with postcolumbian dates and metal objects indicates the presence of status differentiation in late times and, possibly, within the context of direct contact with the Spanish.

CEMETERY AND CEREMONIAL SPACE

El Chorro de Maíta's burial area is located approximately in the center of the archaeological site. Its dimensions (2,000 m^2) are similar to those of the central spaces of many large sites in Banes. The use of central clearings in villages for social exchange and ceremonial activities has been widely reported for Cuba based on revised historical interpretations (Moreira 1999:11; Trincado 1984:49). Considering its location and the fact that no other cleared area has been found that could have functioned as a plaza, the possibility that the cemetery area was used for this purpose cannot be discarded. There is no archaeological evidence for any kind of feature that would delimit this area. In the southern part, Unit 5, domestic remains affecting a burial were located, possibly indicating an encroachment of the residential areas into the burial area around 730 ± 60 B.P. (Beta—148957; charred wood; d 13c/12c = −25 percent). The conditions of the domestic-funeral contact in the remaining edges of the burial area are not clear. There are no concentrations of domestic residuals in the main central area. When they do appear, the deposits are thin and isolated, deposited by natural erosion processes. The fact that this space was kept cleared indicates that its special function was recognized and its dimensions were maintained.

The burial area presents two well-differentiated soil layers. The superficial layer is between 10 and 30 cm thick and consists of a limestone-based brown soil, rich in phosphates and organic matter, with an acid pH. The lower layer is formed by limestone chalk of yellowish color, lacking phosphates and with an alkaline pH. The few skeletons or parts of skeletons present in the first layer had heavy deterioration because of the acidity of the soil. The skeletons in the second layer were better preserved. Only two individuals were buried in the upper layer. It is logical to think that the indigenous people preferred to bury their relatives at deeper levels to avoid the effects of decomposition. However, it may also indicate an intention to preserve the remains linked with the cult of the ancestors (Rodríguez Arce 1989:4). Pané (1990:37) reports the conservation of bones of the ancestors inside some *zemies* (idols). Using historical references, Vega (1987:5) describes a range of preservation techniques that include baskets with bones and skulls set in protected places of the houses, bodies dried over fire, cotton idols covering a skull, and skulls from burials protected by ceramic vessels. The location of the burials was not only an area for the disposal of the dead but also a physical place where the ancestors were preserved.

The available dates for the burials indicate the special use of this area for five centuries. Independent of the continuity of the cemetery, the symbolic meaning of this space as the ancestors' residence and an area of social contact would have encouraged a long-lived tradition. Starting with an analogy to South American groups, Siegel (1989) and Oliver (1992; cited by Curet and Oliver 1998:229–230) have presented the hypothesis that the structuring of Puerto Rico's Saladoid villages around the plazas where burials are clustered represents the axis that connects the world of the living with the world of the ancestors. Considering the relationship of the Saladoid presence in later cultural developments in the Greater Antilles, it is possible to apply this reasoning to the case of El Chorro de Maíta. This cemetery could represent a ceremonial grouping of the ancestors that worked as the *axis mundi* of community life. The cemetery plaza suggests the central role of ceremonies and rituals that accords with the wider deployment of visible religious iconography at the site.

It is notable that the central part of Unit 3 (Zone A) possesses the largest number of burials (see Figure 7.3). This space is near the center of the burial area, according to the site structure determined at the present time. Although the actual layout of the site is not known, it is possible that Zone A was at some time the central focus of the settlement. Such supposition is in agreement with some South American data on the existence of a central element (e.g., post, plaza, icon) that, according to Lathrap (1985; cited by Curet and Oliver 1998:230), contributes a dynamic equilibrium to the cosmos and works as a link between the natural and supernatural worlds. Bearing this evidence in mind, we can conclude that this area has an exceptional symbolic value that emphasizes the location of the burials. This could explain why 80 percent of the children and the great majority of the burials with objects are located there. Since the dated skeletons are located in this area, this symbolic value must have been acknowledged for the whole range of the site's occupation.

In the cemetery of El Chorro de Maíta, the burials are not marked, and many times they are disturbed by other burials, suggesting that the most important thing is to place the body in this special location and not a specific position within it. According to Bloch and Parry (1982; cited by Curet and Oliver 1998:228), this low level of individualization of the dead is related to communal practices intended to reinforce the symbolic unity of the group. Another element that supports the communal character of the cemetery is the fact that some individuals were buried in a careless manner and in positions (such as supine) that perhaps suggest rejection or disapproval of some individuals. It is also significant that the presence of women is common, when it would be expected (based on ethnohistorical analogy) that they did not control any position of power in these communities. Such situations and the limited number of ornamental objects indicate that people with a wide range of social status were buried in this cemetery and not only the elite.

The presence of cemeteries in centralized, unformalized spaces and the lack of individual grave markers at Saladoid sites in Puerto Rico have been considered as evidence of egalitarian social relationships (Curet and Oliver 1998:229). In the case of El Chorro de Maíta, the possibility of a similar situation, at least in certain elements of the social structure, has also to be evaluated.

DISCUSSION

The cemetery of El Chorro de Maíta shows the coexistence of forms of institutionalized social inequality and elements of community cohesion, characteristic of egalitarian groups. Elements of egalitarian profile are associated with the structure of the burial area and are temporally consistent with the other features. They consist of the nonformalization of the cemetery and the individual burials and in the leveling effect associated with the act of locating all the burials in a common space. Inside the cemetery are people with sumptuary and symbolic objects that distinguish them from the rest of the population. These burials appear early on, but it is unclear when children accompanied with such objects began to be buried in this area as an expression of the process of hereditary status transmission and of the institutionalization of social inequality.

In spite of the lack of precise details regarding the chronology of the burials and the development toward institutionalized social inequality, it is evident that such a process resulted in the existence of a well-structured elite. The presence of this elite corresponds with indicators of leadership visible in other aspects of the settlement and related to (1) the control of a large set of body ornaments and ceremonial objects not consumed in mortuary practices; (2) the organization and development of an economy that allowed the maintenance of a possibly large population with adequate levels of health and nutrition; (3) the procurement of exotic raw materials of limited circulation such as metals or the acquisition of objects elaborated with these raw materials and used selectively in mortuary rites; and (4) the apparently dominant position of the settlement in relationship to neighboring sites.

When this inequality was incorporated into the cemetery, it seems to have been linked to important ceremonial aspects, perhaps associated with legitimization of the social hierarchy. The concentration of aspects related to social inequality in the most important zone of the cemetery reinforces this interpretation because this area possesses a strong symbolic value. Inequality, however, goes farther than this and includes the supernatural world, creating different types of ancestors organized in a hierarchy themselves which then reinforces the existence of a hierarchy in the world of the living. From this perspective, there is an insertion of inequality within the communal mechanisms, probably by leaders intending to use them to their own benefit, as seems to have occurred among agricultural groups in Puerto Rico (Curet and Oliver 1998).

Funeral caves are present near El Chorro de Maíta, but at the moment there is no evidence of their use by inhabitants of the site. Neither are there indications of additional burials under house floors or in mounds outside the cemetery area. However, we can not exclude other funeral forms parallel to the use of the cemetery, as is pointed out by Siegel for Puerto Rico (1999:217–220). The simultaneity of communal and domestic (private) burials reported by Siegel represents a coexistence of egalitarian and hierarchical elements. At El Chorro de Maíta evidence of such coexistence is provided in the space of the cemetery and suggests, as in Puerto Rico, the emergence of an elite.

Considering the information at hand, our knowledge about how the communal elements coexisted and related to the institutionalization of social inequality remains imprecise. It is necessary to know the different instances of this coexistence and the correlation of those elements with other aspects of the site to understand the preeminence of one or the other and to determine to what degree egalitarian relationships had deteriorated. In any case, it seems clear that the process of hierarchization was under way and that we are seeing a society in transition. A hierarchical structure was emerging with groups whose leading position was transmitted in a hereditary way and reinforced by means of ceremonies and preferential access to symbolic and sumptuary elements. The presence of the El Chorro de Maíta group suggests a more complex society with interregional links, probably representing an incipient chiefdom.

ACKNOWLEDGMENTS

We would like to acknowledge the support of Dr. Betty J. Meggers of the Smithsonian Institution, who provided the analysis for the radiocarbon dates used in this work. We are also grateful to Lic. Carlos Peña Rodríguez, who assisted with the English translation; to the artist Antonio Cruz Bermúdez, who facilitated the drawings of artifacts from El Chorro de Maíta; to José R. Oliver and Juanita Saenz for providing information on the metal objects; and to L. Antonio Curet for his suggestions on different aspects of this work.

8 / Mythical Expressions in the Ceramic Art of Agricultural Groups in the Prehistoric Antilles

Pedro Godo

When the archaeology of Cuba reoriented its perspective in the 1960s to the methodological and conceptual foundations of historical materialism, the priority of research became knowledge of the socioeconomic and general infrastructural processes of our indigenous communities. It was not until the 1980s that investigations of the superstructural sphere were definitively revived. In my case, motivated by the works of Arrom (1975), López Baralt (1977), Alegría (1978), Dacal Moure (1972), Guarch Delmonte and Rodríguez Cullel (1980), García Arévalo (1989), Rives (1985), Guarch Delmonte (1987), and other authors, I wanted to explore the artistic/mythical milieu with the purpose of going beyond the simple effort to associate common figurative images with the mythic zemies, individuals, and animals appearing in the relations of Friar Pané (1990 [1498]) from Hispaniola.

Going beyond the description of traditions and the unreliable interpretations of historical observers, I became interested in investigating the abstract or geometric expressions of higher complexity. This inevitably led to approaching the semiotics of artistic forms, to consider them as carriers of information through the use of symbols and systems of symbols. Beginning this kind of endeavor required at least an elementary theoretical preparation through the works of Saussure (1973), Eco (1972), Lévi-Strauss (1970), and other authors. The history of my work on this topic, presented here, represents only the beginning of a long-term research project.

THE TURTLE: THE FEMALE AND MOTHER OF HUMANITY

My first entry into this research brought me to the topic of the mythical turtle materialized in the ceramics of El Morrillo (Godo 1985), a well-excavated, late-period site in western Cuba (A.D. 1360) (Payarés 1980). The lack of incising on the rims or shoulder panels of ceramic vessels was distinctive in this collection, composed of thousands of ceramic fragments, including 3,885 sherds from nondisturbed areas (24 m^2 and an average depth of 0.45 m). Among the modeled handles, only six examples re-created the traditional zoomorphic images (frogs, bats, and turtles), and no sign of anthropomorphism was observed. However, of a total of 54 handles collected in the site, 63 percent were distinguished by their curved forms and their tendency to project toward the center or the ends of the vessels. One specimen was key for the reconstruction of what I have suggested to be a series of figures representing the turtle theme (Figure 8.1a). In the center portion of the handle appears a head, out from which project some lateral appendages reinforced by incised linear decorations that may represent the front extremities of the animal.

In other examples, the head of the turtle seems to have disappeared while the handle maintains its projections and a general structure (Figures 8.1b–h). Their numeric dominance over other types of handles corresponds to a strong synthesis, resembling types such as the coil or cleat lug handles (Figure 8.2) identified by Rouse (1942) and the Cuban archaeologists of the Grupo Guamá (Junta Nacional de Arqueología y Etnología 1951; see also Dacal Moure, Chapter 2, and Berman et al., Chapter 3). Clearly, the turtle element was identifiable in pieces with nonfigurative forms and held a special place in the particular context of El Morrillo pottery. It is the most popular theme in the ceramics of this coastal site, where agriculture was significantly supplemented by the marine economy, particularly through a large consumption of *Chelonias* or sea turtles. Although a thorough faunal analysis has not been conducted, the excavation reports mention the presence of large quantities of sea turtle remains, third only to the amount of sea shells and *jutías* (a large native rodent). During the excavations, Payarés (1980) observed this pattern throughout the archaeological deposits. Sea turtles appear to have contributed a larger biomass to the diet than any other faunal species recovered from the site. Therefore, the turtle did not represent a protected or taboo figure but perhaps a community emblem of group self-identification.

In the last few years, I have extended the results of El Morrillo to the study

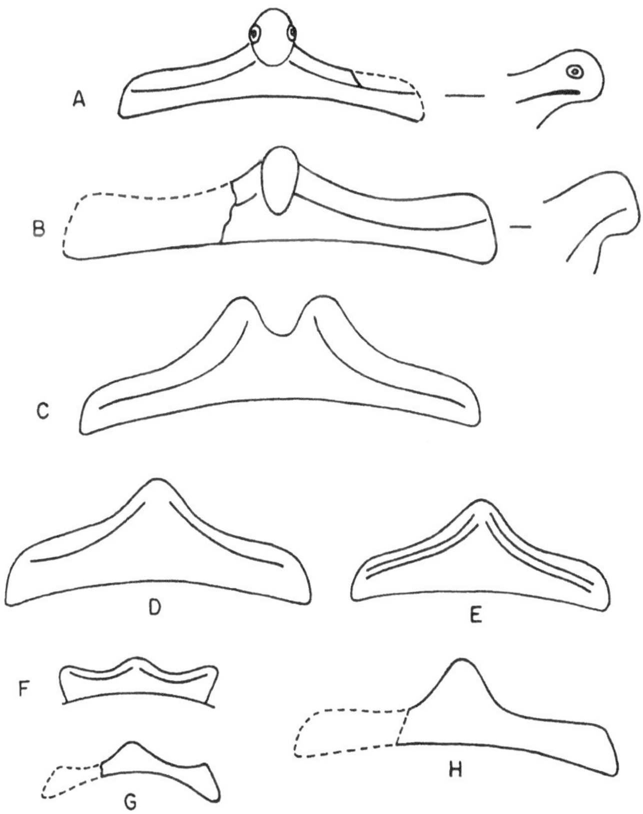

8.1. Examples of turtle theme handles from El Morrillo

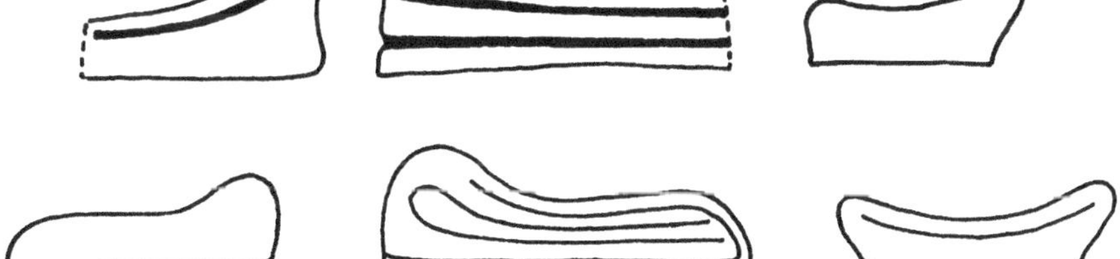

8.2. Syncretism of the coil handle and turtle theme from El Morrillo

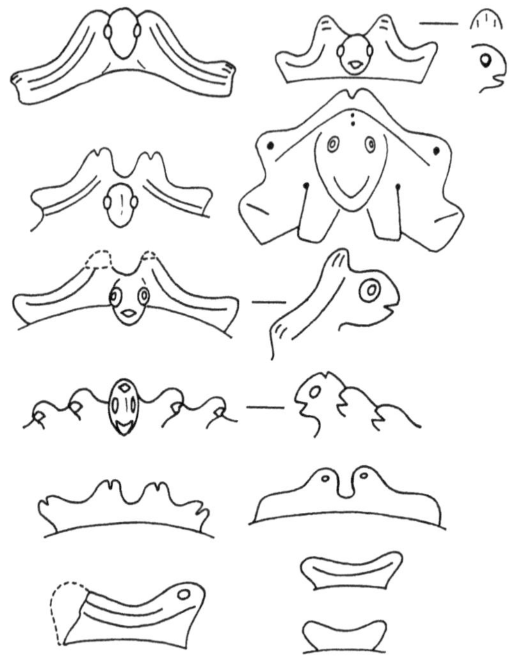

8.3. The basic turtle representational unit and its variations. Examples from sites in central and eastern Cuba.

of collections from five other sites from central and eastern Cuba where turtle designs are abundant in the assemblages of symbolic artifacts. They, too, include figurative and schematic imagery that does not seem to respond to an evolutionary line but to a system of representations. Stylized zoomorphic expressions and more abstract syntheses coexist in the unprovenienced collections. For this reason, at the moment it is not possible to suggest an evolutionary sequence of the artistic forms from the simplest ones to the more complex ones, but certainly a system of representations can be defined by combining these artistic forms.

These forms, and sometimes more elaborated images, exhibit the head of the turtle in the center and rounded projections with small incisions on one end, representing the lateral extremities. The projections, either integrated into the structure of the handle or isolated as in their simplest expression, show some variation at the terminus. In a condensed form, these simplified extremities come to represent the entire turtle motif (Porebski 1994). The turtle sign is active and transformative in its semiotic function, as when the figurative parts (paws, head, mouth, eyes) evoke the whole animal (Figure 8.3).

We also see individuals represented together in one or two pairs, sometimes accompanying the main turtle-head image, sometimes without it. These figures may refer to one of the mythical stories mentioned by Pané (1990 [1498]). In this myth, Demanián Caracaracol, one of the four mythical *caracaracol* twin-heroes, carries a turtle on his back. After removing her, the four twins live with her and take her as a mate. They and their descendants may represent the original turtle-people.

We should be able to assume that the society that created these images generally agreed upon their symbolic significance. These figurative ceramic handles can be characterized as a popular channel for the transmission of messages and themes in a sociocultural communication between originators and receivers (Moles 1973). Among the typology of handles already mentioned, in cases where part of the vessel has survived, the turtle is present in a supine position, perhaps as a metaphor for the common sexual position of females among humans. This is in contrast to the myth, where the turtle is above Demanián. As is well known, the association of turtles with women is a recurrent theme in mythologies throughout the Americas. Perhaps one reason for this is because of the great reproductive capacity of turtles. The sexual relationship between the turtle and the caracaracoles twins is seen in Caribbean myth, an issue discussed extensively by Stevens-Arroyo (1988). In terms of the feminine symbolism, López Baralt (1977) has argued that the female turtle extracted from Demanián's back is a mythical response to the lack of women and the need to create a new generation after the "great flood" produced by the caracaracoles twins. In the myth, this new generation is born after intercourse with the turtle.

While at the end of the story presented by Pané the twins build a house and care for the turtle, in the version presented by Pedro Mártir de Anglería (Pané 1990 [1498]:103), a woman is born from Demanián's back, and it is with her that the twins procreate. Based on these associations, Arrom's (1975:142) argument that the turtle represents the "mythical mother of humanity" seems plausible.

However, another possibility arises. It should be kept in mind that indigenous people preferred to capture turtles on the beach during spawning by turning them face up so that they were immobilized, just as they are observed in the pottery. Therefore, if I apply the approach of Lévi-Strauss (1970) who says that objects reach their definitive existence by means of the integration of their decorative and utilitarian function, then the vessel is the turtle itself that zealously guards its symbolic significance in the antithesis death-life. This duality is expressed in the position of their capture (death) and in the vessel as food and container of foods (life), as the female in a mythical marriage, and as the mother of humanity.

THE FROG, GIVER OF BREAD

The next theme to consider is the mythical frog or, to put it a better way, the different batraciform characters that can be objectively isolated in decorative forms. The first inquiries of Godo and Celaya (1990) also began in the 1980s (undertaken before learning of the invaluable contribution made by Petitjean Roget [1978]) and addressed this topic in the ceramics of the Lesser Antilles. In comparing a small sample of decorated *burenes,* or cassava griddles, with other artifacts, the prevalence of a stylized and schematic image of the frog became apparent. This image could be traced to the motif of the frog's rear extremities and its variants, including the line and point enclosed in an oval design that represents the flexion and geometric motifs, most often a set of concentric circles (Figures 8.4 and 8.5). Why is the frog present on the burenes, in an evident relationship with agriculture? Since the stories presented by Pané did not offer the answer to this question, we looked to a possible connection with variants of a South American myth shared by Arawak and Carib elsewhere (Alegría 1978; Lévi-Strauss 1978; López Baralt 1977). An old frog-woman, adoptive mother of the twins, sent them every day to hunt or fish, and whenever they returned they invariably found the cassava bread already prepared. They decided to discover the secret of the frog-woman. Hiding one day, they observed that she took the dough from a white stain on her back and then cooked it on the burén. In one version of the myth, the frog scratches her neck and vomits fire. The story concludes with the twins acquiring the cassava and the fire either by stealing them or by burning the old woman in the forest or in the clearing of a field.

Using these and other versions documented in the works of Alegría (1978), Lévi-Strauss (1978), and López Baralt (1977), we interpreted the expression of the myth in the burenes as a case of unity and inversion in the mythical-artistic realm. In the story, the frog is under the cassava; it is either on her skin or above her body. In the burén, the frog is on the *casabe* (cassava bread) and transferred to the food, which is consecrated by the fire and by contact with the decorative image. After observing duplications of the batrachiform images or motifs in the burenes and in other pieces, we developed a hypothesis of an Antillean version of the myth with a similar structure, but where the myth performs a transformation of the twins into frogs themselves, after they sacrifice their frog-mother.

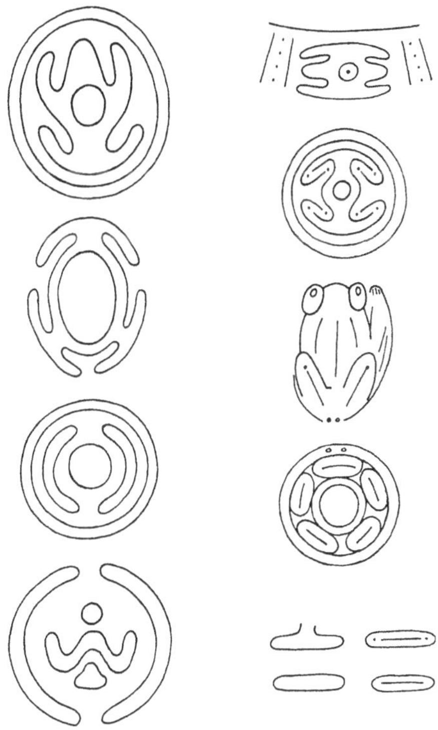

8.4. Batrachiform designs on *burenes* or clay griddles (*right column*) and other artifacts (*left column*) (after Arrom 1975: Figure 60; Godo and Celaya 1990:170–172; Harrington 1975: Figure 86).

In the past few years, I have identified new designs in burenes where the image of the frog is simplified into motifs or geometric expressions through a process of schematization of the batrachian elements (Figure 8.6). Petitjean's (1978) study helps us understand the central motif of the back legs and its derived representations, including the most complex one that constitutes a double spiral, presumed to combine four distinct elements (Figure 8.7).

If the motif of the back leg evokes the whole animal, then its duplications indicate multiple individuals in numbers of two and four. These groupings I interpret as twin-frogs. The zoomorphic transfiguration of the twins is very evident in mythical references. In one version, Shikie' mona and Ivreke were born from two fish spawns and raised by Kawao, the woman-frog, who at the end of the story is transformed into a fish (López Baralt 1977). In addition, Oliver (1998) has convincingly identified the twin-frogs in the iconogra-

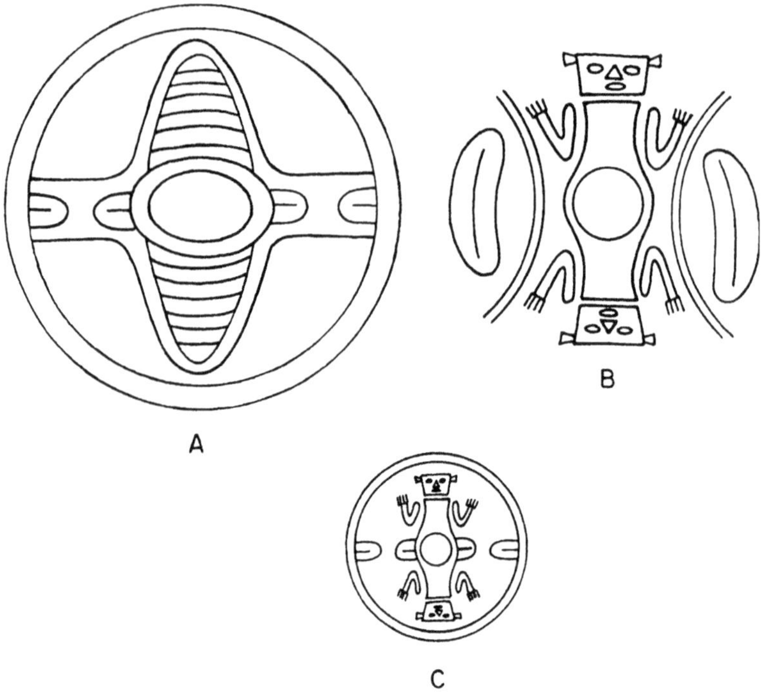

8.5. Batrachiform designs: (a) complex batrachiform representation duplicated on a *burén* or clay griddle from Cuba (after Godo and Celaya 1990:180); (b) note the presence of twins and the similar structure and design to the previous burén (a) (after Chanlatte 1984: Lámina 37); (c) structural arrangement of ceramic designs from Sorcé, Puerto Rico, compared with the design of a Cuban burén (a).

8.6. Reconstruction of the design on *burenes* or clay griddles associated with the schematization of batrachians

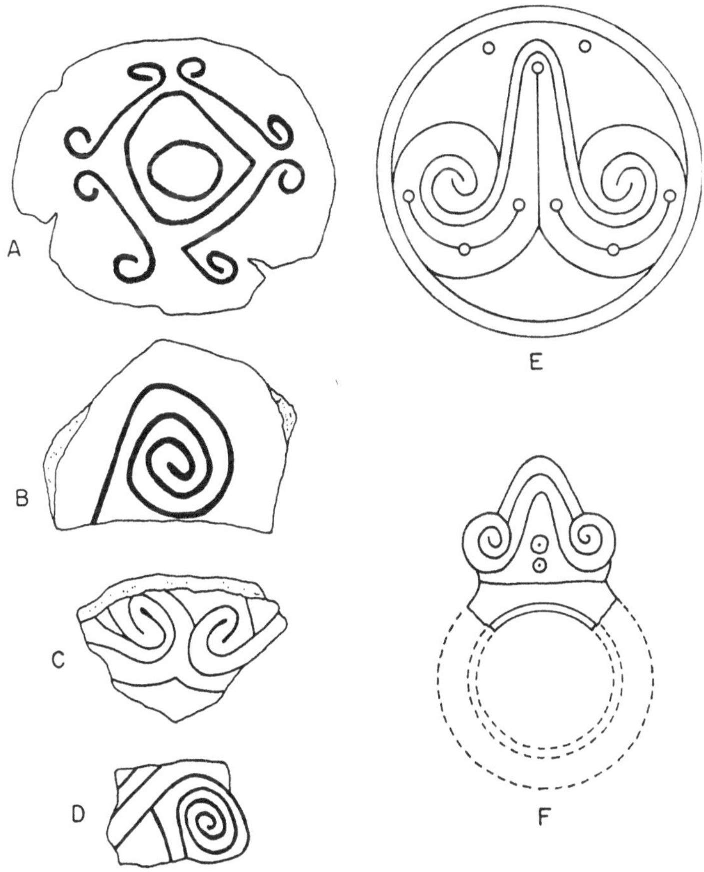

8.7. Batrachiform designs: (a) *burén* or clay griddle with interior incised design associated with aboriginal communities having Saladoid ceramics (after Chanlatte and Narganes 1983: Lámina 15); (b) fragments of burenes with the double spiral design, variety of the frog leg representation from Sardinero, Cuba (after Trincado et al. 1973:119); (c) fragments of burenes with the double spiral design, variety of the frog leg representation from La Rosa, Cuba (after Godo and Celaya 1990:177); (d) from Bellevue, Jamaica (after Medhurst 1977: Figure 7-A); (e) shell disk from the La Rosa site (after Godo and Celaya 1990:177); (f) shell pendant from Playa Carbó, Cuba, with representations of the frog with spiral flexed legs.

phy of the ceremonial center at Caguana in Puerto Rico. I believe that other anthropomorphic representations are clearly present in some of the figurative examples (Figures 8.5b and 8.8).

Geometric forms such as circles, triangles, rhombuses, and others are not just simple ornaments. In my opinion, they are minimal iconographic units

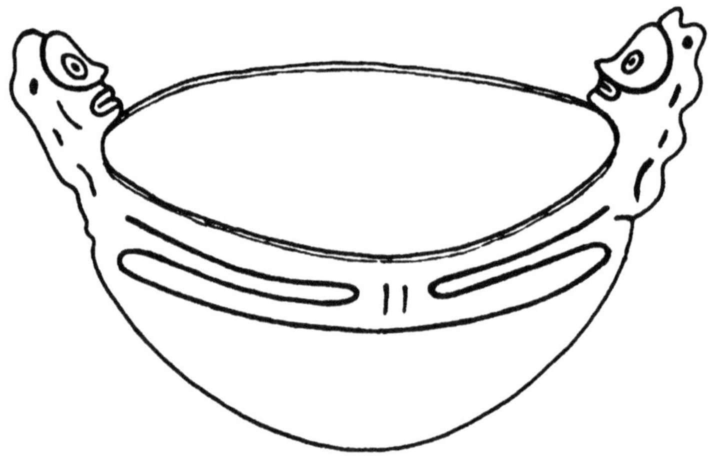

8.8. Ceramic vessel with anthropomorphic handles (twins) and paneled motifs of frog legs from a cave in Baracoa, Cuba. After Tabío and Rey 1966:253.

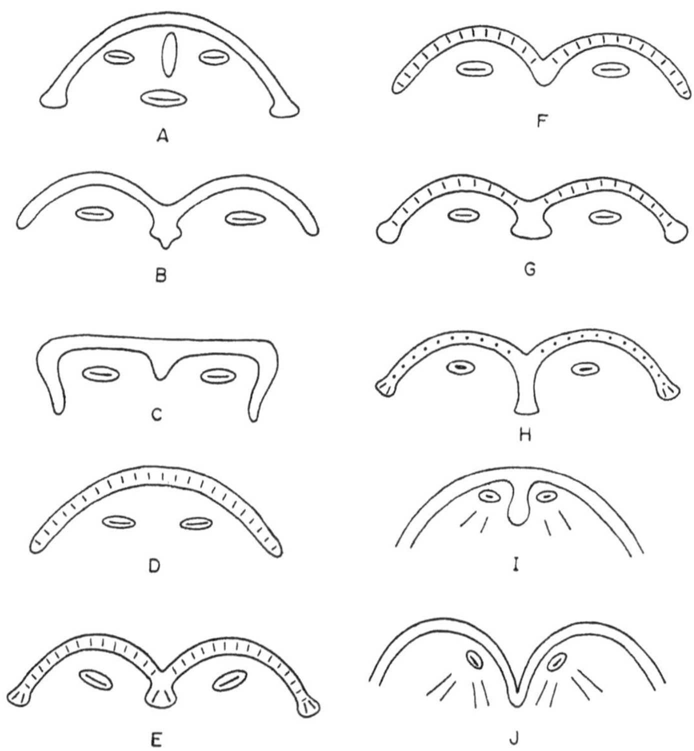

8.9. Anthropomorphic images of crying/raining. After Celaya and Godo 2000:72.

that alone, according to Olmos (1991), do not possess a meaning. It is when they are combined with the rest of the elements of the design that they acquire a meaning and become proper symbolic units. Possible examples of this interpretation are the circle on the body of the frog or in the middle of the burén and the cassava and the rhombus-like body of the frog with the circle-cassava superimposed in the example of Puerto Rico (Figure 8.7a). Nevertheless, the single designs of concentric circles, triangles, rhomboids, and other compositions of geometric character are observed in a large sample of burenes, possibly representing iconic syntagmas of the same topic, since the reference context is the burén. As in the case of the turtle vessels, the burén is both the frog itself and the history of the twins in the origin myth of systematized agriculture.

THE CRYING FIGURE

My last topic is related to a crying figure commonly found in ceramics from eastern Cuba. In the collection from Loma del Indio, Celaya and Godo (2000) reconstructed about 30 varieties of this character (see examples in Figures 8.9, 8.10, and 8.11), generically identified by a face under a simple or double arch that extends to the sides, suggesting the presence of limbs. The tears, when present, are shown as single, double, or triple incisions and rarely as punctation. In the process of artistic synthesis some features (nose, mouth, tears) were lost and others persisted, such as the eyes, the appliqué in the form of arches, or smaller strips of clay that evoke the image, even though other more clearly figurative elements are missing.

These crying faces, which have also been found in media other than ceramics, are usually called the *llora-lluvias* (cry-rains) and traditionally have been identified with the *zemi* Boinayel. Arrom (1975) has suggested that this zemi was the provider of rain and, according to the myth, its companion was Márohu, its complementary opposite whose name can be translated as "without clouds" or "spirit of the clear skies." Several bicephalous entities and similar double figures or twins have been connected to these zemies.

After considering the iconographic heterogeneity among the anthropozoomorphic figures, Celaya and Godo (2000) have questioned the identification of the mythical Boinayel with the archaeological crying figures (Figure 8.11). In the case of the anthropozoomorphic figure, the individual is related to the previously mentioned coil or cleat-lug handles that represent a synthesis of the turtle or another handle type similar to the representations of owls, where the emphasis is on the beak and the eyes are shown as perforations or depres-

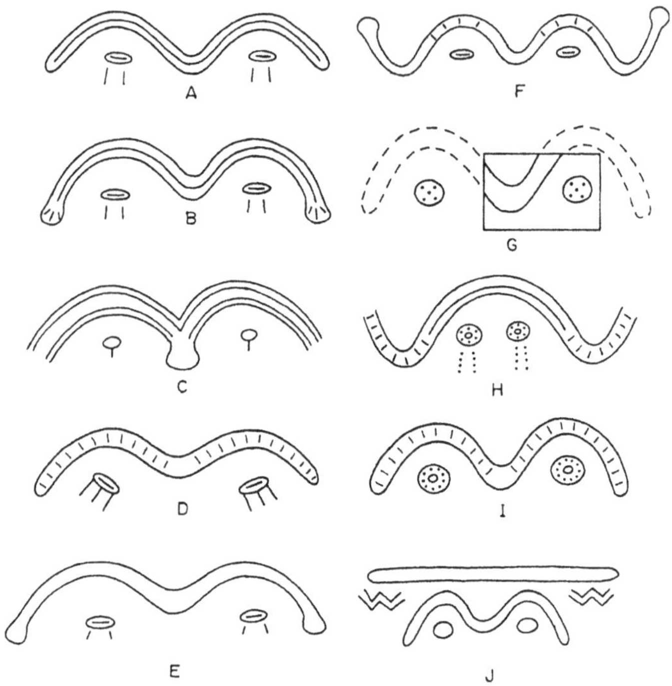

8.10. Anthropomorphic images of crying/raining. After Celaya and Godo 2000:73.

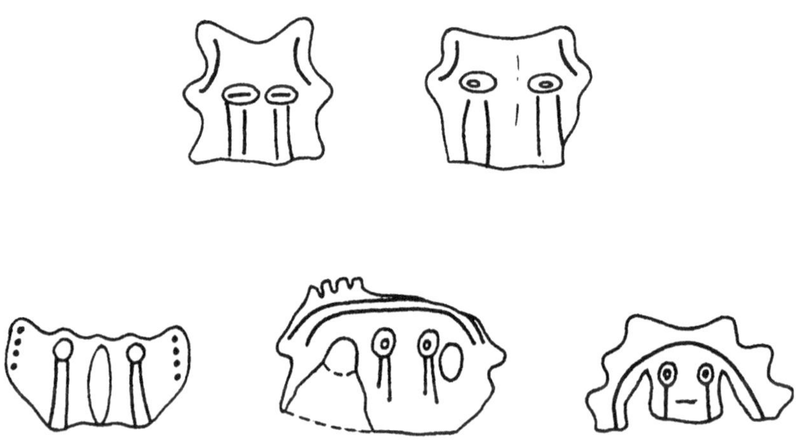

8.11. Images of crying/raining with anthropozoomorphic features. After Celaya and Godo 2000:77–79.

sions. This evidence of human-animal isomorphism tends to complicate the identification of the character. Although Pané (1990 [1498]) indicates that representations of Boinayel and Márohu were visited by indigenous people when rain was scarce, he does not make any specific reference to tears. The figures were simply described as zemies made of stone, with their hands tied and with evidence of sweating. It is possible that in myth they were twins, but this does not mean that they can be matched to the artistic forms of the crying twins nor can they be related to water, since this would contradict the etymology of Márohu.

Far from being a standardized representation, the repertoire of images of these crying figures is extensive and variable in its artistic forms, raw materials, and type of artifact. In addition to its particular expression in ceramics, it is found in petroglyphs in a simplified form with the face represented schematically. It is also present on lithic artifacts and on wooden idols associated with the *cohoba* ceremony, where it is more characteristically shown with ear ornaments, hair dressing, a band or ribbon over the head, and other decorations that seem to impart a degree of social distinction. In Cuba, there is at least one additional example among the *guaizas* or shell masks that normally emphasize the human face (Figure 8.12a).

Another example is a very particular type of small pendant idol that has also been related to Boinayel, which is an armless squatting figure. Some variations have eyes, others have incisions on the face that look like tears. In general, they exhibit a prominent nose or snout and a headdress or turban (Figure 8.12b). Rodríguez Arce (2000) believes that they are pieces with an anthropomorphic body and the face of a bat, but it is also possible to recognize the intention of the artisan to reproduce indeterminate beings with a broad anthropomorphic conception. In other words, they have human bodies and animal faces.

I believe that in this typology of pendants, the headdress or turban is very important because, in its most elaborate expression, it presents binary motifs such as the incised line enclosed by an oval. Arrom (1975) presents an example of this same motif with a crying individual wearing a headdress (Figure 8.12c). Pendants of twins with these same elements that have been identified at the site of El Morrillo (Figure 8.12d) at first sight look like a complex geometric composition. However, it is actually a dual anthropomorphic image with an incomplete and dismembered anatomic structure. The double dental arrangement can be observed in the central idol, and on both sides the extremities have eyes of idols. Their headdresses repeat the binary motif. Another version

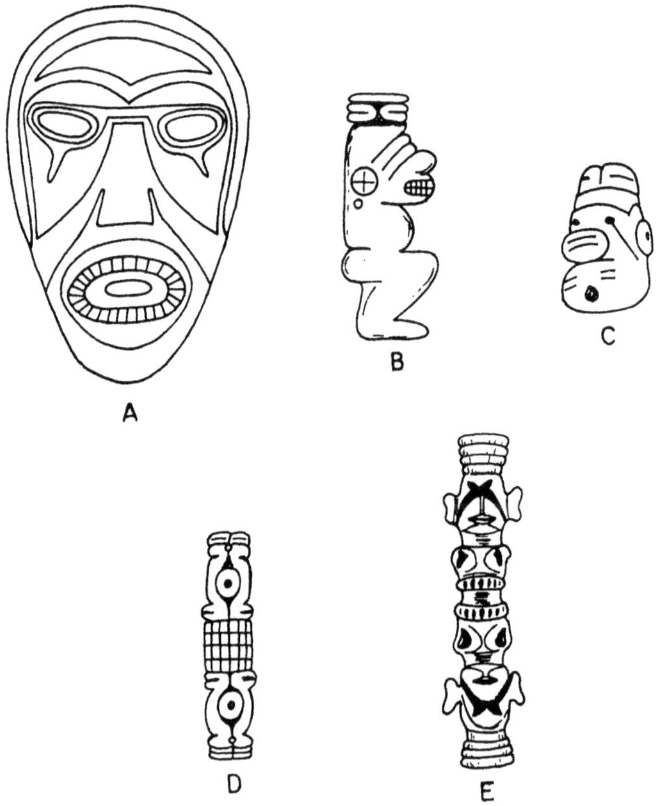

8.12. Crying figure designs: (a) shell *guaiza* (plaque or mask) with tearful face from Playa Carbó, Cuba; (b) type of pendant with headdress (Oriente region of Cuba); (c) small idol with tears from Santo Domingo (after Arrom 1975:70); (d) opposed twins with incomplete and dislocated anatomy and headdress (El Morrillo); (e) twins with headdresses and furrows on the face from Santo Domingo (after Alegría 1978:122).

of this type has a more complete structure, suggesting opposite twins with headdresses. If their faces are incised with lines it is possible that they also are crying figures (Figure 8.12e). Therefore, the variability of these raining or crying characters is too complex always to be identified with the Boinayel described in the ethnographic chronicle of Friar Pané.

DISCUSSION

With these results, which I consider preliminary, I include myself among the optimists working toward a cognitive archaeology that will allow us to have access to the field of indigenous thought and cosmology. I align myself with Navarrete (1990), who values the importance of ceramic decorations and their symbolic codes as an expression of ethnicity; with Curet (1991), when he outlines the utility of studying symbols used by the chiefly elite and symbols that identify political groups; and with Oliver's (1998) efforts to decipher the "syntaxes" (motifs, designs), "semantics" (meanings), and pragmatisms (function or use) of the petroglyphs and ceremonial center at Caguana. I support all of those who work in this vein. It will be of great importance to consolidate an archaeological semiology that integrates general findings from the archaeological contexts. In that way, the textual interpretations of artistic forms would be justified by their social and ideological roots.

As a starting point, I think we need to establish a database of images that, preferably, could be contextualized in time and space and that could be manipulated with statistical treatment. Obviously, the objective is not simply to store and classify the data but to convert it into a documentation of the historic trajectory of artistic forms and the social practices of the people that produced them. We should not evaluate the record of the images and their symbolic meaning through the lens of our own conceptual categories or from ethnocentric perspectives. The theoretical and methodological interpretation of the structured texts involves approaching the cosmology of the indigenous people in the terms of their own system of representations, one that belongs to a concrete cultural tradition. It is necessary to decipher the particular mechanisms of the productions of symbols and the systems of symbols as suggested by Saussure (1973:60) in order to get to know their meaning and the "laws that govern them." In our case, this refers to the specific nonlinguistic symbols articulated in a system, their relations, and their meanings.

I owe many debts in my research to Olmos (1991), who has worked with the Iberic iconography, especially regarding the development of a corpus of images for the reconstruction of the original paradigms and interpretation of the systems of representations. Olmos also argues for the necessity of cataloguing minimal formal units, even ones that many times are considered simple decorative elements but that, in certain contexts, combined with other elements, generate truly meaningful units. In this respect, it is important to recall the criteria developed by García Arévalo (1989) for symbolic geometric units that acquire their contextual meaning when found articulated with quite figurative representations in particular objects.

Although not conclusive, my analysis has applied these principles to the motifs and themes in our history of turtles, frogs, and crying figures. In the same way, I have contributed to the study of artistic expression as "text" and its potentials for transforming the original mythico-poetic messages into other new messages. I refer, for example, to the hypothesis of the myth of the mother frog and the twins, and the possible transfiguration of the twins into frogs, or the unpredictable varieties of the crying figure that seem to respond to thematic cycles of higher complexity.

Here I have readapted the theoretical basis of the Tartu-Moscow School and of its main spokesman, Y. Lotman (1982, 1994), who considers creativity an act of communication (sender-receiver) and of information exchange during which the initial message is transformed into a new one. This orientation surpasses the strict definition of semiotics as the study of communication, situating it in an effort to write a history of human culture itself. From this perspective, the semiotics of art has to be understood within the context of a general semiotics. Only then can we achieve a basic knowledge of indigenous artistic forms in their broader cultural context or as social products. In this way, we can follow the trail of artistic evidence as an indicator of the economic conditions that created them and of their repercussions in the transformation of communal society.

9 / Subsistence of *Cimarrones*

An Archaeological Study

Gabino La Rosa Corzo

In the western region of the island of Cuba, two mountain ranges of relative low elevation extend from east to west between the provinces of Havana and Matanzas.[1] The one to the north is named Alturas del Norte de La Habana-Matanzas and the one on the south Alturas del Centro de La Habana-Matanzas. The archaeological sites that are the focus of this investigation are located in the first of these ranges (Figure 9.1). The plains and rolling hills that surround these mountain ranges served as a geographic base for a slave-based plantation economy that began to expand and intensify in the early nineteenth century.[2] In the study area, this process of expansion peaked in the second and third decades of the century, greatly altering the landscape by covering the plains almost entirely with new economic units. Despite this economic "boom," the higher elevations of the nearby mountain ranges remained uninhabited.

These depopulated mountain regions defined the margins of agricultural expansion and the settlements of a rapidly increasing slave population.[3] Because of their inhospitable environment, the mountains were not incorporated in a direct way into the productive process. They remained mostly covered with forest and practically unknown. These uncultivated spaces attracted slaves who saw in them the possibility of temporary refuge and the chance to alleviate themselves of the severe regime of servitude to which they were subjected.

The work presented here is part of a larger project that examines the system of resistance of escaped slaves sheltered in numerous regions in these high-

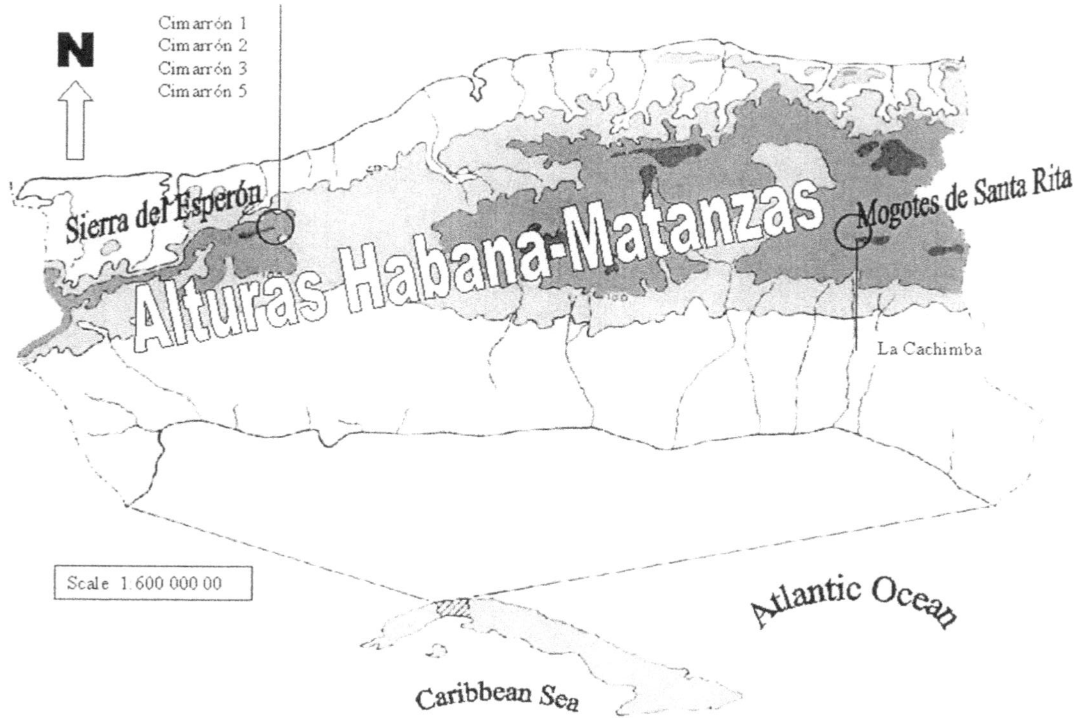

9.1. Map of Cuba showing the location of the sites discussed

lands. The purpose here is to analyze subsistence remains from 5 out of 25 sites discovered in these mountain ranges.

CIMARRÓN SPACE

The elevations of the Alturas del Norte de La Habana-Matanzas have a morphology defined by conical karstic formations. These formations produce steep slopes that rise up abruptly from the surrounding plain, although not as high as the eastern mountain ranges of the island. The Alturas del Norte are covered with thick vegetation, cut by deep canyons, ravines, and valleys, and pocketed with overhangs and caverns.

According to an 1849 report submitted by a local authority from El Naranjal in the province of Matanzas, the eastern end of the these mountains "is very rough and the ascent to them quite dangerous due to the cliffs." He goes on to say that from those elevations the cimarrones, or escaped slaves, "can see all the movements in the surrounding area perfectly and they flee immediately because they have developed the custom of having lookouts watch for movements; their defense strategy is to escape for other parts" (Archivo Histórico Provincial de Matanzas, I Gobierno Provincial, Leg. 13, no. 66). In an 1852 letter from the governor of the city of Matanzas addressed to the Capitán General of the island, the governor asserts that these mountains had become habitual dens for cimarrones, "since they have many inaccessible parts *where no human foot has set down,* almost all of them difficult to access, and where dogs are normally useless" (Archivo Nacional de Cuba [ANC], Gobierno Superior Civil, Leg. 1416, no. 55225; emphasis added).

Based on many historical descriptions such as these, a search for archaeological evidence has been undertaken during the past few years in the Alturas del Norte de La Habana-Matanzas, so far resulting in the recording of 25 sites that suggest the presence of small groups of fugitive slaves. Within these elevations, all the sites consist of overhangs and caves that served as temporary shelters to isolated groups of *cimarrones.*[4]

Some of the archaeological patterns that characterize this type of human shelter have been examined in previous studies and their particularities analyzed within the context of historical archaeology (La Rosa 1999, 2001). The presence of work tools, weapons, and glass and ceramic containers originating from nearby haciendas, combined with the existence of artifacts manufactured by escaped slaves such as ceramic pots, rustic smoking pipes, and objects of personal appearance such as wooden combs, have shed light on several interesting aspects of cimarrón daily life. Until now, however, subsistence remains have not been analyzed even though the study of faunal remains has become an important standard of modern archaeological investigations (Gutiérrez and Iglesias 1996; Jiménez and Cooke 2001).

Convinced that the analysis of these remains recovered from excavations of cimarrón shelters could provide evidence for the use of faunal resources and cultural factors linked to this use, the author selected five sites located in the westernmost and central areas of the mountain range for study. According to the artifact analysis, the occupations of these sites have been dated to the first half of the nineteenth century.[5]

The sites were selected based on the criteria that excavation of most of the living areas and all stratigraphic levels had been complete, reliable excavation records were available, and there was little evidence of postdepositional disturbance. Four sites were selected from the easternmost end of the Alturas del Norte of La Habana-Matanzas, an area also known as Sierra del Esperón. The first site, called Cimarrón 1, is a small cave with a single entrance, a living area of 3 × 4 m, and two hearths. One of the hearths contained abundant food remains; the other had glass and ceramic vessels, a rustic smoking pipe, and the remains of a shackle. This site is located on the northern slopes of the Sierra. The Cimarrón 2 site consists of a rock shelter measuring 14 × 5 m and has one hearth located near one of the shelter's three entrances. The hearth contained food remains, one machete, one knife, and ceramic and glass containers. The third site, Cimarrón 3, consisted of a rocky overhang on the edge of the north face. While the occupation area is of only about 1 m^2, the position of the site is advantageous as an observation point. In a hearth that covered most of the site, food remains and fragments of glass and ceramic containers were unearthed. Cimarrón 5, the fourth site in this part of the survey area, consists of a cave 13 × 5 m located on the south side of the highest area of the mountain ranges. The site produced food remains and fragments of a rustic handmade ceramic that has been the subject of previous studies by the author (La Rosa 1999). The fifth site, La Cachimba, located in the central part of the mountain range, is a large cavern with several entrances, an interior space of 4 × 3 m, two hearths and abundant remains of ceramics and glass, and two rustic smoking pipes (La Rosa 1991a, 1999).

Since the sites are located in extremely inaccessible locations and do not seem to have suffered measurable postdepositional alterations, detailed attention was paid to the exact location of the faunal and food remains within the restricted spaces of the caves and overhangs. This type of information allowed us to define the use of space, recover all possible evidence, identify food sources, and determine the sequence of the processing (butchering) of the game. After identifying the faunal elements, the presence of a variety of species was evaluated and their relationship within the sample was determined. The identification of the zoological species and their anatomical elements was performed by paleontologist Williams Suárez of the Museo de Historia Natural de la Habana, but the analysis and the ethnohistoric interpretation of these data are the responsibility of the author.

IDENTIFICATION OF THE FAUNAL REMAINS

A total of 1,167 elements of faunal remains were recovered in the study, 840 (72 percent) of which were identified, while the rest constituted fragments too small for categorizing. Cimarrón 5 produced the highest number of remains (Table 9.1) with 298 elements, followed by La Cachimba with 278 elements and Cimarrón 2 with 182. Cimarrón 1 and 3 produced lower numbers (Figure 9.2). Significantly, Cimarrón 5, La Cachimba, and Cimarrón 2 were in fact the most isolated and protected sites within the highlands, conditions that must have allowed runaways to remain in these locations for longer periods of time. Cimarrón 1 and Cimarrón 3 were sites of smaller size and are located on the hillsides of the ranges, at elevations intermediate between the plain and the highest parts of the mountains. Figure 9.3 shows the minimum number of individuals (MNI) for each species obtained in all the sites. Species that stand out in the sample include the large native rodent *hutía* (*Capromys* sp.) (16 individuals), pig (*Sus scrofa*) (10), chicken (*Gallus gallus*) (8), cow (*Bos taurus*) (6), and duck (*Cairina moschata*) (6). Present in lower numbers are dog (*Canis familiaris*) (2), horse (*Equus caballus*) (1), and *majás* or the Cuban boa (*Epicrates angulifer*) (also 1).

Figure 9.4 shows the distribution of faunal remains for all sites allowing the comparison of species and MNI for each shelter. Cows, pigs, and hutías are present in almost all of the shelters, while ducks were located in only three of them and chicken in two. On the other hand, the two samples of dogs came from Cimarrón 1, the horse from Cimarrón 2, and the majá or Cuban boa from Cimarrón 5. Since no relationship between the represented species and the degree of accessibility of the shelters was confirmed, the representativeness of species within the sample may correspond to other casual factors.

Of the total of 840 bones identified taxonomically, 93 percent belong to bones or fragments of less than 10 cm. Paleontological studies confirm that the

Table 9.1. Number of Remains (**NISP**) and Minimum Number of Individuals (**MNI**) in the studied sites.

Sitio	COW (Bos taurus)		PIG (Sus scrofa)		DUCK (Cairina moschata)		MAJÁ (Epicrates angulifer)		HUTÍA (Capromys sp.)		CHICKEN (Gallus gallus)		HORSE (Equus caballus)		DOG (Canis familiaris)		TOTAL	
	NISP	MNI	NISP	MNI	NISP	MNI	NISP	MNI	NISP	MNI	NISP	MNI	NISP	MNI	NISP	MNI	NISP	MNI
Cimarrón 1	12	**1**	13	**2**	5	**2**	0	**0**	10	**3**	13	**5**	0	**0**	6	**2**	59	**15**
Cimarrón 2	96	**2**	24	**2**	3	**1**	0	**0**	21	**4**	20	**3**	18	**1**	0	**0**	182	**13**
Cimarrón 3	1	**1**	21	**1**	0	**0**	0	**0**	1	**1**	0	**0**	0	**0**	0	**0**	23	**3**
Cimarrón 5	0	**0**	211	**3**	0	**0**	64	**1**	23	**4**	0	**0**	0	**0**	0	**0**	298	**8**
La Cachimba	186	**2**	25	**2**	59	**3**	0	**0**	8	**4**	0	**0**	0	**0**	0	**0**	278	**11**
Total	295	**6**	294	**10**	67	**6**	64	**1**	63	**16**	33	**8**	18	**1**	6	**2**	840	**50**

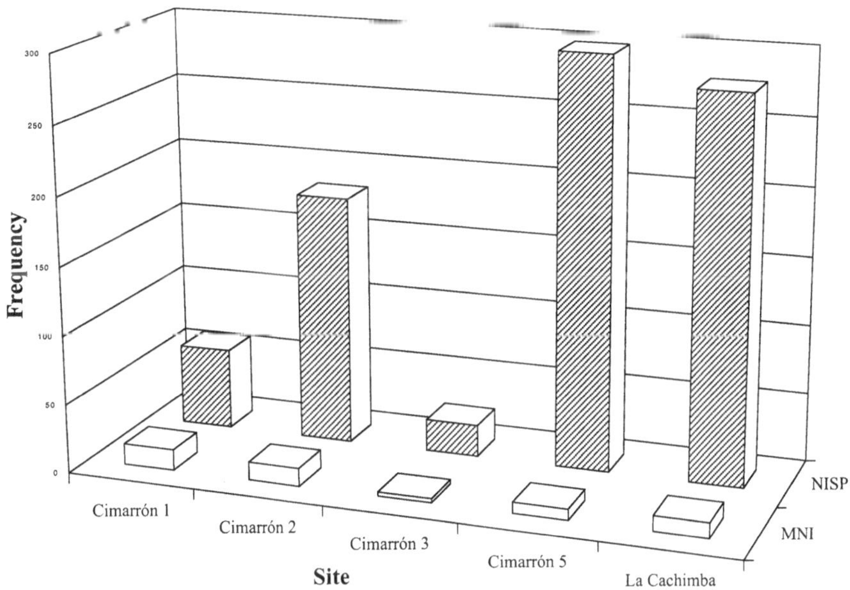

9.2. Total number of remains (NISP) and minimum number of individuals (MNI)

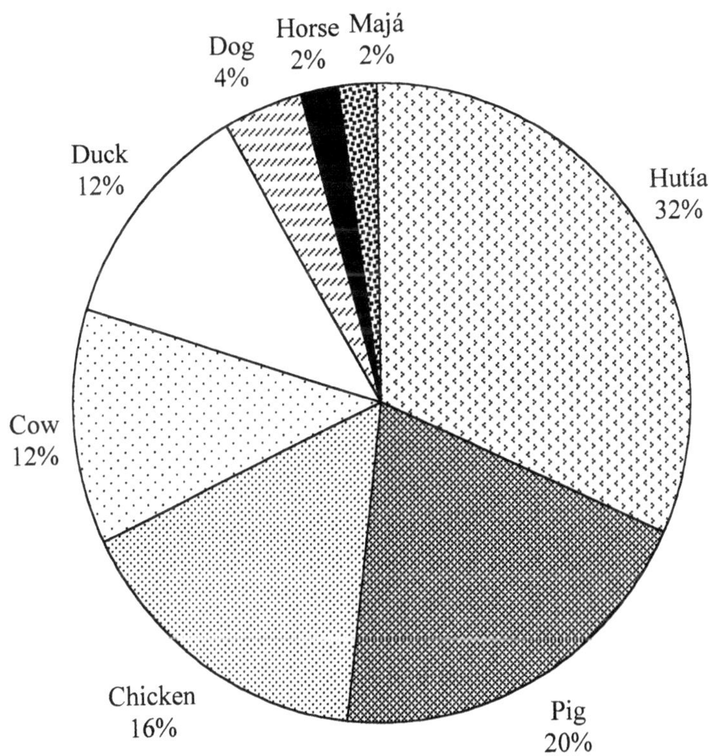

9.3. MNI by species in all the studied sites

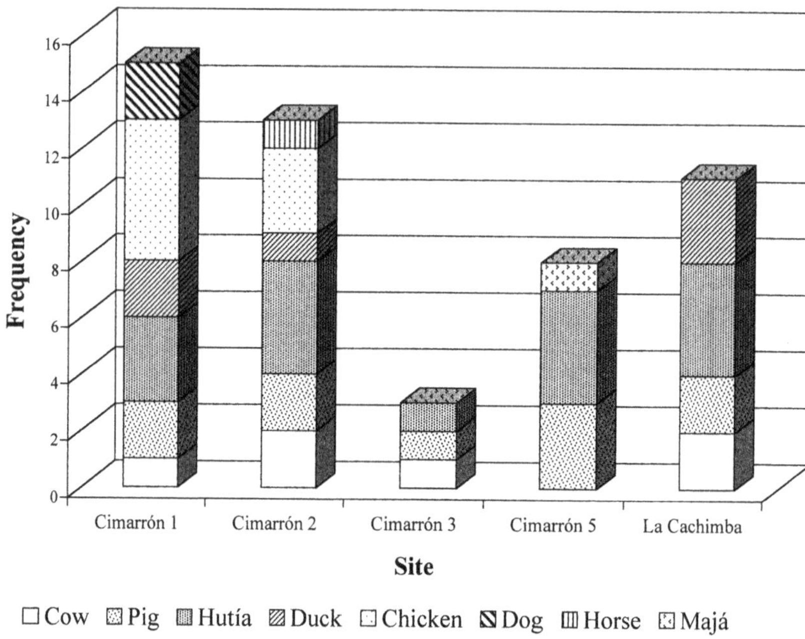

9.4. Distribution of MNI by species for each of the studied sites

bones of the larger mammals usually fracture more often than those of smaller size (Morales Muñiz 1989:389), a tendency that is present to a certain degree in the studied sample. However, the degree of fracture and the regularity of the sizes, cutting marks, and types of fractures seem to indicate that the reduction of large bones was related more to food preparation techniques. The relationship of this index between the five sites is illustrated in Figure 9.5.

The degree of completeness of the bone remains can provide additional information about the food preparation habits of the cimarrones. Of the 840 identified bones, 629 (75 percent) were broken into fragments, and 211 (25 percent) were complete elements. However, included in this last category were bones of various small species such as hutía, chicken, duck, dog, majá, and juvenile pig. Figure 9.6 illustrates the fact that, in general, fragments or small-sized bones prevailed in the sites.

Since the presence of charred bones could be indicative of the habits of meat consumption, all of the identified remains were subjected to a detailed examination. The results indicated that of the 840 identified remains, 47 (6 percent) presented light indications of burning and 53 (6 percent) were highly burnt (Figure 9.7). The total number of remains with indications of

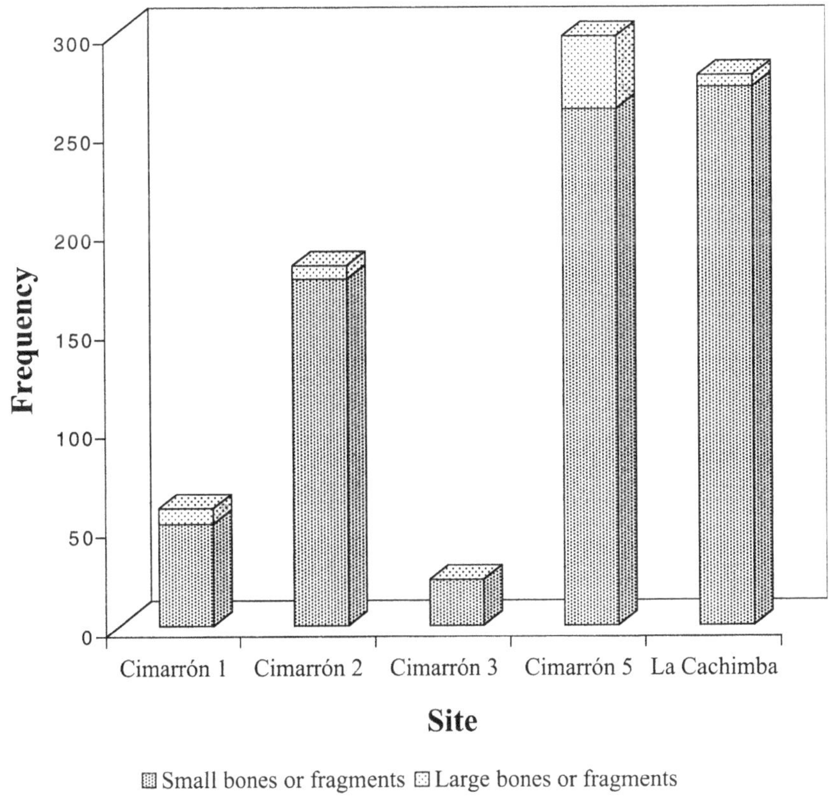

9.5. Distribution of bone and fragment sizes by site

burning was 100, or 12 percent of the sample, indicating that burnt elements were not prevalent. In fact, the great majority of burnt bones are vertebrae, phalanges, tarsals, and calcaneus, which suggests that they were burned when thrown near the hearth, where they were found by our team, and not by the process of food preparation. The small size of the burned bones and their location in the hearth, together with the fact that the rest of the bones, including the large ones, did not present any evidence of burning and were located dispersed within the shelter, suggest that most of the food was not cooked by direct exposure to the fire. The abundant presence of ceramic vessels in the hearths and in the rest of the area of occupation also supports the use of containers for cooking. All this suggests that despite the poor subsistence economy and marginal state of these groups, they retained soup-based cooking traditions from Africa and the plantations that they escaped. Figure 9.8 shows the distribution of burnt bones by site.

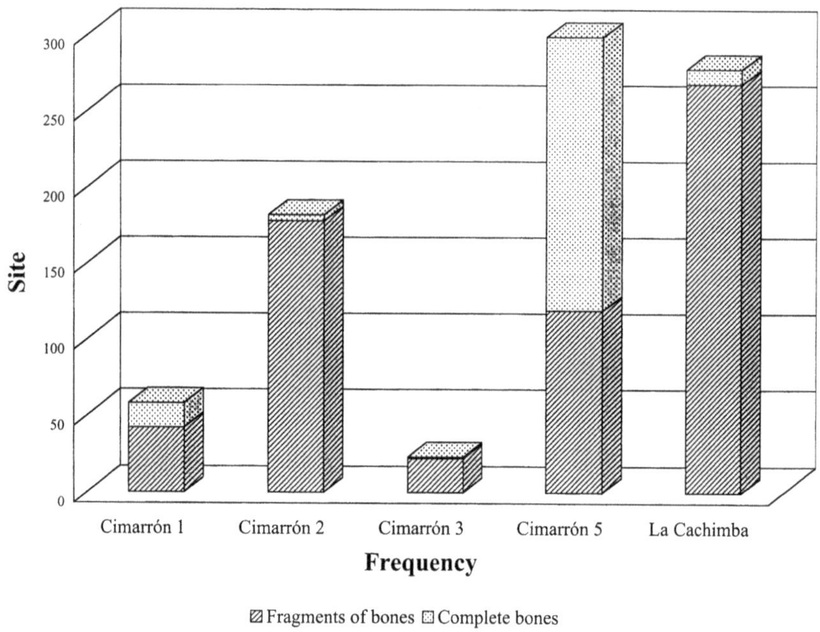

9.6. Degree of completeness of the bones identified by site

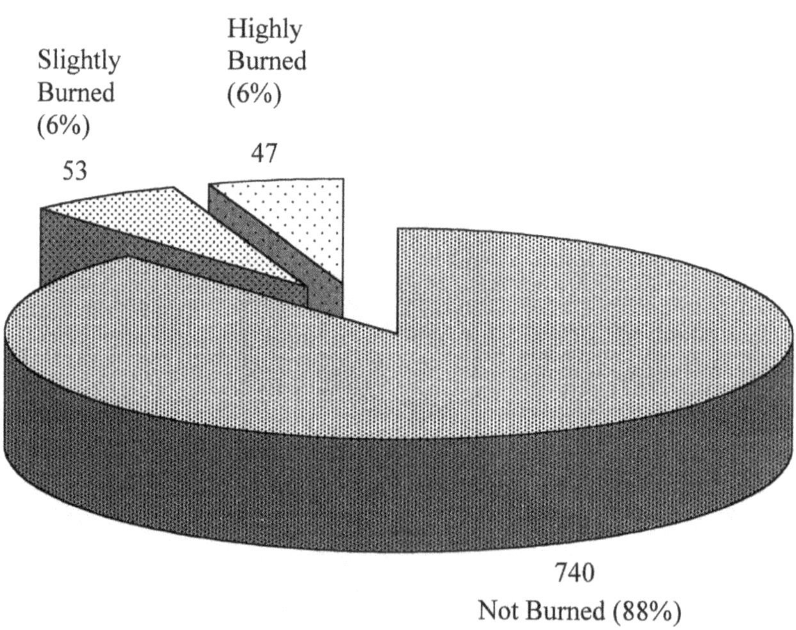

9.7. Distribution of burn marks in all sites

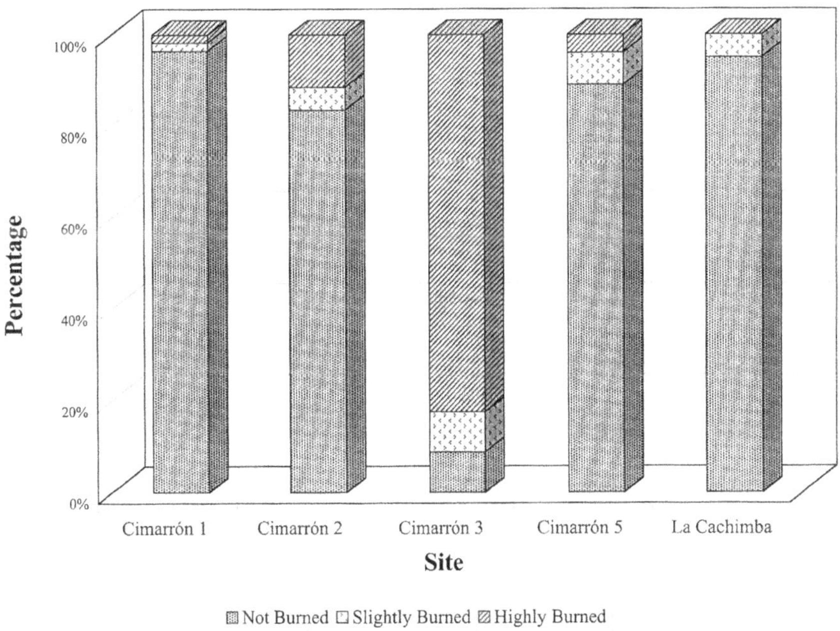

9.8. Distribution of burn marks by site

One of the most interesting pieces of evidence about human activities that can be obtained from faunal remains is butchering or cutting marks. Of the total of 840 bones identified anatomically, 83 (10 percent) presented this type of modification. Figure 9.9 shows the proportion of the types of marks in the sample. The two sites with the largest number of bones with butchering marks were Cimarrón 1 with 12 and La Cachimba with 48. Within the different types of butchering marks, fractures and cuts intended to fracture the bones were most prominent, followed by evidence of disarticulation and defleshing, and lastly those related to portion cuts.

DISTRIBUTION OF FAUNAL REMAINS WITHIN THE FLOOR PLAN OF THE SITES

A characterization of the modes of meat consumption by groups that occupied these natural shelters during the first half of the nineteenth century can be obtained from the distribution of faunal remains inside the sites. With this purpose in mind, the spatial locations of the faunal remains were recorded and correlated to individual bones and the species they represented.[6] This sys-

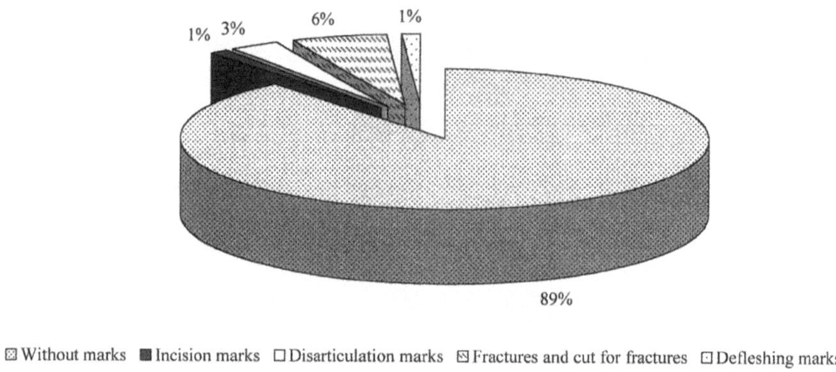

9.9. Butcher marks by site

tem reveals the marginal and persecuted character of the small groups that camped in these sites. Hearths were the spaces with the richest evidence, where the largest quantity of faunal remains was deposited. However, the rest of the food remains were dispersed around or at a distance from the fire pit as a consequence of having been thrown as waste, or in areas affected by natural agents such as erosion, small animals, and irregularities in the topography of the cave floor. Given the elevation of the shelters, with the exception of Cimarrón 2 and La Cachimba, whose natural ceilings reached more than 2 m, the hearths in the rest of the sites were in living areas of barely 1.20 m in height. This second measurement suggests that when preparing and consuming their food, individuals necessarily had to be in a squatting position, and movement inside the shelter had to be done in the same position.

At the Cimarrón 1 site, the remains were concentrated around the hearth, at the entrance of the shelter, and in areas impacted by natural agents in front of the entrance. A second sterile hearth was located in the innermost part of the shelter, inviting us to speculate on its use by the individuals who used the site as a temporary shelter. It is important to note that numerous testimonies of the time mention how African slaves habitually used hearths for night heating.[7] If it is true that this part of the cave was used as a sleeping area, it could be speculated, based on the shelter's size, that the number of individuals who occupied the site should not have been more than three or four persons.

Cranial bones were collected only in the case of one hutía, two dogs, two pigs, and three ducks. No bones pertaining to this part of the skeletons were collected for the rest of the species and individuals. This phenomenon could be related to the selection of the parts of the animals, since it is possible that the heads of large prey like horses and cows were discarded before returning to camp. This is not the case of pigs' heads, which were customarily consumed on the surrounding plantations, or those of the hutías or birds captured in the local regions, the transportation of which would have caused little inconvenience.

While in general the recovered remains tend to be patterned, depositional and preservation factors should not be dismissed because not all available fauna are represented in the sample, nor were all the animals consumed as food necessarily deposited at these five sites. In addition, the remains may have suffered fragmentation and degradation over more than a century and a half. In the case of the cow and the two pigs, the skeletal elements are represented by portions of medium to high nutritional value, according to Morales Muñiz (1989), suggesting a pattern of preference by cimarrones for some body parts rather than preservation bias.

The Cimarrón 2 site is located inside a narrow canyon in the highest part of the Sierra del Esperón and consists of a shelter, barely 14 m long and 5 m wide at its center, formed by the detachment of a large rock from the wall. It has three entrances. The climb to the site is difficult, and it is impossible that animals such as pigs, cows, or horses could have ascended to it, suggesting that the faunal remains were transported to the site after butchering. This site and La Cachimba and Cimarrón 5 were the most inaccessible and hidden shelters of the studied sample. Here also skeletal remains of food species were concentrated mostly around the hearth, and the parts represented attest to a nutritional pattern similar to the Cimarrón 1 site. The only difference was that horse remains were found at this site instead of dog bones. Similarly, the represented parts attest to the use of portions of medium to high nutritional yield.

With a small size of about 1 m^2, the Cimarrón 3 site consists of a rocky eave located in the abrupt slope of the north hillside of the Sierra del Esperón. The hearth was found on top of rocks deposited with the purpose of leveling the natural inclination of the shelter floor. The remains collected from this hearth were a fragment of a cow femur, numerous remains of the most edible parts of a pig, and the vertebra of a hutia. Evidently this was not a campsite for groups of cimarrones, but its strategic position makes it an ideal site for a lookout manned by one or two individuals. From this spot, the whole north area of the mountain range and the coast are visible, an area that at that time included seven sugar plantations and four coffee plantations.

The next site studied, Cimarrón 5, a rocky shelter 10 m long and 5 m wide, was located close to the summit at the western end of the Sierra del Esperón. Its main entrance faces east, but the site can be accessed through a difficult entrance located 10 m below. Thus, the cave consists of three levels that are connected to each other by small passageways. The highest and roomiest part served as a shelter to a small number of individuals who filled part of the floor with stones to level it and to close one of the corridors that communicated with the lower level. The rustic hearth used for cooking meats was placed on this pebble floor. Although the stone in-filling served as a base for the hearth, it did not prevent numerous subsistence remains thrown toward the fire from filtering through the rocks. For this reason, some of the remains were collected in the lower levels denominated as an *área de arrastre,* or a low area where artifacts accumulated due to the inclination of the surface, small animals, or erosion. The evidence was concentrated mostly around the hearth and in the área de arrastre below it. In general, alimentary patterns followed the same trends defined at the other sites; three pigs were identified in the recovered remains. The hutía (4 individuals) and one majá or Cuban boa suggest a greater use of autochthonous fauna compared to the other sites. The prevalence of pig was remarkable, since almost all skeletal parts were represented in the recovered sample, including mandibles.

The last of the sites selected for the study, the cave of La Cachimba, is located in one of the innermost living areas of an enormous cavern having three possible entrances. This cave is located in one of the Mogotes de Santa Rita, north of Madruga, and corresponds to the central part of the Alturas del Norte de La Habana-Matanzas. Although this shelter possesses the same alimentary pattern in terms of the consumption of animal meat, the skeletal remains of ducks were widely represented in the sample, as well as a single case of a mature cow, represented by almost the whole skeleton but not the head. Contrary to the other studied sites, the faunal remains were more spatially dispersed inside the enclosure.

The main butchering marks that were identified in the samples represented cuts made to separate the parts of the animal, break the bones into fragments, or remove the flesh.

DISCUSSION

The particular composition of the food remains of groups that used these caves as shelters during the first half of the nineteenth century reflects the character of their subsistence economy. Pigs, chickens, cows, ducks, dogs, and horses were domestic animals introduced by Spanish settlers, and they were a common feature on any plantation or farm at that time in Cuba. Letters from slave and hacienda owners from the western region of the island that complain to authorities about the constant robbery of domestic animals by cimarrones sheltered in the nearby forests and mountains are common in the colonial period. It is interesting to point out that of the 50 individuals identified in the faunal remains, 42 percent were juvenile (n=21). This indicator is one expression of the predatory character of these groups that survived, in great measure, on the resources of the haciendas, who were victims of their night forays. The abundant remains of hutías and of a majá or Cuban boa demonstrate that these human groups also used the natural resources offered by the forest, an alimentary tradition that in the case of Cuba goes back to the skilled exploitation of aboriginal groups.[8]

The presence of two juvenile dogs in the collection does not necessarily reflect the imperatives of subsistence. The first occasion in which the existence of dog remains was reported from cimarrón sites was during excavations conducted in a cave located in the Pan de Matanzas, part of the Alturas del Norte de La Habana-Matanzas (La Rosa Corzo and Ortega 1990). Those remains were found in the fire pit and had slight burning and cutting marks. This pattern was repeated at the Cimarrón 1 site, with the remains of two juvenile individuals. This pattern may not simply correspond to subsistence needs that forced an indiscriminate use of all food sources but may go back to traditions from the continent of origin. While it has been affirmed since the eighteenth century that the Ararás[9] slaves belonging to the Ewe-Fon cultures, whose main place of origin is Benin, might exchange two pigs for a dog and consume it roasted (Labat 1979:176), it has also been stated that in some cultures, such the Yoruba, these habits are linked to certain rites and cults (Beier 1961:15).

Finally, an interesting topic for consideration is the possible differences between the dietary practices of slaves and cimarrones, as well as of the persistence of some African traditions in the alimentary habits of the latter. In Cuba, most of the historians who have studied the question of slave diet have generally agreed in evaluating it favorably. Moreno Fraginals considered it "an exceptionally rich diet" (1986:59).[10] Pérez de la Riva (1981:176) also considered it ample. More recently, in a study on slaves from military fortifications, F. Pérez Guzmán (1997:120) concludes that their diet "included enough food and calories to guarantee slaves and prisoners sufficient nutrition."

It is necessary to keep in mind that all these historical studies were based primarily on the documentation of the time, especially documentation of a legal character, which logically reflects the interest of the slaveowners in caring for slaves as valuable property. But what the Royal Decrees and Orders specified, and what the *hacendados* (planters) actually did could be two different things, as demonstrated in some testimonies from the same time period. Dumont, a Frenchman who served as a doctor to numerous estate slaves, characterized their diet as faulty (Dumont 1865:500). During the middle of the nineteenth century, the Swede Federica Bremer on numerous occasions witnessed the way slaves were fed and became convinced that while an owner was forced to feed his slaves, he proceeded "however he wanted," because "what law could make him to count?" (Bremer 1980:79). The English consul Richard Madden described irregularities and violations at different plantations and qualified slave food as of "very little nutritious matter, of bad taste, and worse scent" (1964:169). Also, one particular report (coincidentally regarding a plantation near the sites included in this study) states officially that the great slave rebellion of 1833 on the Salvador coffee plantation, located between the north coast and the Sierra del Esperón in the province of Havana, was likely caused by the hunger that slaves had been experiencing (ANC, Miscelánea, Leg. 540/B). Given these contradictions, the application of archaeological methods can shed some light with new data. In the past few years several archaeological studies have focused their attention on this question (Ferguson 1992). Some studies conducted on the remains of numerous slave plantations in Barbados have demonstrated the presence of nutritional stress (Armstrong 1999:181). Therefore, the study of slave diet, and especially of cimarrones, should not be limited to descriptions in historical sources. The complementarity of archaeological methods can provide a new perspective on this subject.

Using historic documentation, it has also been argued that no significant differences existed between the diet of slaves and cimarrones (Laviña 1987:214). However, archaeology can demonstrate otherwise. The variety of sources of foods rich in protein, and the fresher and more diverse sources of meat compared to those obtained in the slave quarters, offered the fugitive slave better advantages than simple freedom. Another item of interest refers to the argument (again based on documentary evidence) that the cimarrón diet lacked any African traditional elements (Laviña 1987:214). However, the apparent consumption of dog meat suggests otherwise.

The evidence and arguments presented here only scratch the surface of the issues related to the study of cimarrones. In the future, these studies should be expanded on the basis of new archaeological techniques. For example, the study of the use of other food resources such as fruits, vegetables, and seeds should not be based on documentary information alone but should also be expanded using interdisciplinary methods. A hearth found in a site not included in this study has produced evidence for the presence of corncobs, indicating that modern techniques of paleobotany have much to contribute to this topic. Slave diet, especially that of the cimarrones, constitutes a controversial and unique territory in which archaeology can achieve firmer inferences than historical studies, flesh out the nature of the problem, and rectify some earlier generalizations.

NOTES

1. From west to east, the highest elevations are Sierra del Esperón at 250 m above sea level, Loma del Grillo at 321 m, Loma Palenque at 327 m, and El Pan de Matanzas at 381 m.

2. According to a plan consulted in the Fondo de Mapas y Planos del Archivo General de Indias (Archivo de Indias, Mapas y Planos, Santo Domingo, 335), the sugar factories existing in 1766 were concentrated on the plains of southern Havana. But in the first decades of the nineteenth century, the development of the sugar and coffee plantations demanded the clearing of new territories. The extensive character of exploitation under this system produced a rapid depletion of nutrients in the soil and of wood (used as fuel) from the forests. In the last decade of the eighteenth century, the collapse of Haitian production caused an increase in the demand for sugar and coffee on the international market, resulting in the eastward expansion of plantations in Cuba. This expansion began in all of the plains from the western end of Havana up to Colón, in Matanzas. Almost immediately, the expansion reached the valleys of the central region.

3. In the year 1841, during one of the decades of pronounced development in slave plantation agriculture, the western region had 321,274 slaves (representing 73.6 percent of the total number of slaves of the island), 650 *ingenios* or sugar factories (representing 53.15 percent), and 1,141 coffee plantations (representing 62 percent of those in operation that year) (Comisión de Estadísticas 1842). In 1857, sugar produced by the ingenios of Matanzas, Cardenas, and Colón represented 55.56 percent of the exports, or 436,030 metric tons that year (Moreno Fraginals 1986:141).

4. Similar studies were undertaken in the Cuchillas del Toa, in the eastern region of the island, leading to the identification of numerous remains of villages established by fugitive slaves. These villages are known in Cuba as *palenques* (La Rosa Corzo 1991b, 2003b).

5. The occupation phases of the shelters were established from their association with chronological frameworks based on the production and use of tools such as

machetes and a hoe, a shackle, buttons, and especially glass containers (bottles and *damajuanas* or demijohn), vitreous stoneware bottles, and ceramic olive jars. These artifacts were found inside the shelters where human activity centered around the fire pits, which were always the richest areas in items of material culture.

6. This systematic has been applied with excellent results in studies of zooarchaeological remains of colonial sites by Laura Beovide (1995) and Pintos and Gianatti (1995). For my part, I followed the criteria suggested by Morales Muñiz (1989).

7. On this topic, folklore writer Cirilo Villaverde affirmed that in 1839 slaves maintained the fire perennially and that "they sleep and spend long hours of the night around its heat" (Villaverde 1961:18). Federica Bremer, who visited numerous slave-based plantations of Cuba in the middle of the nineteenth century, asserted that the Africans of the island could not live without fire, "even amid the hottest heat spell; and they like to light it in the floor, in [the] middle of the rooms" (Bremer 1980 [1851]:190).

8. Many historical sources document the predilection that Africans and their descendants acquired for the consumption of fresh hutía meat which they used to expand their alimentary rations from the slave haciendas. They also had a preference for *tasajo* (salted meat imported from Buenos Aires) and for *bacalao* (salted codfish).

9. *Arará* is an ethnic denomination and not the name of an ethnic group. The term was used by slave traders to identify slaves from the regions of Togo and Benin but that included people from numerous ethnic groups such as the Ewe, Fon, Adja, and Ayizo.

10. This well-known authority on Cuban slave plantations assumed that the daily meat consumption of an adult slave was higher than 200 g, providing 70 g of animal protein, 13 g of fat, and 382 calories in addition to the daily 500 g of flour, which he considered more than enough for daily labor.

10 / An Archaeological Study of Slavery at a Cuban Coffee Plantation

Theresa A. Singleton

In the nineteenth century, Cuba became known as the "Pearl of the Antilles" because it was the largest, most prosperous island of the Caribbean. This prosperity was derived from the exploitation of slave labor in the production of staple crops. Cuba imported more than one million enslaved Africans over three centuries of transatlantic slave trade. The vast majority of Africans, however, came during the nineteenth century, making the island the greatest slaveholding colony of Spanish America and the center of the nineteenth-century transatlantic slave trade to the Caribbean (Bergad et al. 1995:38). Although sugar monoculture fueled Cuba's plantation economy, the role of coffee has often been overlooked in the development of Cuban slavery because it was a secondary crop. Yet coffee was particularly important to the prosperity of the early nineteenth-century economy of western Cuba in the provinces of Havana, Matanzas, and Pinar del Rio. By 1830, investments in coffee production were equal to those in sugar, and the number of enslaved workers on coffee plantations equaled the number on sugar plantations (Bergad et al. 1995:29). Thus, coffee cultivation played a significant role in the formation of plantation slavery in western Cuba.

Since 1999, I have undertaken an archaeological project at Cafetal del Padre (Figure 10.1) in collaboration with the Gabinete de Arqueología (Bureau of Archaeology), Office of the Historian for the City of Havana. I was initially drawn to this site because of a masonry wall 3.35 m high that encloses the location of the former slave village (Figures 10.2–10.4). The imposing wall intrigued me because it represented an extreme example of a slaveholder ex-

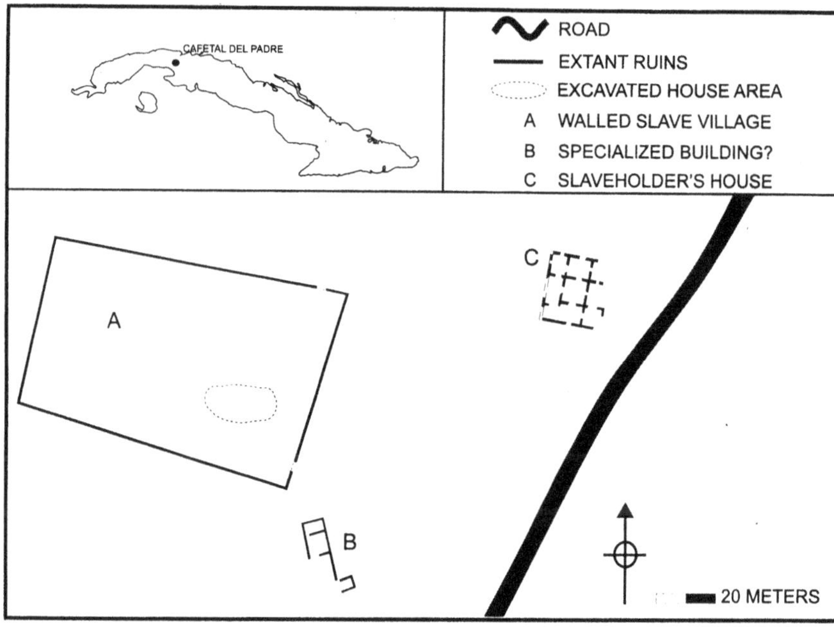

10.1. Map of the Cafetal del Padre

erting control over the living spaces of enslaved people. The use of such wall enclosures is not discussed in the historiography of Cuban slavery or in other slave societies of the Americas. The enclosure raises questions about the character of Cuban slavery, particularly methods used in the management and surveillance of enslaved workers (Singleton 2001b). The primary goal of the larger study, however, focuses less upon why Cuban slaveholders adopted this prison-like approach to slavery and more upon how enslaved people responded to these conditions. Despite the overwhelming domination that slaveholders wielded over slave workers, enslaved people struggled to control a modicum of their destiny (Berlin 1998:2–4). Archaeology is particularly equipped to unveil material aspects of slave agency by providing insights into the everyday lives of slave men and women, including the ways they fashioned their domestic spaces, produced food and finished products for themselves and for sale to others, and created religious and recreational practices that could provide a mental and spiritual release from the oppression of enslavement. This chapter briefly summarizes the project objectives and ongoing work at Cafetal del Padre.

10.2. Picture of the wall surrounding the slave village at the Cafetal del Padre

10.3. Picture of the wall surrounding the slave village at the Cafetal del Padre

10.4. Picture of the wall surrounding the slave village at the Cafetal del Padre

HISTORICAL BACKGROUND OF CAFETAL DEL PADRE

Cafetal del Padre is located today in Havana Province approximately 75 km southeast of the City of Havana near the town of Madruga. At an average elevation of 160 m above sea level, El Padre is situated in a subregion of western Cuba consisting of rolling hills, plateaus, and low-lying mountains known as the Alturas de Bejucal-Madruga-Limonar (Nuñez Jiménez 1959:109–114). This lush terrain is quite scenic; the plantation itself has been described as "possessing a beautiful natural balcony" (Alvarez Estévez 2001:60), with panoramic vistas of the surrounding area.

When Cafetal del Padre was operating as a coffee plantation, it was known as Santa Ana de Viajacas, and the O'Farrills, a distinguished and powerful family of nineteenth-century Cuba, owned it. Richard O'Farrell (the Irish surname O'Farrell was later Hispanicized to O'Farrill), the Irish progenitor of the family, born on the island of Montserrat in the eastern Caribbean, came to Cuba around 1715 (Franco Ferrán 1986:7). He made his fortune in the slave trade, and his descendants in turn invested in land and enslaved laborers. Richard's son, Juan José, acquired large tracts of land and owned one of the largest sugar plantations in Cuba during 1780s (Bergad 1990:14). Juan José's seventh child, Ignacio O'Farrill y Herrera, a Catholic priest, inherited the tract of land, approximately 1,000 acres, that became the coffee plantation, as well as an adjacent *potrero* (a stock-raising farm) and other landholdings from his parents (Archivo Nacional de Cuba [ANC] Protocolo de Salinas, 1788; ANC Escribanía Mayor de la Real Hacienda, legajo 142, No. 2662, 1834). At some later time, presumably after Ignacio's death, the cafetal became known simply as El Padre, meaning "the father" or "the priest."

In 1829, Ignacio O'Farrill began mortgaging his properties to pay back a loan of 60,000 pesos he used to develop two sugar plantations, La Concordia, located in the nearby district of Tapaste, and San Juan de Nepomuceno, located in the same district as the cafetal (ANC Salinas, 1829, 1262–1263). Ignacio had difficulty repaying these loans, and when he died in 1838 his estate had accumulated considerable debt. Two probate inventories taken of his estate, one in 1838 and another in 1841, provide most of the written information about the operation of the cafetal, including descriptions of the *dotación* (the slave population), the number and kinds of plantation buildings, the number of coffee plants, the types of other cultivated crops, fruit trees, and animals, and the kinds of furnishings and other household objects left in the great house.

After the padre's death, the coffee plantation continued to operate on a reduced scale with one-fourth of the slave force utilized by Ignacio O'Farrill. In 1844 a hurricane destroyed the coffee works, and the remaining enslaved community was relocated to the sugar plantation San Juan de Nepomuceno, where 40 laborers from the cafetal had been placed earlier (ANC Escribanía Archivo de Galletti, legajo 240, 1838–1839). From 1844 to 1853, La Real Hacienda (the Royal Treasury) of Cuba took over the administration of Ignacio O'Farrill's estate until the debts and back taxes were settled. The sugar plantations were eventually sold, and coffee cultivation was never restored at the cafetal. At some later point, the coffee plantation ceased to exist and was subdivided into *sitios,* or small subsistence farms (ANC Gobierno General, legajo 652, expediente 27528, 1862).

ARCHAEOLOGICAL INVESTIGATIONS AT CAFETAL DEL PADRE

Ruins of three structures made of *mampostería*—a construction material consisting of stone, rubble, and a lime-based mortar—are located on the site of El Padre today (Figure 10.1). These structures include the great house, a wall enclosure surrounding the site of the slave village, trapezoidal in shape (104 m on its longest side and 71.5 m on the widest) and measuring 3.35 m in height, and a specialized building of unknown function tentatively designated as an *almacén* (warehouse). Archaeological testing has been undertaken around each of the ruins, but excavations within the slave village have been the primary focus of the archaeological research thus far (Figure 10.5). Probate inventories of the plantation (ANC Galletti, legajo 245, expediente 1, 1838–1839; ANC Galletti, legajo 934, expediente 6, 1841) confirm that the area within the wall enclosure was indeed the site of the slave village containing from 30 to 45 *bohíos*—wood frame buildings, walled with cane, clay, or clapboards and roofed with thatch.[1] The bohíos at Cafetal del Padre used for housing enslaved workers were constructed of *guano y embarrado,* mud- or clay-walled buildings with thatched roofs of palm, while those used for outbuildings such as the overseer's kitchen and the chicken house were made of *guano y estantes de madera* (clapboards) with palm roofs (ANC Galletti, legajo 934, expediente 6). Although excavations have not yielded archaeological remains of preserved mud or daub as has been the case in other excavations of clay-walled slave dwellings (Armstrong 1999; Wheaton and Garrow 1985), the small amount of recovered nails suggests that wood was not the primary material used to build the walls of the slave bohíos.

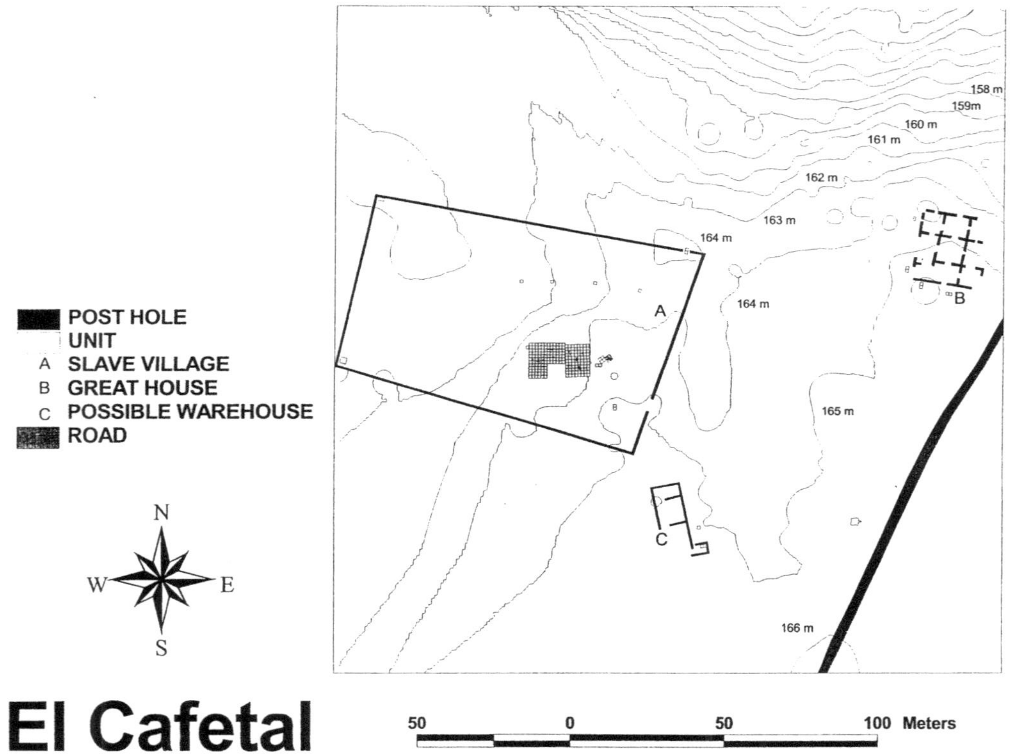

10.5. Map of the Cafetal del Padre showing the location of the excavation units

Excavations at the El Padre slave village were conducted initially to examine how enslaved workers lived in their quarters and modified these spaces to suit their needs. A second objective is to evaluate the extent to which the enslaved community at El Padre participated in independent economic activities of their own interests: Did they produce food or craft items for themselves or for trade? What kinds of objects did they purchase? With whom did they trade? Students of slavery refer to these economic activities as the internal or informal economy, or the slaves' economy (herein I use the term informal slave economy). A final objective is to analyze the meanings and usages of objects beyond what they were originally intended by manufacturers or others who created them (Thomas 1991:28–29). Capturing and understanding these meanings present ongoing challenges to archaeologists.

Before launching full-scale excavations, it was necessary to establish the site's integrity. The slave village had obviously been farmed after its abandonment; therefore, we needed to know whether any undisturbed remains of slave houses or other structures and deposits could be located and identified. While clearing the site of its thick vegetation prior to subsurface testing, the excavation team identified a small posthole cut through the limestone outcropping. I had observed similar posthole construction in the excavations of slave houses on the island of Monteserrat in the eastern Caribbean. In building slave houses on Montserrat, short posts called "knogs" were placed in these holes and used in combination with stones to raise and support a wooden floor aboveground (Howson 1995:105–106; Pulsipher and Goodwin 1999:18). Thus, the small posthole was an encouraging indicator that archaeological remains of slave bohíos were preserved at El Padre. Later in the first field season, we found 18 more postholes of varying sizes associated with the initial post, forming a rectangular pattern measuring approximately 5 × 7 m. In subsequent field seasons numerous postholes have been uncovered, totaling over 100 to date, but it has been difficult to determine the size, shapes, and orientation of the structures or where one structure ends and another begins. Despite this problem, four structures have been tentatively identified.

Recovered artifacts are primarily of interest in the study of the slave village, for they indicate the kinds of objects enslaved people produced, acquired, and used. It is often difficult to document from written sources alone the items acquired by enslaved people through informal trade networks. Thus, archaeological findings allow us to see enslaved people as both producers and consumers within the informal slave economy of nineteenth-century Cuba. Artifacts also provide temporal indicators for when the site was occupied. The vast majority of the artifacts date between 1800 and 1860, a time range consistent with the years when the site was operating as a coffee plantation.

INTERPRETING SLAVERY AT CAFETAL DEL PADRE

All of the primary written sources associated with the cafetal are public records, found primarily in notarial and probate archives. Many of these records date from after the death of Ignacio O'Farrill, when the plantation was frequently described as being in "a ruinous state." Unfortunately, no personal records kept by O'Farrill have surfaced. Therefore, to gain insights into the plantation's more prosperous times, we must rely on inferences drawn from the archaeological record in combination with these and other written sources. My approach to understanding these sources is guided by Allison Wylie's notion of "conjoint use of evidence," which neither privileges nor treats an evidential resource as a given nor assumes one source has epistemic priority over another (1999:29). Rather, it is the working back and forth with multiple sources that has permitted me to offer the following interpretation of slavery at the cafetal.

The Slave Population

Information on the enslaved labor force at the cafetal comes from the plantation inventories. In 1838, there were 77 enslaved men, women, and children living on the plantation. According to the manager of the cafetal, the dotación consisted of 81 enslaved persons prior to taking the inventory, but four of them ran away after Ignacio O'Farrill's death (ANC, Galletti, legajo 245, 1). The inventory provides a list of the names, ages, and *naciones* (ethnic affiliation or place of birth) of each of the enslaved laborers. Of the total number 53 were enslaved men and 24 were women. This sex ratio of 2:1 is comparable to that found on other coffee plantations studied in Matanzas Province (González Fernández 1991:171). Sex imbalances favoring men over women could be even more pronounced on sugar plantations, and dotaciones comprised entirely of slave men are known to have existed (Moreno Fraginals 1978:2:39; Paquette 1988:60). Only five children are listed, two boys and three girls, all under the age of five years. The small number of children is consistent with analyses indicating Cuban slave populations did not increase through natural reproduction, making chronic importation of African laborers necessary to sustain the slave population (Bergad et al. 1995:36).

The term *nación* refers to the ethnic or cultural affiliation of an African-born slave man or woman. These ethnic labels were products of the slave trade that loosely correspond to ethnolinguistic groups in Africa. Slave traders often created these labels on the basis of departure points from which victims of the transatlantic slave trade were taken. For example, *Minas* refers to Elmina, first a Portuguese and later a Dutch trading post on the Gold Coast, the Atlantic shore of present-day Ghana. Similarly, "*Araras*" refers to Fon-speaking Africans taken from the kingdom of Andrah or Allada on the Slave Coast, the present-day Republic of Benin. Although many of these ethnic designations often have little or no historical meaning in Africa, they became ways in which Africans defined themselves in the Americas and how Europeans distinguished among them. Africans organized mutual aid and religious organizations based on these ethnicities throughout Latin America (Singleton 2001a:184n.3). In Cuba, these organizations were known as *cabildos de naciones*; in nineteenth-century Cuba some 100 African ethnicities were recognized, and more than 20 ethnically based cabildos maintained their cultural identities into the twentieth century (Ortiz 1921). Cabildos were primarily an urban Afro-Cuban institution, and their influence on enslaved Cubans living on plantations is unclear. Nonetheless, naciones played significant roles in ritual performances and other religious activities on plantations, such as funerals (see, e.g., Barcia Paz 1998:26–28).

The enslaved community at Cafetal del Padre belonged to the following naciones: 16 Carabalí (Igbo and Ibibo-speaking people of southeastern Nigeria), 17 Congo (Ki Kongo speakers of Angola and the Democratic Republic of the Congo), 12 Ganga (a Mande-speaking people from Upper Senegal), 12 Lucumí (Yoruba-speaking people of southwestern Nigeria), 5 Maená (a Mande-speaking people from Senegambia area), 4 Mina (Akan-Ewe peoples of southern Ghana and Togo), 11 *Criolla* (born in Cuba).[2] The distribution of naciones indicates that no one group was in the majority. This situation may have resulted from deliberate efforts to prevent one group from overpowering the others and from organizing ethnically based insurrections.

The Informal Slave Economy

Excavations at the El Padre slave village have shed light on the ways in which enslaved workers participated in independent economic activities. The independent slave economy included such activities as producing food for themselves as well as for sale to others; raising livestock; producing finished goods (e.g., baskets, furniture, or pottery); marketing their own products; and consuming or saving the proceeds obtained from these activities (Berlin and Morgan 1991:1). On many of the British islands, enslaved people traded items through institutionalized markets, held typically on Sundays. The ability of enslaved laborers to buy and sell items was much more restricted in Cuba than on other Caribbean islands. Provision ground products had a limited market and were often sold to the plantation itself (Scott 1985:149–150). Similarly, some slave-purchased items were acquired from stores established on the plantation for the purpose of selling goods to the slave community. These stores are better known in the second half of the nineteenth century on large sugar estates (Scott 1985:194). The extent to which similar stores existed earlier on coffee plantations is unknown, and no store is mentioned or listed on the inventories of Cafetal del Padre. Reverend Abiel Abbott describes such a shop at the coffee plantation Angerona in 1828: "He [the slaveowner] furnishes a shop in the apartment of the building next to the mill, with everything they wish to buy that is proper to them; cloth, cheap and showy, garments gay and warm, crockery; beads, crosses, guano, or the American palm that they make neat hats for themselves, little cooking pots, etc. He puts everything at low prices, and no peddler is permitted to show his wares on the estate" (Abbott 1829:141).

Although this plantation shop may have been unique to Angerona, Abbott's description offers useful insights for understanding Cuba's informal slave economy in several ways. First, it identifies the kinds of objects enslaved Cubans purchased on plantations. Second, it indicates that traveling peddlers were another, and perhaps the primary, source for slave-purchased goods. And, third, it hints at the influence exerted by slaveholders on the selection of items made available to enslaved people. Therefore, the degree of slave choice in making purchases was perhaps more limited on Cuban plantations than in other slave societies.

Despite the utility of Abbott's description of slave-purchased objects, it provides a lens into only one kind of economic exchange, the plantation shop in Cuba's informal slave economy. Presumably there was a range of economic exchanges, including purchasing from traveling peddlers, rural stores and taverns and exchanges with other enslaved people. Objects available from a plantation shop were most likely those that met with the slaveholder's approval. Yet archaeological investigations at El Padre slave village yielded remains of items slaveholders were unlikely to approve, such as alcoholic beverages. According to Laird Bergad, authorities in Matanzas province complained constantly about enslaved persons purchasing liquor illegally (1990:238).

Tobacco pipes also occur in large quantities at El Padre and, like alcoholic beverages, were probably not provisioned to the enslaved community. All of the pipe bowls are mold-made and were presumably mass-produced imports. Several of the bowls are similar to those manufactured in the Cataluña region of Spain (Arrazcaeta Delgado 1987). Maroon sites have yielded both locally made and imported pipes. The latter are believed to have been purchased from rural stores when the maroons were enslaved (La Rosa Corzo and Pérez Padrón 1994:128).

Many of the objects recovered from the El Padre slave village are remarkably similar to, and in some cases identical to, those artifacts found at slave sites both in the United States and elsewhere in the Caribbean, such as English tablewares and blue glass beads from Bohemia (present-day Czech Republic). The major differences are in the ceramic assemblages. All of the coarse earthenwares are of either Spanish or Spanish-American origin. They include majolicas such as Triana blue-on-white and polychrome from Spain and Aucilla polychrome from Mexico; utilitarian wares such as El Morro, possibly imported or made locally in Cuba; and red-slipped pottery from Mexico and Central America.

Only two sherds of hand-built pottery comparable to either colono wares (Ferguson 1992) or the Afro-Caribbean wares (e.g., Armstrong 1999; Petersen et al. 1999) have been identified. Referred to as *criolla* ware in Cuba, this pottery has been recovered from numerous colonial-period sites dating between the sixteenth and nineteenth centuries, but it has been primarily associated with people who are identified as Amerindian or of mixed Amerindian and African heritage. Even as late as the 1830s, a Spaniard visiting Cuba noted a family of potters living in Guanabacoa, a present-day suburb of Havana city, self-identified as "Indians" and producing earthenware cooking pots, jars, and bowls (Andueza 1841:159). The two fragments recovered from El Padre were apparently from a large, globular vessel known as a *pote* used for preparing slow-cooked foods (Lourdes Domínguez, personal communication, 2002), in much the same way colonoware was used in the southern United States. The sherds are heavily charred, indicating that this vessel was well used.

With only two fragments, it is not possible to make a case for slave production of criolla pottery at El Padre. It is more likely that the users of this vessel acquired it through trade. Pottery-making was perhaps unnecessary for enslaved workers at El Padre or at other Cuban plantations because of the availability of a variety of utilitarian earthenwares and iron pots for cooking. However, the absence of pottery-making may also speak to slave demography in Cuba and sex ratios at El Padre. The production of Afro-Caribbean wares has been generally attributed to females. As mentioned, the slave trade to Cuba was heavily oriented to the procurement of males (Bergad et al. 1995:27).

Household and personal objects, including ceramics, iron kettles, beads, tobacco pipes, brewed beverages, and a few decorative items such as a metal fragment from a parasol, attest to the fact that the enslaved community participated in the internal economy as consumers. It is unclear how they were able to earn money to purchase or produce items to barter for these items. Gardening appears to have been the primary way enslaved laborers produced commodities for trade throughout the Americas. In Cuba, as on other Caribbean Islands, enslaved workers were often granted provision grounds known as *conucos.* The extent to which slaveholders provided slave workers with conucos varied through time and from plantation to plantation. Housing the enslaved community in bohíos as opposed to *barracones*—masonry structures containing prison-like cells for slave habitation—facilitated small backyard food production of garden crops and keeping animals such as pigs and chicken.

Meat products apparently were scarce food resources for the occupants at the El Padre slave village. Written accounts emphasize the kinds of plant food enslaved Cubans were provided. Many plantations reserved a small amount of land for the cultivation for slave food of crops such as *yuca* (manioc), *malanga* (a starchy tuber similar in both texture and taste to African yams), sweet potatoes, or plantains (González Fernández 1991:173). All these crops were grown at the cafetal in addition to corn (ANC 1841). Animal food remains recovered archaeologically are usually a reliable indicator of the approximate amount of meat consumed. In the case of the El Padre slave village, however, fewer than 100 fragments of animal bones were recovered, and these came from plow-zone deposits rather than trash pits. The small sample size combined with the mixed archaeological context make the faunal assemblage inappropriate for zooarchaeological calculations that could estimate the amount of consumable meat or the contribution of meat to the diet. The recovery of such a small amount of animal bone is surprising considering that a stock-raising farm, also belonging to Ignacio O'Farrill, was adjacent to the cafetal.

Perhaps the small amount of recovered animal bone is an indication that slave community had little or no access to livestock raised in the potrero but consumed salted or preserved fish and meats containing little or no bone. It is impossible to determine the kinds of foods that were distributed to the enslaved community without slaveholder ledgers or other records indicating what foods were purchased for them. Most of the identifiable bone is pig (*Sus scrofa*), an animal typically raised in house or barnyard situations rather than herded like cattle (*Bos taurus*), sheep (*Ovis aries*), or goat (*Capra hircus*) (Reitz and Wing 1999:285–286). Joseph Dimock, a nineteenth-century visitor to Cuba, observed that enslaved Cubans were permitted to "raise chickens, a pig, and sometimes a mare" (1998 [1846]:96). Therefore, the recovered food remains were more likely from slave-owned animals than those raised on the stock-raising farm. Discrete trash deposits containing organic refuse, however, have not yet been uncovered at the El Padre slave village, so any definitive statement regarding slave diet at the cafetal must await additional excavations.

Craft production offered enslaved people another possibility for making items for their own use and for trade. Abiel Abbott observed enslaved Cubans making hats from palm leaves in the quote cited, and it is likely that they made other items from these leaves. Unfortunately, it is difficult to document the making of basketry and other textiles from archaeological sources. While the archaeological evidence for craft production at the El Padre slave village is slim compared to African-American sites that have yielded evidence of pottery-making, wood-working, button-making, or iron-working, a few artifacts suggest craft-making activities. Glass scrapers offer one possibility. These artifacts made from broken bottle glass are similar to those found at other sites occupied by people of African descent (Armstrong 2003; Wilkie 1996). These scrapers could be used for a variety of purposes, but they are most often associated with wood-working. Another possibility of craft production is the reuse of discarded pipe bowls for smoothing or polishing. The interior surfaces of several recovered pipe bowl fragments exhibit considerable wear resembling that found on objects used for smoothing or polishing materials such as wood, bone, hide, or possibly pottery. The wear appears to have occurred after the pipe bowls were broken and were no longer usable for smoking.

Expressive Culture

The most curious artifacts recovered from the El Padre slave village are ceramic discs measuring 8–15 mm. They appear to have been made by smoothing the edges of broken ceramics into rounded forms. Perhaps the pipe bowl fragments were used to make these artifacts. Similar discs have been found at a variety of sites in other world areas, for example, at post–European contact sites in Africa (Gerard Chouin, personal communication, 2001) and at Spanish missions in California (Lourdes Domínguez, personal communication,

2002). They have been found on several slave sites in the Americas, including Tennessee (Russell 1997:75), Jamaica (Armstrong 1990:137–138), and Montserrat (Pulsipher and Goodwin 1999:17, 30n.57). These artifacts have been interpreted as gaming pieces, and in the Caribbean they are associated with games of chance. Lydia Pulsipher and Conrad Goodwin describe a gambling game that modern Montserratians play that they call "Chiney Money" in which three ceramic disks are thrown on a table and the arrangement in which the pieces land determines the thrower's score.

How these ceramic discs were used in Cuba is unknown. Throwing objects (e.g., cowries, beads, or seeds) and using the arrangement in which the objects fall to determine the course of action is a key principle of divination in African-influenced religions in the Americas. I have observed modern-day practitioners of the Afro-Cuban religion Santería use pieces of coconuts in this way. The number and arrangement of the white interiors versus the brown exteriors of the coconut pieces that land facing upward indicate how the person seeking advice is to proceed. In a similar vein, all of the ceramic discs are decorated on the exterior side and undecorated on the interior side. It is possible that in Cuba these discs were used in a fashion similar to the coconut fragments and other objects used in divining. Gambling games, however, should not be ruled out as a possibility for the use of these artifacts in Cuba. *Juegos de envite* (betting games) that utilized gaming pieces were played throughout the Spanish colonial empire in the eighteenth and nineteenth centuries (Lourdes Domínguez, personal communication, 2002).

The ceramic discs, tobacco pipes, and ceramic glass bottles that once contained alcoholic beverages are suggestive of slave recreational activities and perhaps religious activities as well. José Antonio Yarini, a Cuban slaveholder, observed enslaved Cubans on his sugar plantation using "a bottle of brandy, a pipe with tobacco, a cudgel belonging to a former overseer, and rooster feathers" in a funeral offering for a deceased slave (Barcia Paz 1998:27). While making a claim that these items were used in religious practices requires finding them in a context suggestive of a religious offering, Yarini's account reminds archaeologists that many of the objects recovered from slave sites had uses other than what appears to be obvious. Objects like the ceramic discs, pipes, and even bottle glass are examples of multivalent artifacts—those containing multiple meanings and purposes (Perry and Paynter 1999:303–304).

Slave Resistance

Slave resistance took many forms in slave societies throughout the Americas, including Cuba. The wall enclosure around the slave village at El Padre was obviously built, first and foremost, to prevent enslaved people from running away, one of the most overt forms of resistance. Enclosing slave bohíos within a wall was mandated in an ordinance issued for Matanzas province after a slave rebellion took place there in 1825. The ordinance required plantations with bohíos to surround and enclose the houses with a palisade 4–5 *varas* high, approximately 3.4–4.25 m (ANC Gobierno Superior Civil [GSC], legajo 1469, expediente 57999, 1825:4). It is unlikely that most slaveholders complied with the ordinance because building such a wall was a major capital expenditure that many simply could not afford. In 1841, the wall enclosure at El Padre was valued at 5,270.70 pesos (ANC Galletti, legajo 934, expediente 6), a substantial amount of money for the time, and the construction of the wall must have been undertaken because it was believed necessary.

The wall enclosure likely served the dual purpose of discouraging enslaved workers from running away and hindering outsiders from entering the slave quarters. Bands of maroons, or runaway slaves, often attacked plantations and, in the process, liberated enslaved workers, took plantation supplies, and destroyed property (Paquette 1988:73–75; see also La Rosa Corzo, Chapter 9). In 1837, the Office of *Pedaneo*—the administrative official for a subdivision of a district—reported that a small party of maroons came to El Padre slave village. However, the maroons did not capture any enslaved people or take any property (Archivo Histórico Provincial de Matanzas [AHPM], Gobierno Provincial O.P. Cimarrones legajo 12, expediente 50, 1837). In fact, the encounter appears to have been a peaceful one, perhaps involving some kind of trade exchange. However, hostile maroon attacks were known and posed a constant threat.

In spite of the wall, slave runaways did occur at Ignacio O'Farrill's plantations. As mentioned, four enslaved persons ran away after Padre O'Farrill's death. In 1841, 45 enslaved workers at O'Farrill's sugar plantation San Juan de Nepomuceno ran far away to an "inaccessible distance in the sierras" (ANC GSC legajo 617, 19712, 1841). All except eight of the runaways returned. Slave catchers known as *rancheadores* captured some of them, others surrendered themselves to the authorities. Some of these runaways possibly originated from the coffee plantation because 40 laborers at the coffee plantation were sent in 1839 to San Juan de Nepomuceno (ANC Galletti, legajo 240, expediente 1).

On a daily basis, slave resistance took place in ways that were far more subtle than running away or inciting revolts. Students of slavery have long discussed the many ways enslaved men and women feigned illness, hid or broke tools, or pilfered property. It is difficult to understand slavery without seriously considering these subtle acts of resistance that were so much a part of the everyday lives of enslaved workers. In this study of Cafetal del Padre, the evidence of subtle resistance must come from the archaeological record, because verbal descriptions of these activities have not survived. At this juncture, the strongest possibility for everyday resistance as seen from the archaeological record of the cafetal was the participation of enslaved workers in the informal slave economy. Many scholars believe that these activities provided bondmen and -women with a semblance of independence that undermined plantation regimes and slaveholder authority (see Berlin and Morgan 1991). Whether this was the case for enslaved Cubans requires more investigation. The informal economy permitted enslaved workers like those at the cafetal to improve their situation beyond that which slaveholders provided. In this sense, they were able to reject some of the inhuman treatment of their enslavers and create a way of life that better suited their needs.

CONCLUSION

Archaeological research at the slave village of El Padre is still ongoing, but already it has produced primary information on how the enslaved community lived within the walled enclosure. They were engaged in many of the same activities as enslaved people elsewhere in the Caribbean and in the Americas. They found ways to supplement their meager plantation rations. Through recreational and religious activities, they created a world removed from daily oppression of enslavement. They participated in the internal economy as both producers and consumers, although the possibilities to do so were considerably more limited and not institutionalized as on other Caribbean islands. The wall enclosure was a constraining device, both literally and metaphorically. It was built to contain slave activities and to prevent maroons and perhaps others from entering the premises. It also symbolized the fear that Cuban slaveholders had of the people they held in bondage and their desire and need to control them in a brutal fashion.

ACKNOWLEDGMENTS

I thank the following persons for their assistance in undertaking this research: Dr. Eusebio Leal Spengler, Roger Arrazcaeta Delgado, Dr. Lourdes S. Domínguez, Lisette Roura Alvarez, Karen Mahé Lugo Romera, Sonia Menéndez Castro, Anicia Hernández Gonzáles, Dania Hernández Perdices, Beatriz Antonia Rodríguez Basulto, Leida Fernandez Prieto, Antonio Qúevedo Herrero, Fidel Navaetes Quiñones, Aldo Primiano Rodríguez, Néstor Martí Delgado, Juan Carlos Méndez Hernández, Adrián Labrada Milán, Alejandro Ramírez Anderson, Jorge Luis García Báez, Jorge Ponce Aguilar, Mark Hauser, Stephan Lenik, Acelia Rodríguez Bécquer, Claudia Roessger, Babette Forster, Amilkar Feria Flores, Jorge Garcell Domínguez, Alejandro Torres Collazo, Ernesto Fong Arévalo, Francisco Simanea Vidal, Rolando Barroso Gutérrez, Germán Barruso Gutiérrez, Melanie Pilecki Estrada, Ismael Pérez Pérez, and Consuelo Bueno Pérez.

NOTES

1. Inventories taken in 1838 and 1841 describe the slave village as consisting of *bohíos* inside an enclosure of *mampostería,* but the total number of slave bohíos varies throughout these documents from 45 to 28. The inconsistencies in the number of slave houses may be related to the fact that many of the houses were not occupied, particularly after 1839 when only 20 enslaved workers were living on the plantation.

2. To determine the corresponding African ethnolinguistic group of these *naciones,* I consulted Ortiz (1988) and Gomez (1998). The nación Maená could not be found in these or other sources and is possibly a misspelling of Maní, a nación frequently found on Cuban slave lists.

11 / Afterword

Samuel M. Wilson

I am honored to be asked to add a note at the end of this valuable and timely volume and full of admiration for the editors and contributors for going to such great effort to make this book possible. It is a significant contribution to Caribbean archaeology, and I hope it will be part of an expanding dialogue between Cuban scholars and others studying the prehistory and history of the Caribbean.

Looking at contemporary culture in the world today, it is worth noting that in many ways the cultural significance of the Caribbean region is dramatically out of proportion to its relative size and population. In art, music, and literature, the Caribbean is a leader and trendsetter, in spite of representing only a tiny fraction of the world's population. Why is that? Perhaps it is because the Caribbean is so full of people with very different histories, cultures, languages, identities, and perspectives. It is a rich and exciting marketplace of ideas, each trying to make itself heard, each trying to translate itself into as many different languages and media as possible. In this exciting milieu, clinging to old orthodoxies or staying within the lines of conservative tradition is generally unproductive. In whatever arena—art, politics, even scholarship—the advantage goes to those with the creativity to see things in new ways or combine old ideas into novel and compelling forms.

At the best of times, this sort of "marketplace of ideas" has been a good description of the international community of Caribbean archaeologists. We have had the privilege of learning from each other and combining our data and insights in new ways. Together we have come to understandings of the past that are richer than we ever could have working in isolation. The International Association of Caribbean Archaeologists has been a sort of "moveable feast" in this regard, holding meetings on a different Caribbean island every two years. (The IACA is known in Spanish as the Asociación Internacional de Arqueología del Caribe, or AIAC, and in French as the Association Internationale d'Archaéologie de la Caraïbe, or AIAC.) Since the early 1960s, the IACA Proceedings have been one of the most important outlets for the publication of archaeological research in the Caribbean.

The problem that this volume helps to address is that an important voice in the dialogue of Caribbean scholarship has been relatively muted, not by choice but by political and economic circumstances. During the long period of estrangement and embargo between the governments of Cuba and the United States, communication between Cuban archaeologists and others working in the Caribbean has been made very difficult. Mail is slow and uncertain, and faxes and telephone calls are expensive and difficult to make. Travel, particularly from the United States, has been made difficult (though not impossible) by Treasury Department restrictions and limited direct air routes. The worst part is that the vast economic disequilibrium between industrialized countries and countries such as Cuba makes it difficult or impossible for Cuban scholars to have extensive contact with researchers in other countries. The case of Cuba is extreme, brought about by the policies of both the U.S. and the Cuban governments. But scholars all over Latin America can relate to the Cubans' dilemma: It is awfully difficult to participate fully in the regional or global scholarly community if that participation requires international travel, telephone and fax budgets, memberships in scholarly organizations, internet access, and access to a well-funded research library with current books and journals. The raw economic inequity of it is frustrating enough, but for many Latin American scholars what is even more intolerable is an attitude of condescension by better-funded scholars. In this regard, there is perhaps some consolation that in the history of Caribbean scholarship, it has been vision and commitment, not economic resources, that are the most valuable.

The barriers to communication and dialogue noted in some of the articles here and in the editors' introduction are real. Nevertheless, as the work in this volume also demonstrates, these difficulties have not resulted in the complete isolation of Cuba. Nor, obviously, has it made archaeological research in Cuba impossible. However great the difficulty, Cuban scholars have been interacting in creative ways with a wide community of archaeologists and historians throughout Latin America, Canada, Europe, and the former Soviet republics.

A growing number of U.S. scholars have been visiting Cuba and collaborating with Cuban colleagues, and it is hoped that this trend will continue. This volume pushes the door open even wider.

I have had the pleasure of visiting Cuba two times in recent years, and, like many others in this volume, I was impressed by the quantity and high quality of the archaeological research going on. I would like to thank my wonderful friend and colleague Dra. Estrella Rey, who opened her home to me and introduced me to her wide community of colleagues, students, and friends. Through Dra. Rey and her colleagues, I saw that despite the continuing hardships, Cuba remains one of the leading islands in the Caribbean in terms of the archaeological research being carried out. What was most clear and promising is that there is a vibrant young generation of Cuban students who are doing fantastic work and are hungry for interaction, dialogue, and collaboration with their counterparts from other countries.

This volume is a sign of great promise for the future of the dialogue between Cuban scholars and the rest of the international community. Shannon Dawdy's efforts in helping to put it together demonstrate the enthusiasm of a young generation of scholars north of the Straits of Florida that is eager to engage in a dialogue with Cuba and the Caribbean. She and Gabino La Rosa and Antonio Curet are to be heartily commended for their efforts in pulling together the symposium from which this volume evolved (and the grant money that made it possible) and the volume itself. The editors and indeed all of the participants in the book should be acknowledged for their generosity of spirit and commitment to the good of our community. For Shannon and Gabino and Antonio, there are certainly other pressing obligations of greater direct benefit to them personally, but nevertheless they put their efforts toward this project, which helps us all.

The dialogue that this volume promotes is badly needed, and the papers collected here will be of great value to a wide audience. It is important to remember that one of the most important and useful parts of the process of dialogue is respectful difference of opinion. It is a lot more difficult to engage in a real dialogue than it is to reproduce complacently the same interpretations and opinions. It is also a lot more valuable. Dialogue is work, and disagreement is even harder work, yet it is the process through which we learn more about the past. As noted, the Caribbean has a long history of being a marketplace of competing voices and ideas, and that is what we desperately need in Caribbean archaeology. This volume is a wonderful and timely contribution to this dialogue.

References Cited

Abbott, A.

1829 *Letters Written in the Interior of Cuba.* Bowles & Dearborn, Boston.

Alegría, R.

1978 *Apuntes en torno a la mitología de los indios Taínos de las Antillas Mayores y sus orígenes suramericanos.* Centro de Estudios Avanzados de Puerto Rico y el Caribe, Museo del Hombre Dominicano.

1980 *Cristóbal Colón y el tesoro de los indios de La Española.* Ediciones Fundación García Arévalo, Santo Domingo.

1981 *El uso de la terminología etno-histórica para designar las culturas aborígenes de las Antillas.* Cuadernos Prehispánicos. Seminario de Historia de América, Universidad de Valladolid, Valladolid.

Alexeiev, V. P.

1986 Acerca de la características craniológicas de la población indígena de Cuba. In *Arqueología de Cuba,* edited by R. S. Vasilievski, pp. 15–22. Novosibirsk Editorial "Nauka" Sección Siberiana. Novosibirsk, Siberia.

Alonso Lorea, J. R.

2001 Ortiz y la Cueva del Templo o el informe de "Don Fernando." *Gabinete de Arqueología, Boletín* 1:45–55.

Álvarez Conde, J.

1956 Arqueología Indocubana. Publicaciones de la Junta Nacional de Arqueología y Etnología. Havana.

Álvarez Estévez, R.

2001 *Huellas francesas en el occidente de Cuba (siglos XVI–XIX).* Editorial José Martí, Havana.

Anderson, B.
1983 *Imagined Communities: Reflections on the Origin and Spread of Nationalism.* Verso, London.

Andrade de Lima, T., and J. López Mazz
2000 La emergencia de complejidad entre los cazadores recolectores de la costa Atlántica meridional sudamericana. *Revista de arqueología americana* 17, 18 and 19:129–175.

Andueza, J.
1841 *Isla de Cuba, pintoresca, histórica, política, mercantil e industrial. Recuerdos y apuntes de dos épocas.* Boix, Madrid.

Angulo, C.
1992 Modos de vida en la prehistoria de la llanura atlántica de Colombia. In *Prehistoria sudamericana: Nuevas perspectivas,* edited by B. J. Meggers, pp. 253–270. Taraxacum, Washington, D.C.

Armstrong, D. V.
1990 *The Old Village and the Great House: An Archaeological and Historical Examination of Drax Hall Plantation, St. Ann's Bay, Jamaica.* University of Illinois Press, Urbana.
1999 Archaeology and Ethnohistory of the Caribbean Plantation. In *I, Too, Am America: Archaeological Studies of African-American Life,* edited by T. A. Singleton, pp. 173–192. University Press of Virginia, Charlottesville.
2003 *Creole Transformation to Freedom: Historical Archaeology of the East End Community, St. Johns, U.S. Virgin Islands.* University Press of Florida, Gainesville.

Arrazcaeta Delgado, R.
1987 Las pipas: un antiguo útil de fumar. Ms. on file, Gabinete de Arqueología, Havana.

Arrom, J. J.
1975 *Mitología y artes prehispánicas de las Antillas.* Siglo XXI, Mexico City.

Arvelo B., L. M.
1995 *The Evolution of Prehispanic Complex Social Systems in the Quibor Valley, Northwestern Venezuela.* Unpublished Ph.D. dissertation, Department of Anthropology, University of Pittsburgh, Pittsburgh.

Bahn, P.
1996 Rock Art. In *The Oxford Companion to Archaeology,* edited by B. Fagan, pp. 593–594. Oxford University Press, New York.

Bahn, P., and J. Vertut
1997 *Journey Through the Ice Age.* University of California Press, Berkeley.

Baker, C. P.
1997 *Cuba Handbook.* Moon Publications, Chico, California.

Barcia Paz, M.
1998 *La resistencia esclava en las plantaciones cubanas (1790–1870).* Vitral, Pinar del Rio, Cuba.

Bate, L. F.
1978 *Sociedad, formación social y cultura.* Ediciones Cultura Popular, Mexico, D.F.

Bauzá, V.
2003 Smithsonian Returns Taino Indian Remains to Descendants in Cuba. *Florida Sun-Sentinel,* 13 January. http://www.rose-hulman.edu/~delacova/taino/taino-reburial.htm.

Beier, U.
1961 La actitud de los Yorubas hacia los perros. *Boletín Mensual del Centro de Estudios del Folklore del TNT* (Havana) 1(8):13–14.

Beovide, L.
1995 Análisis de los restos arqueofaunísticos de la Casa del Diablo, San Miguel, Rocha. In *Arqueología en el Uruguay,* pp. 54–64. Imprenta y Editorial Surcos, Uruguay.

Bergad, L. W.
1990 *Cuban Rural Society in the Nineteenth Century.* Princeton University Press, Princeton, New Jersey.

Bergad, L. W., F. I. García, and M. Barcia
1995 *The Cuban Slave Market.* Cambridge University Press, New York.

Berlin, I.
1998 *Many Thousands Gone: The First Two Centuries of Slavery in North America.* Harvard University Press, Cambridge.

Berlin, I., and P. Morgan (editors)
1991 *The Slaves' Economy: Independent Production by Slaves in the Americas.* Frank Cass, London.

Berman, M. J.
1999 Review of *The Art and Archaeology of Pre-Columbian Cuba* by Ramon Dacal Moure and Manuel Rivero de la Calle. *Museum Anthropology* 23(1):56–57.

Blakey, M.
2001 Bioarchaeology of the African Diaspora in the Americas: Its Origin and Scope. In *Annual Review of Anthropology* 30:387–422. Annual Reviews, Palo Alto, California.

Bloch, M., and J. Parry
1982 Introduction. In *Death and the Regeneration of Life,* edited by M. Bloch and J. Parry, pp. 1–44. Cambridge University Press, London.

Bremer, F.
1980 [1851] *Cartas desde Cuba.* Editorial de Arte y Literatura, Havana.

Brinton, D. G.
1919 The Archaeology of Cuba. *The American Archeologist* 2(10):253–256.

Calvera, J., R. Funes, and F. Cuba

1991 Investigaciones arqueológicas en Cubitas, Camagüey. In *Arqueología de Cuba y de otras áreas antillanas,* pp. 522–548. Centro de Antropología. Editorial Academica, Havana.

Calvera, J., E. Serrano, and M. Rey

1996 El sitio arqueológico Los Buchillones. *El Caribe arqueológico* 1:59–67.

Cassá, R.

1992 *Los indios de las Antillas.* Editorial Mapfre, Madrid.

Castro, F.

1975 Discurso con motivo de la velada conmemorativa de los cien años de lucha, 10 de octubre de 1968, Bayamo, Cuba. In *Discursos de Fidel Castro, compilación,* vol. 1. Editorial de Ciencias Sociales, Havana.

Celaya, M., and P. P. Godo

2000 Llora lluvia: expresiones mítico-artísticas en la alfarería aborigen. *El Caribe Arqueológico* 4:70–84.

Centro Nacional de Cultura–Restauración de Monumentos

1984 *Cuatro textos internacionales sobre conservación y restauración de monumentos.* Proyecto Cuba 81 PNUD, UNESCO, CNRS, Havana.

Chakrabarti, D. K.

1997 *Colonial Indology: Sociopolitics of the Ancient Indian Past.* Munshiram Manoharlal, New Delhi.

Chanlatte, L. A.

1984 *Catálogo. Arqueología de Vieques.* Centro de Investigaciones Arqueológicas. Universidad de Puerto Rico, Río Piedras, Puerto Rico.

Chanlatte, L. A., and Y. M. Narganes

1983 *Vieques–Puerto Rico. Asiento de una nueva cultura aborigen antillana.* Santo Domingo, Dominican Republic.

Childe, V. G.

1947 Archaeology as a Social Science. In *Third Annual Report,* pp. 49–60. University of London, Institute of Archaeology, London.

Collazo, G.

1998 Taíno Finds. *Archaeology* 51(5). http://www.archaeology.org/found.php?page=/9809/newsbriefs/taino. html.

Comisión de Estadísticas

1842 *Resumen del censo de población de la Isla de Cuba a fin del año 1841.* Imprenta del Gobierno por S.M., Havana.

Córdova, A.

n.d. Estudio arqueológico de la variante cultural Mayarí. Ms. on file, Departamento de Arqueología, Centro de Antropología, CITMA, Havana.

Coronil, F.

1995 Introduction to the Duke University Press Edition. In *Cuban Counterpoint,*

Tobacco and Sugar, by Fernando Ortiz, pp. ix–lvi. Duke University Press, Durham, North Carolina.

Correia, M.

2002 Terminología, desenvolvimento e identidad nacional. *Actas del VI simpósio ibero-americano de terminología.* Ediçoes Colibri Lisbon, Portugal. http://www.iltec.pt/eng/conteudo.html

Culin, S.

1902 The Indians of Cuba. *Bulletin of the Free Museum of Science and Art of the University of Pennsylvania* 3(4):185–226.

Curet, L. A.

1991 El cacicazgo en el registro arqueológico: modelos y variables arqueológicas. In *Actas del Decimotercer Congreso Internacional de Arqueología del Caribe,* edited by E. N. Ayubi and J. B. Haviser, pp. 15–21. Reports of the Archaeological-Anthropological Institute of the Netherlands Antilles, no. 9, Curaçao, Netherlands Antilles.

Curet, L. A., and J. R. Oliver

1998 Mortuary Practices, Social Development, and Ideology in Precolumbian Puerto Rico. *Latin American Antiquity* 9(3):217–239.

Dacal Moure, R.

1972 Notas sobre las figurinas aruacas de la prehistoria cubana. *Revista de la Universidad de la Habana* 196–197:85–116.

1978 *Artefactos de concha en las comunidades aborígenes cubanas.* Museo Antropológico Montané, Universidad de la Habana, Havana.

1986 *Playita, un sitio protoagrícola en las márgenes del río Canímar, Matanzas, Cuba.* Museo Antropológico Montané, Universidad de la Habana, Havana.

Dacal Moure, R., and O. Collado López

1975 Indice analítico de la Revista de arqueología y etnología. *Ciencias Serie No. 9, Antropología y Prehistoria No. 4.* Universidad de la Habana, Havana.

Dacal Moure, R., and M. Rivero de la Calle

1986 *Arqueología aborígen de Cuba.* Editorial Gente Nuevo, Havana.

1996 *The Art and Archaeology of Pre-Columbian Cuba.* Translated by D. R. Watters and D. H. Sandweiss. University of Pittsburgh Press, Pittsburgh.

Davis, D. D.

1996 Revolutionary Archeology in Cuba. *Journal of Archaeological Method and Theory* 3(3):159–188.

Deacon, T. W.

1997 *The Symbolic Species.* W. W. Norton & Company, New York.

Deagan, K.

1987 *Artifacts of Spanish Colonies of Florida and the Caribbean, 1500–1800.* Smithsonian Institution Press, Washington, D.C.

De Booy, T.

1915 Pottery from Certain Caves in Eastern Santo Domingo, West Indies. *American Antiquity* 17:69–97.

1919 *Santo-Domingan Kitchen Midden and Burial Ground.* Indian Notes and Monographs, vol. 1, no. 2. Museum of the American Indian, Heye Foundation, New York.

Dimock, J.

1998 [1846] *Impressions of Cuba in the Nineteenth Century: The Travel Diary of Joseph J. Dimock.* Scholarly Books, Wilmington, Delaware.

Domínguez, J.

1993 Cuba since 1959. In *Cuba: A Short History,* edited by L. Bethell, pp. 95–148, 160–166. Cambridge University Press, Cambridge.

Domínguez, L.

1980 Cerámica de transculturación en el sitio colonial Casa de la Obrapía. In *Cuba arqueológica II.* Editorial Oriente, Santiago de Cuba.

1981 Arqueología del sitio colonial Casa de la Obrapía de la Puerta. Habana Vieja. *Santiago* 41:63–82. Havana.

1988 La importancia de la excavación arqueológica en la restauración de monumentos. In *Documentos (1).* Centro de Restauración, Conservación y Museología, Ministerio de Cultura, Havana.

1991 *Arqueología del centro-sur de Cuba.* Editorial Academia, Havana.

1998 La ciudad encontrada. *Opous Habana* 2:58–63.

Domínguez, L., and J. Febles

1981 Primera expedición arqueológica soviético-cubana: excavaciones en Siberia. *Revista Bohemia* 73(5):90–91.

Domínguez, L., J. Febles, and A. Rives

1994 Las comunidades aborígenes de Cuba. In *Historia de Cuba: La colonia, evolución socioeconómica y formación nacional.* Editora Política, Havana.

Dubelaar, C. N.

1995 *The Petroglyphs of the Lesser Antilles, the Virgin Islands, and Trinidad.* Publications of the Foundation for Scientific Research in the Caribbean, no. 35. Amsterdam.

Dumont, H.

1865 Investigaciones sobre enfermedades de los negros que no padecen la Fiebre Amarilla. Estudio particular de la enfermedad "Hinchazón" de los negros y chinos. In *Anales de la Real Academia de Ciencias Médicas, Físicas y Naturales de La Habana,* pp. 493–522. Imprenta del Tiempo, Havana.

Eco, H.

1972 Tratado de semiótica general. *Nueva imagen,* p. 512. Lumen, Barcelona.

Escobar Guío, F., and J. J. Guarch Rodríguez

1991 Hipótesis sobre una nueva región del arte rupestre en Cuba. *Estudios arqueológicos 1989,* pp. 48–56. Editorial Academia, Havana.

Fabian, J.
1983 *Time and the Other: How Anthropology Makes Its Object.* Columbia University Press, New York.

Fairbanks, C.
1972 "The Cultural Significance of Spanish Ceramics." In *Ceramics in America,* edited by I. Quimby, pp. 141–174. University of Virginia Press, Charlottesville.

Fane, D., I. Jackins, and L. M. Breen
1991 *Objects of Myth and Memory, American Indian Art at the Brooklyn Museum.* University of Washington Press, Seattle.

Febles, J.
1982 *Estudio tipológico y tecnológico del material de piedra tallada del sitio arqueológico Canímar I, Matanzas, Cuba.* Editora de la Academia de Ciencias de Cuba, Havana.
1991 Estudio comparativo de las industrias de la piedra tallada de Aguas Verdes (Baracoa) y Playitas (Matanzas): Probable relación de estas industrias con otras del S.E de los Estados Unidos. In *Arqueología de Cuba y otras áreas antillanas,* edited by M. A. Rodríguez, pp. 312–370. Editorial Academia, Havana.
1995 *Taíno. Arqueología de Cuba.* Centro de Antropología, Havana, Cuba. CEDISAC, Havana, Cuba (CD-ROM).

Ferguson, L. G.
1992 *Uncommon Ground. Archaeology and Early African America, 1650–1800.* Smithsonian Institution Press, Washington, D.C.

Fernández Leiva, O.
1992 Desarrollo del pensamiento arqueológico en Cuba. In *Arqueología en América Latina hoy,* edited by G. G. Politis, pp. 32–44. Biblioteca Banco Popular, Bogota.

Fernández Ortega, R., and J. B. González Tendero
2000 Los petroglifos de la Cueva de Patana, Maisí, Guantánamo. *El Caribe Arqueológico* 4:45–52.
2001a Dos personajes mitológicos en los petroglifos de la Caverna de Patana (Maisí, Guantánamo), Cuba. *Boletín del Museo del Hombre Dominicano* 28(29):133–145.
2001b Dos personajes mitológicos en los petroglifos de la Caverna de Patana (Maisí, Guantánamo), Cuba. http://repestreweb.tripod.com/patana.htm

Fewkes, J. W.
1904 Prehistoric Culture of Cuba. *American Anthropologist* 6(5):585–598.
1907 The Aborigines of Puerto Rico and the Neighboring Islands. In *Annual Report of the Bureau of American Ethnology for 1903–1904,* no. 25. Smithsonian Institution, Washington, D.C.

Flannery, K.

1973 Archaeology with a Capital "S." In *Research and Theory in Current Archaeology,* edited by C. L. Redman, pp. 47–53. Wiley, New York.

Ford, J.

1969 *A Comparison of Formative Cultures in the Americas. Diffusion or the Psychic Unity of Man.* Smithsonian Institution, Washington, D.C.

Forster, N., and H. Handelman

1985 "Food Production and Distribution in Cuba: The Impact of the Revolution." In *Food, Politics, and Society in Latin America,* edited by J. C. Super and T. C. Wright, pp. 174–198. University of Nebraska Press, Lincoln.

Fowler, D. D.

1987 Uses of the Past: Archaeology in the Service of the State. *American Antiquity* 52(2):229–248.

Franco Ferrán, J. L.

1986 Esquema histórico sobre la trata negrera y la esclavitud. In *La esclavitud en Cuba,* pp. 1–10. Instituto de Ciencias Históricas. Editorial Academia, Havana.

Funari, P. P.

1995 The archaeology of Palmares and its contribution to the understanding of the history of African-American culture. *Historical Archaeology in Latin America* 7:141.

2000 *Desafios da destruicao e conservacao do patrimonio cultural no Brasil.* Campinas, Brazil.

Gamble, L., P. Walker, and G. S. Russell

2001 An Integrative Approach to Mortuary Analysis: Social and Symbolic Dimensions of Chumash Burial Practices. *American Antiquity* 66(2):185–211.

García Arévalo, M. A.

1989 *Los signos en el arte taíno.* Serie Monográfica, no. 25. Ediciones García Arévalo, Santo Domingo, Dominican Republic.

Gathercole, P., and D. Lowenthal (editors)

1990 *The Politics of the Past.* One World Archaeology 12. Unwin Hyman, Winchester, Massachusetts.

Gnivecki, P. L.

1998 Review of *The Art and Archaeology of Pre-Columbian Cuba* by Ramón Dacal Moure and Manuel Rivero de la Calle. *Latin American Antiquity* 9(3): 275–276.

Godo, P. P.

1985 Complejo sincrético cultural de El Morrillo. Paper presented at the Primer Evento Científico de las BTJ, Instituto de Ciencias Históricas, Academia de Ciencias de Cuba, Havana.

1997 El problema del protoagrícola de Cuba: discusión y perspectivas. *El Caribe arqueológico* 2:19–30.

Godo, P. P., and M. Celaya

1990 Expresiones mitológicas en los burenes de Cuba. *Anuario de arqueología 1988*, pp. 152–184. Editorial Academia, Havana.

Goggin, J.

1968 *Spanish Majolica in the New World.* Yale University Publications in Anthropology, no. 72. Yale University Press, New Haven.

Gomez, M.

1998 *Exchanging Our Country Marks: The Transformation of African Identities in the Colonial and Antebellum South.* University of North Carolina Press, Chapel Hill.

González Fernández, D.

1991 La economía cafetalera cubana: 1790–1860. *Arbor* (Madrid) (July–August) 139 (547–546):161–179.

Goodwin, C.

1978 The History and Development of Osteology in the Caribbean Area. *Revista interamericana* 8(3):463–494.

Gould, S. J.

1996 Up Against the Wall. *Natural History* 105:16–22.

Graham, E., D. M. Pendergast, J. Calvera, and J. Jardines

2000 Excavations at Los Buchillones, Cuba. *Antiquity* 74:263–264.

Greer, J.

2001 Rock Art and Rock Art Research in Worldwide Perspective: An Introduction. In *Handbook of Rock Art Research,* edited by D. S. Whitley, pp. 665–706. Altamira Press, Walnut Creek, California.

Guarch Delmonte, J. M.

1972 Excavaciones en el extremo oriental de Cuba. *Serie arqueológica No. 1.* Academia de Ciencias de Cuba, Instituto de Arqueológica, Havana.

1973 El ajuar no-cerámico de los Taínos de Cuba. *Serie arqueológica No. 3.* Academia de Ciencias de Cuba, Instituto de Arqueológica, Havana.

1974 Ensayo de reconstrucción etno-histórica del Taíno de Cuba. *Serie arqueológica No. 4.* Academia de Ciencias de Cuba, Instituto de Arqueológica, Havana.

1978 *El Taíno de Cuba: Ensayo de reconstrucción etno-histórica.* Academia de Ciencias de Cuba, Instituto de Ciencias Sociales, Havana.

1987 *Arqueología de Cuba: Métodos y sistemas.* Editorial de Ciencias Sociales, Havana.

1990 *Estructura para las comunidades aborígenes de Cuba.* Ediciones Holguín, Holguín.

1994 *Yaguajay, Yucayeque, Turey.* Publicigraf, Holguín.

1996 La muerte en las Antillas: Cuba. *El Caribe arqueológico* 1:12–25.

2003 The First Caribbean People: Part I. The Paleoindians in Cuba and the Circum-Caribbean. In *General History of the Caribbean,* vol. 1, *Autochthonous Societies,* edited by J. Sued Badillo, pp. 93–117. UNESCO Publishing and Macmillan Publishers Ltd., London and Oxford.

Guarch Delmonte, J. M., and A. Querejeta Barceló

1992 *Cuban Aboriginal Mythology: Deities and Characters.* Publicigraf, Havana.

Guarch Delmonte, J. M., and C. Rodríguez Cullel

1980 Consideraciones acerca la morfología y desarrollo de los pictogramas cubanos. *Cuba arqueológica No. 2,* pp. 53–76. Editorial Oriente, Cuba.

Guarch Delmonte, J. M., C. Rodríguez, and R. Pedroso

1987 Investigaciones preliminares en el sitio El Chorro de Maíta. *Revista de historia de Holguín* 3:25–40.

Guarch Delmonte, J. M., E. Rey, J. Febles, et al.

1995 Historia de los aborígenes de Cuba (según datos arqueológicos). In Taíno. Arqueología aborigen de Cuba (CD-ROM). Centro de Antropología, CENEDIT, México.

Guarch Rodríguez, E., and J. J. Guarch Rodríguez

1999 Caracterización de las regiones pictográficas de la Provincia Holguín. *El Caribe arqueológico* 3:95–101.

Gutiérrez Usillos, A., and R. Iglesias

1996 Identificación y análisis de los restos de fauna recuperados en los Conventos de San Francisco y Santo Domingo de Quito, siglos XVI–XIX. In *Revista española de antropología americana* 26:77–100. Universidad Complutense, Madrid.

Harrington, M. R.

1921 *Cuba Before Columbus.* 2 vols. Indian Notes and Monographs, Museum of the American Indian, Heye Foundation, New York.

1935 *Cuba antes de Colón.* Translated by A. Del Valle and F. Ortiz. Colección de Libros Cubanos, vol. 32. Cultural S.A., Havana.

1975 *Cuba antes de Colón.* Collección de Libros Cubanos, Vol. 32. Havana. Reprint.

Harrington, S. M.

1999 Taíno Stilt Village. *Archaeology* 52(6). http://www.archaeology.org/found.php?page=9911/newsbriefs/taino.html.

Herrera Fritot, R.

1939 *Informe sobre una exploración arqueólogica a Punta del Este, Isla de Pinos, realizada por el Museo Antropológico Montané de la Universidad de la Habana: Localización y estudio de una cueva con pictografías y restos de un ajuar aborigen.* Publicaciones de la Revista de la Universidad de la Habana, Havana.

Hinsley, C. M.

1981 *The Smithsonian and the American Indian, Making a Moral Anthropology in Victorian America.* Smithsonian Institution Press, Washington, D.C.

Hoffmann, W. J.

1888 Pictographs and Shamanistic Rites of the Ojibwa. *American Anthropologist* 3:209–229.

Holmes, W. H.

1894 Caribbean Influences on the Prehistoric Ceramic Art of the Southern States. *American Anthropologist* 7:71 79.

Hoopes, J. W.

1994 Ford Revisited: A Critical Review of Chronology and Relationships of Earliest Ceramic Complexes in the New World, 6000–1500 B.C. *Journal of World Prehistory* 8(1):1–49.

Howson, J.

1995 *Colonial Goods and the Plantation Village: Consumption and the Internal Economy in Montserrat from Slavery to Freedom.* Ph.D. dissertation, New York University, New York. University Microfilms, Ann Arbor.

Huckerby, T.

1914 Petroglyphs of Saint Vincent, British West Indies. *American Anthropologist* 16(2):238–244.

1921 *Petroglyphs of Grenada and a Recently Discovered Petroglyph in St. Vincent.* Indian Notes and Monographs, Museum of the American Indian, Heye Foundation, New York.

Izquierdo Díaz, G., and A. Rives Pantoja

1990 Tendencias de desarrollo del arte rupestre en Cuba. In *Estudios arqueológicos: Compilación de temas,* pp. 28–45. Editorial Academia, Havana.

James, C.

2000 Introduction. In *The Cultures of the Hispanic Caribbean,* edited by C. James and J. Perivolaris, pp. 1–8. University Press of Florida, Gainesville.

Jardines, J. E., and J. Calvera

1999 Estructuras de las viviendas aborígenes en Los Buchillones. *El Caribe arqueológico* 3:44–52.

Jiménez, M., and Y. R. Cooke

2001 Análisis faunístico de los restos excavados en las casas de Terrin (Panamá La Vieja): Una aproximación a la dieta y a la ecología. In *Arqueología de Panamá La Vieja,* CD-ROM edition. Universidad de Panamá, Panamá.

Johnson, P. T.

1988 Cuban Academic Publishing and Self-Perceptions. In *Cuban Studies* 18, edited by C. Mesa-Lago, pp. 103–122. University of Pittsburgh Press, Pittsburgh.

Jouravleva, I.

n.d. *Origen de la alfarería de las comunidades protoagroalfareras de la región central de Cuba.* Departamento de Antropología, CITMA, Havana.

Jouravleva, I., and N. Gonzáles

2000 Nuevos resultados acerca de la cerámica del sitio Arroyo del Palo. Ms. on file, Departamento de Antropología, CITMA, Havana.

Junta Nacional de Arqueología y Etnología

1951 *Reunión en mesa redonda de arqueólogos del Caribe.* Havana.

Kepecs, S.

2002 Saving Old Havana. *Archaeology* 55(2):42–47.

Kitchen, W.

1998 From Croatia to Cape Town: The Future of the World Archaeology Conference. *Antiquity* 72(278):747–750.

Kohl, P. L.

1998 Nationalism and Archaeology: On the Constructions of Nations and the Reconstruction of the Remote Past. *Annual Review of Anthropology* 27: 223–246.

Kohl, P. L., and Clare Fawcett (editors)

1995 *Nationalism, Politics, and the Practice of Archaeology.* Cambridge University Press, New York.

Kozlowski, J. K.

1972 *Industria lítica de "Aguas Verdes," Baracoa, Oriente, Cuba.* Ciencias Serie no. 9. Antropología y Prehistoria no. 1. Universidad de la Habana, Havana.

1974 *Preceramic Cultures in the Caribbean.* Zeszyty Naukowe Uniwersytetu Jagiellonskiego, 386 Prace Archeologiczne, Zesz. 20. Krakow.

1975 *Las industrias de la piedra tallada de Cuba en el contexto del Caribe.* Serie Arqueológica, no. 5. Editorial Academia, Havana.

Kozlowski, J. K., and B. Ginter

1975 *Técnica de la talla y tipología de los instrumentos líticos.* Editorial Pueblo y Educación, Instituto Cuba del Libro, Havana.

Krieger, H. W.

1933 The Early Indian Cultures of Cuba in the Smithsonian Institution. Explorations and Fieldwork (1932):49–52. Unpublished papers, Smithsonian Institution.

2002 Manuscripts. http://www.siris.si.edu.we

Labat, R. P.

1979 [1722] *Viajes a las islas de La América.* Editorial Casa de Las Américas, Havana.

La Rosa Corzo, G.

1991a La Cueva de la Cachimba: Estudio arqueológico de un refugio de cimarrones. In *Estudios Arqueológicos,* pp. 57–84. Editorial Academia, Havana.

1991b *Los palenques del oriente de Cuba: Resistencia y acoso.* Editorial Academia, Havana.

1994 Tendencias en los estudios sobre arte rupestre de Cuba: Retrospectiva crítica. *Revista Cubana de Ciencias Sociales* 29:135–152.

1995 *Arqueología en sitios de contrabandistas.* Editorial Academia, Havana.

1999 La huella africana en el ajuar del cimarrón. *El Caribe arqueológico* 3:109–115.

2000 Perspectivas de la arqueología histórica en Cuba en los umbrales del siglo XXI. *Revista bimestre cubana* (Havana) (January–June), época II, 87(12): 124–125.

2001 La arqueología en el estudio de la resistencia esclava. Paper presented at the Intercongress on the African Diaspora, Jacob Gelt Center Institute, Curaçao, Netherlands Antilles.

2003a La orientación este de los entierros aborígenes en cuevas de Cuba: Remate de una fábula. *Latin American Antiquity* 14(2):143–157.

2003b *Runaway Slave Settlements in Cuba: Resistance and Repression.* University of North Carolina Press, Chapel Hill.

La Rosa Corzo, G., and O. Ortega

1990 Refugios cimarrones en el Pan de Matanzas. In *Carta informativa* no. 6, Epoca III. Academia de Ciencias de Cuba, Havana.

La Rosa Corzo, G., and J. Pérez Padrón

1994 La resistencia esclava en la Sierra del Grillo: Estudio arqueológico. In *Estudios arqueológicos compliación de temas, 1990,* pp. 101–128. Editorial Academia, Havana.

Las Casas, B. de

1951 *Historia de las Indias.* 3 vols. Fondo de Cultura Económica, Mexico City.

Lathrap, D. W.

1985 Jaws: The Control of Power in the Early Nuclear American Ceremonial Centers. In *Dumbarton Oaks Early Andean Ceremonial Centers,* edited by C. Donnan, pp. 241–267. Dumbarton Oaks, Washington, D.C.

Laviña, J.

1987 Alimentación y cimarronaje en Vuelta Abajo. In *Revista boletín americanista* (Barcelona) 29(37):203–214.

Leal Spengler, E.

1986 *Regresar en el tiempo.* Editorial Letras Cubanas, Havana.

1995 *Andar . . . Havana.* Oficina del Historiador de la Ciudad. Editorial Gedepsa, Madrid.

Lévi-Strauss, C.

1970 *Antropología estructural.* Editorial de Ciencias Sociales, Havana.

1978 *Mitológicas 2. De la miel a las cenizas.* Fondo de Cultura Económica, México City.

López Baralt, M.

1977 *El mito taíno: Raíz y proyecciones en la amazonia continental.* Ediciones Huracán, Río Piedras, Puerto Rico.

Lorenzo, J. L.

1976 *Hacia una arqueología social. Reunión en Teotihuacan, Octubre de 1975.* Instituto Nacional de Antropología e Historia. México City.

Lotman, Y. M.

1982 El arte como lenguaje. In *Estructura del texto artístico,* pp. 17–46. Ystmo, Madrid.

1994 Para la construcción de una teoría de la interacción de las culturas (aspecto semiótico). *Revista criterios* 32 (7–12):117–130.

Lumbreras, L. G.

1974 *La arqueología como ciencia social.* Ediciones Histar, Lima, Perú.

MacCurdy, G. G.

1902 Twenty Years of Section H Anthropology. *Science* 15:532–534.

MacNeish, R.

1992 The Beginning of Agriculture in the New World. *Revista de Arqueología Americana* 6:7–34.

Madden R.

1964 [1849] *La Isla de Cuba: Sus recuerdos, progresos y perspectivas.* Consejo Nacional de Cultura, Havana.

Martínez Gabino, A. G.

1990 Presencia aborigen en cuevas de las costa norte del este de La Habana. *Anuario de Arqueología 1988,* pp. 133–151. Editorial Academia, Havana.

Martyr de Angleria, P.

1944 [1530] *Décadas del Nuevo Mundo.* Colección de Fuentes Para la Historia de América. Edición Estel, Buenos Aires.

McGuire, R. H.

1992 *A Marxist Archaeology.* Academic Press, New York.

Medhurst, C.

1977 Bellevue Phase II. *Archaeology–Jamaica* 77(3):1–11.

Meggers, B.

1987 Oscilación climática y cronología cultural en el Caribe. In *Actas del Tercer Simposio de la Fundación de Arqueología del Caribe,* edited by M. Sanoja, pp. 23–54. Washington, D.C.

Meggers, B., and C. Evans

n.d. *Aspectos arqueológicos de las tierras bajas de Suramérica y las Antillas.* Cuadernos del CENDIA, vol. 258, no. 4. Universidad Autónoma de Santo Domingo, Santo Domingo.

Meggers, B., C. Evans, and E. Estrada

1965 *Early Formative Period of Coastal Ecuador: The Valdivia and Machalilla Phases.* Smithsonian Contributions to Anthropolgy no. 1, Washington, D.C.

Meltzer, D.
1985 North American Archaeology and Archaeologists, 1879–1934. *American Antiquity* 50(2):249–260.

Meskell, L. (editor)
1998 *Archaeology Under Fire: Nationalism, Politics, and Heritages in the Eastern Mediterranean and Middle East.* Routledge, London.

Miguel, O.
1949 Descubrimiento y excavación de un montículo funeral en el potrero El Porvenir. In *Revista de arqueología y etnología* 8–9:175–194.

Miller, D.
1980 Archaeology and Development. *Current Anthropology* 21(6):709–726.

Moles, A.
1973 *Sociodinámica de la cultura.* Editorial Progreso, Moscow.

Montané, L.
1918 El indio cubano de la Ciénaga de Zapata. In *Cuatro años en la Ciénaga de Zapata,* edited by Juan Antonio Casculluela, pp. 115–146. Imprenta y Papelería La Universal de Ruiz y Cía., Havana.

Morales Muñiz, A.
1989 Zooarqueología. In *Paleontología* 10:381–410. Consejo Superior de Investigaciones Científicas, Madrid.

Moreira, L. M.
1999 *La sociedad comunitaria de Cuba.* Editorial Felix Varela, Havana.

Moreno Fraginals, M.
1978 *El ingenio. Complejo económico social cubano del azúcar.* 3 vols. Editorial de Ciencias Sociales, Havana.
1986 *El ingenio. Complejo económico social cubano del azúcar.* 2d ed. Editorial de Ciencias Sociales, Havana.

Moscoso, F.
1986 *Tribu y clases en el Caribe antiguo.* Ediciones de la Universidad Central del Este, Santo Domingo.

Nastri, J.
2003 (Pre)history, Identity, and Construction of the Past: The Experience of Early Americanist Archaeology. Paper presented at 5th World Archaeological Congress, Washington, D.C.

Navarrete, R.
1990 Cerámica y etnicidad. *Gens* (Caracas, Venezuela) 4(2):59–97.

Noelke, V. H. McK.
1974 *The Origin and Early History of the Bureau of American Ethnology, 1879–1910.* Unpublished Ph.D. dissertation, Department of Anthropology, University of Texas, Austin.

Núñez Jiménez, A.

1948 *Nuevos descubrimientos arqueológicos en Punta del Este, Isla de Pinos.* Publicaciones de la Universidad de La Habana (Separata), Havana.

1959 *Geografía de Cuba.* Lex, Havana.

1961 *20 Años explorando a Cuba: Historia de la Sociedad Espeleológica de Cuba.* INRA, Havana.

1967 *Cuevas y pictografías: Estudios espeleológicos y arqueológicos.* Edición Revolucionaria, Havana.

1975 *Cuba: Dibujos rupestres.* Editorial de Ciencias Sociales, Havana.

1980 *40 Años explorando a Cuba: Historia documentada de la Sociedad Espeleológica de Cuba.* Editorial Academia, Havana.

1985 *Arte rupestre de Cuba.* Editorial Jaca Book Spa, Italy

1990 *Medio siglo explorando a Cuba.* 2 vols. Imprenta Central de las FAR, Havana.

1994 *En canoa: Por el mar de las Antillas.* Patronato de la Ciudad Colonial de Santo Domingo. Collección Quinto Centenario, Santo Domingo.

Oliver, J. R.

1992 The Caguana Ceremonial Center: A Cosmic Journey Through Taíno Spatial and Iconographic Symbolism. Paper presented at the 10th International Symposium, Latin American Indian Literatures Association, San Juan, Puerto Rico.

1998 *El centro ceremonial de Caguana, Puerto Rico: Simbolismo iconográfico, cosmovisión y el poderío caciquil taíno de Boriquén.* International Series 727. British Archaeological Reports, Oxford.

2000 Gold Symbolism among Caribbean Chiefdoms: Of Feathers, Cibas, and Guanín Power among Taíno Elites. In *Precolumbian Gold: Technology, Style and Iconography,* edited by C. McEwan, pp. 196–219. British Museum Press, London.

Olmos, R.

1991 Nuevos enfoques y propuestas de lectura en el estudio de la iconografía ibérica. In *Nuevos enfoques en arqueología,* edited by A. Vila, pp. 209–230. Consenjo Superior de Investigaciones Científicas, Madrid.

Orser, Charles E., Jr.

1994 Toward a global historical archaeology: an example from Brazil. *Historical Archaeology* 28(1):5–22.

Ortiz, F.

1921 *Los cabildos africanos.* La Universal, Havana.

1922a Historia de la arqueologiia cubana. *Cuba Contemporánea* 30(117):5–35.

1922b *Historia de la arqueología indocubana.* Imprenta El Siglo XX, Havana.

1935 *Historia de la arqueología indocubana.* 2d ed. Colección de libros cubanos, vol. 32. Cultural, Havana.

1943 *Las cuatro culturas indias de Cuba.* Biblioteca de Estudios Cubanos, vol. 1. Editores Arrellano, Havana.

1988 *Los negros esclavos.* Editorial de Ciencias Sociales, Havana.

Osgood, C.

1942 *The Ciboney Culture of Cayo Redondo, Cuba.* Yale University Publications in Anthropology, no. 25. Yale University Press, New Haven.

Oyuela-Caycedo, A. (editor)

1994 *History of Latin America.* Worldwide Archaeology Series. Avebury (Ashgate Publishing Ltd.), Aldershot, Great Britain.

Oyuela-Caycedo, A., A. Anaya, C. G. Elera, and L. M. Valdez

1997 Social Archaeology in Latin America: Comments to T. C. Patterson. *American Antiquity* 62(2):365–374.

Pané, R.

1984 *Relación acerca de las antigüedades de los indios.* 5th ed. Siglo XXI Mexico City.

1990 *Relación acerca de las antigüedades de los indios.* Editorial de Ciencias Sociales, Havana.

Panichev, V. A.

1986 Nuevos fechados por C-14 obtenidos para los monumentos arqueológicos de Cuba. In *Arqueología de Cuba,* edited by R. S. Vasilievski, pp. 167–169. Novosibirsk Editorial "Nauka" Sección Siberiana. Novosibirsk, Siberia.

Paquette, R. L.

1988 *Sugar Is Made with Blood: The Conspiracy of La Escalera and the Conflict Between Empires over Slavery in Cuba.* Wesleyan University Press, Middletown, Connecticut.

Parezo, N.

1987 The Formation of Ethnographic Collections: The Smithsonian Institution in the American Southwest. In *Advances in Archaeological Method and Theory,* vol. 10, edited by M. B. Schiffer, pp. 1–45. Academic Press, New York.

Patterson, T. C.

1994 Social Archaeology in Latin America: An Appreciation. *American Antiquity* 59(3):531–537.

1995 *A Social History of Archaeology in the United States.* Harcourt Brace College, Fort Worth, Texas.

Payarés, R.

1980 Informe de los trabajos de salvataje en El Morrillo. *Cuba Arqueológica II,* pp. 77–90. Editorial Oriente, Cuba.

Pendergast, D. M.

1997 Up from the Shallows. *Rotunda* 30(2):28–31.

1998 The House in the Water. *Rotunda* 31(2):26–31.

Pendergast, D. M., E. Graham, R. J. A. Calvera, and M. J. Jardines

2001 Houses in the Sea: Excavation and Preservation at Los Buchillones, Cuba. In *Enduring Records: The Environmental and Cultural Heritage of Wetlands,* edited by B. A. Purdy, pp. 71–82. Oxbo Books, Oxford.

2002 The Houses in Which They Dwelt: The Excavation and Dating of Taino Wooden Structures at Los Buchillones, Cuba. *Journal of Wetland Archaeology* 2:61–75.

Pérez, L. A., Jr.

1995 *Cuba: Between Reform and Revolution.* Oxford University Press, New York.

1999 *On Becoming Cuban: Identity, Nationality and Culture.* University of North Carolina Press, Chapel Hill.

Pérez de la Riva, F.

1981 *La Isla de Cuba en el siglo XIX vista por los extranjeros.* Editorial de Ciencias Sociales, Havana.

Pérez Firmat, G.

1989 *The Cuban Condition: Translation and Identity in Modern Cuban Literature.* Cambridge University Press, Cambridge.

Pérez Guzmán, F.

1997 *La Habana, clave de un imperio.* Editorial de Ciencias Sociales, Havana.

Perpiñá, A.

1889 *El Camagüey: Viajes pintorescos por el interior de Cuba y por sus costas, con descripciones del país.* Publicación de J. A. Bastinos, Barcelona.

Perry, W., and R. Paynter

1999 Artifacts, Ethnicity and the Archaeology of African Americans. In *I, Too, Am America: Archaeological Studies of African-American Life,* edited by T. A. Singleton, pp. 299–310. University Press of Virginia, Charlottesville.

Petersen, J. B., D. R. Watters, and D. V. Nicholson

1999 Continuity and Syncretism in Afro-Caribbean Ceramics from the Northern Lesser Antilles. In *African Sites Archaeology in the Caribbean,* edited by J. Haviser, pp. 157–195. Markus Wiener, Princeton, New Jersey.

Petitjean Roget, H.

1978 *L'art des Arawak et des Caraibes des petites Antilles. Analyse de la décoration de céramiques.* Les Cahiers du CERAG No.35. Centre d'Etudes Regionales Antilles-Guyane, French Guayana.

Pichardo Moya, F.

1956 Los aborígenes de las Antillas. Fondo de Cultura Económica, Mexico City.

1971 *Documentos para la historia de Cuba.* Vol. 1. Editorial de Ciencias Sociales, Havana.

1990 *Caverna, costa y meseta.* Editorial Ciencias Sociales, Havana.

Pintos, S., and C. Gianatti

1995 Arqueofauna de los constructores de Cerritos "Quebra y Requiebra." In

Arqueología en el Uruguay, pp. 79–91. Imprenta y Editorial Surcos, Uruguay.

Plog, S., F. Plog, and W. Wait

1978 Decision Making in Modern Surveys. In *Advances in Archaeological Method and Theory*, edited by M. B. Schiffer, pp. 383–421. Academic Press, New York.

Politis, G.

2003 The Theoretical Landscape and the Methodological Development of Archaeology in Latin America. *Latin American Antiquity* 14(2):115–142.

Politis, G., G. Martínez, and M. Bonomo

2001 Alfarería temprana en sitios de cazadores-recolectores de la región pampeana Argentina. *Latin American Antiquity* 12(2):167–181.

Porebski, M.

1994 Semiótica e icónica. *Revista criterios* (Havana) 32(7–12):275–286.

Price, T. D., and G. M. Feinman

1995 Foundations of Prehistoric Social Inequality. In *Foundations of Social Inequality*, edited by T. D. Price and G. M. Feinman, pp. 3–11. Plenum Press, New York.

Pulsipher, L., and C. Goodwin

1999 "Here Where the Old Time People Be": Reconstructing Landscapes of Slavery and Post-Slavery Era in Monteserrat, West Indies. In *African Sites Archaeology in the Caribbean*, edited by Jay Haviser, pp. 9–33. Markus Wiener, Princeton, New Jersey.

Radio Habana

2002 Archaeological Artifacts Found in Villa Clara. http://www.hartford-hwp.com/archives/41/309.html, April 23.

Rangel Rivero, A.

1994 Historical Aspects of the Montané Anthropological Museum of the University of Havana. *Museum Anthropology* 18(1):61–64.

Reitz, E. J., and E. J. Wing

1999 *Zooarchaeology*. Cambridge Manuals in Archaeology. Cambridge University Press, New York.

Renfrew, C., and P. Bahn

1993 *Arqueología: Teorías, métodos y práctica*. Ediciones AKAL, Madrid.

Rey, E.

1970 *Las peculiaridades de la desintegración de las comunidades primitivas cubanas*. Serie Antropológica no. 5. Academia de Ciencias de Cuba, Havana.

Rímoli, R. O., and J. Nadal

1980 Cerámica temprana de Honduras del Oeste. In *Boletín del Museo del Hombre Dominicano* 15:17–82.

1983 *El horizonte ceramista temprano en Santo Domingo y otras Antillas*. Editorial de la UASD, Santo Domingo.

Rivero, A. R.

1994 Historical Aspects of the Montané Anthropological Museum of the University of Havana. *Museum Anthropology* 18(1):61–64.

Rivero de la Calle, M.

1960 *Caguanes: Nueva zona arqueológica de Cuba.* Departamento de Investigaciones Antropológicas, Universidad Central de Las Villas, Santa Clara.

1966 *Las culturas aborígenes de Cuba.* Editora Universitaria, Havana.

1985 *Nociones de anatomía humana aplicadas a la arqueología.* Editorial Científico-Técnica, Havana.

Rivero de la Calle, M., and A. Núñez Jiménez

1958 *Excursiones arqueológicas a Camagüey.* Departamento de Investigaciones Antropológicas e Investigaciones Geográficas, Universidad Central de Las Villas, Santa Clara.

Rives, A.

1985 Los instrumentos de piedra tallada y su reflejo en las manifestaciones superestructurales antillanas. *Revista Biblioteca Nacional* 76, Época (Havana) 3:157–169.

Rodríguez Arce, C.

1987 Informe del proceso de interpretación del material arqueozoológico del sitio Chorro de Maíta. Ms. on file, Departamento Centro Oriental de Arqueología, Holguín.

1989 Las costumbres funerarias de los aborígenes agricultores de la Provincia Holguín, Cuba. Ms. on file, Departamento Centro Oriental de Arqueología, Holguín.

2000 Apuntes sobre la figura del murciélago en la iconografía prehispánica de Cuba. *El Caribe Arqueológico* 4:94–99.

Rodríguez Ferrer, M.

1876–1877 *Naturaleza y civilización de la grandiosa Isla de Cuba.* 2 vols. Imprenta J. Noguera, Madrid.

Romero, L.

1995 *La Habana arqueológica y otros ensayos.* Editora Letras Cubanas, Havana.

Ross, M.

2001 Emerging Trends in Rock Art Research: Hunter-Gatherer Culture, Land and Landscape. *Antiquity* 75:543–548.

Rostain, S., and R. D. Moure

1997 Shape and Function of Tanki Flip Shell, Stone, Coral, and Bone Artefacts on a Comparative Level. In *The Archaeology of Aruba: The Tanki Flip Site,* edited by A. H. Versteeg and S. Rostain, pp. 265–278. Publications of the Archaeological Museum Aruba 8. Publications of the Foundation for Scientific Research in the Caribbean Region 141, Aruba.

Rouse, I.

1942 *Archaeology of the Maniabon Hills, Cuba.* Yale University Publications in Anthropology no. 21. Yale University Press, New Haven.

1992 *The Tainos: Rise and Decline of the People Who Greeted Columbus.* Yale University Press, New Haven.

Rouse, I., and J. Cruxent

1961 *Arqueología cronológica de Venezuela.* Vol. 1. Unión Panamericana, Washington, D.C.

Rovira, B.

1985 *La arqueología histórica en Panamá.* Instituto Nacional de Cultura, UNESCO, PNUD, Panama City.

1991 Reflexiones acerca de la arqueología histórica, definiciones, problemas y una propuesta para su estudio. *Hombre y cultura, Revista del Centro de Investigaciones Antropológicas* 1(1):1–30. University of Panama, Panama.

Russell, A. E.

1997 Material Culture and African-American Spirituality at the Hermitage. *Historical Archaeology* 31(2):63–80.

Sandweiss, D. H., and D. R. Watters

1993 Cuban Prehistory—A New Connection. *Carnegie Magazine* 61(8):9.

Sanoja, M.

1988 La formación de cazadores recolectores en Venezuela. In *Actas del Segundo Simposio de la Fundación de Arqueología del Caribe.* Washington, D.C.

2001 Cerámica tipo formativo de Camay, estado Lara, Venezuela: Primer informe. *El Caribe arqueológico* 5:2–18.

Sanoja, M., and I. Vargas

1974 *Antiguas formaciones y modos de producción en venezuela.* Monte Avila Editores, Caracas, Venezuela.

1995 *Gente de la canoa.* Fondo Editorial Tropykos, Caracas.

Saussure, F.

1973 *Curso de lingüística general.* Editorial de Ciencias Sociales, Havana.

Savranski, I.

1983 *La cultura y sus funciones.* Editorial Progreso, Moscow.

Schiffer, M. B.

1976 *Behavioral Archaeology.* Academic Press, New York.

Scott, R.

1985 *Slave Emancipation in Cuba: The Transition to Free Labor, 1860–1899.* Princeton University Press, Princeton, New Jersey.

Scott, R., A. Oyuela, and P. Carmichael

1991 A Comparison of the Earliest Ceramic Technologies of Ecuador and Colombia. Paper presented at the 56th Annual Meeting of the Society for American Archaeology, New Orleans.

Shepherd, N.
2002 The Politics of Archaeology in Africa. *Annual Review of Anthropology* 31:189.

Siegel, P. E.
1989 Site Structure, Ceramics, Demography and Social Complexity in the Early Ceramic Age of the Caribbean. In *Early Population Lifeways and Adaptive Strategies in the Caribbean,* edited by P. E. Siegel, pp. 193–245. BAR International Series 506. British Archaeological Reports, Oxford.
1999 Contested Places and Places of Contest: The Evolution of Social Power and Ceremonial Space in Prehistoric Puerto Rico. *Latin American Antiquity* 3:209–238.

Siegel, P. E., and K. P. Severin
1993 The First Documented Prehistoric Gold-Copper Alloy Artifact from the West Indies. *Journal of Archaeological Science* 20:67–79.

Silberman, N. A.
1995 Promised Lands and Chosen Peoples: The Politics and Poetics of Archaeological Narrative. In *Nationalism, Politics, and the Practice of Archaeology,* edited by P. L. Kohl and C. Fawcett, pp. 249–262. Cambridge University Press, New York.

Singleton, T. A.
2001a An Americanist Perspective on African Archaeology: Toward an Archaeology of the Black Atlantic. In *West Africa during the Atlantic Slave Trade,* edited by C. R. DeCorse, pp. 179–184. Leicester University Press, London.
2001b Slavery and Spatial Dialectics on Cuban Coffee Plantations. *World Archaeology* 33(1):98–114.

Smith, B. D.
1995 The Origins of Agriculture in the Americas. *Evolutionary Anthropology* 3(5):174–184.

Squier, E. G.
1860 *Discovery of Ancient Tumuli in the Island of Cuba.* American Ethnological Society, Washington, D.C.

Statutes of the Academy of Sciences of Cuba
2001 www.cuba.cu/ciencia/acc/estatutos-ingles.htm

Stephens, J. L.
1841 *Incidents of Travel in Central American, Chiapas and Yucatan.* Harper and Brothers, New York.

Stevens-Arroyo, M. A.
1988 *Cave of the Jagua: The Mythological World of the Tainos.* University of New Mexico Press, Albuquerque.

Suárez del Portal, R.
1997 *La Habana, ciudad viva.* Oficina del Historiador de la Ciudad, Havana.

Suchlicki, J.

2001 *Historical Dictionary of Cuba.* 2d ed. Scarecrow Press, London.

Sued-Badillo, J. (editor)

2003 *General History of the Caribbean,* vol. 1, *Autochthonous Societies.* UNESCO Publishing and Macmillan Publishers Ltd., London and Oxford.

Tabío, E.

1978 *La comunidad primitiva . . . ¿Uno o varios modos de producción? Revolución y cultura 73:7–13.* Havana.

1984 Nueva periodización para el estudio de las comunidades aborígenes de Cuba. In *Islas* (Universidad Central de las Villas) (May–August), 78:37–52.

Tabío, E., and J. M. Guarch

1966 *Excavaciones en Arroyo del Palo.* Departamento de Antropología, Academia de Ciencias de Cuba, Havana.

Tabío, E., and E. Rey Betancourt

1966 *Prehistoria de Cuba.* Departmento de Antropología, Academia de Ciencias de Cuba, Havana.

1979 *Prehistoria de Cuba.* Editorial de Ciencias Sociales, Havana.

1985 *Prehistoria de Cuba.* Editorial de Ciencias Sociales, Havana.

Taylor, C.

1990 *Aplicaciones de los estudios de paleonutrición en el sitio agroalfarero Chorro de Maíta, Banes, Holguín.* Master's thesis, Universidad de La Habana, Havana.

Taylor, T.

1988 Mainz 1987: The State of World Archaeology. *Current Anthropology* 29(4): 671–679.

Thomas, N.

1991 *Entangled Objects: Exchange, Material Culture and Colonialism in the Pacific.* Harvard University Press, Cambridge, Massachusetts.

Torre, J. M.

1841 Mapa de la Isla de Cuba y tierras circunvecinas según las divisiones de los naturales. In *Memorias de la Sociedad Económica de La Habana* 13:18–67.

Torres, P., and M. Rivero de la Calle

1972 Paleopatología de los aborígenes de Cuba. *Serie espeleológica y carsológica 32.* Academia de Ciencias de Cuba, Havana.

Trigger, B.

1984 Marxism and Archaeology. In *On Marxian Perspectives in Anthropology: Essays in Honor of Harry Hoijer, 1981,* edited by J. Maquet and N. Daniels, pp. 59–97. Undena Publications, Malibu, California.

1989 *A History of Archaeological Thought.* Cambridge University Press, Cambridge.

Trincado, M. N.

1984 *Introducción a la protohistoria de Cuba.* Editorial Oriente, Santiago de Cuba.

Trincado, M. N., N. Castellanos, and G. Sosa

1973 *Arqueología de Sardinero.* Editorial Oriente, Santiago.

Ubelaker, D.

1991 *Human Skeletal Remains. Excavation, Analysis, Interpretatation.* Manuals on Archaeology 2. Taraxacum, Washington, D.C.

Ulloa Hung, Jorge

2002 Archaeology and Rescue of the Aboriginal Presence in Cuba and the Caribbean. *KACIKE: Journal of Caribbean Amerindian History and Anthropology. Special Issue,* edited by L. Guitar. New Directions in Taino Research. http://www.kacike.org/UlloaEnglish.html

Ulloa Hung, J., and R. Valcárcel Rojas

2002 *Cerámica temprana en el centro del oriente de Cuba.* Viewgraph, Santo Domingo.

Urbanowicz, C. F.

1992 Four Field Commentary. *Anthropology Newsletter* 33(9):3.

Valcárcel, R.

1999 Banes precolombino. Jerarquía y sociedad. *El Caribe arqueológico* 3:84–89.

2002a *Banes precolombino. La ocupación agricultora.* Ediciones Holguín, Holguín.

2002b Reporte de composición metálica de objetos asociados a entierros en el sitio arqueológico Chorro de Maíta. Ms. on file, Departamento Centro Oriental de Arqueología, Holguín.

Valcárcel, R., C. Rodríguez, M. Labrada, and P. Cruz

2002 Informe de exploración arqueológica en el Cerro de Los Muertos, Yaguajay, Banes. Ms. on file, Departamento Centro Oriental de Arqueología, Holguín.

Vargas, I.

1987 Sociedad y naturaleza: Mediaciones y determinaciones del cambio social. In *Actas del Tercer Simposio de la Fundación de Arqueología del Caribe.* Taraxacum, Washington, D.C.

2001 Institucionalización de la arqueología en la Habana Vieja. *Gabinete de Arqueología, Boletín* 1:22–28.

Vasconcellos Portuondo, D.

2001 Dr. Luis Montané y Dardé. *Gabinete de Arqueología, Boletín* 1:110–112.

Vasilievski, R. S. (editor)

1986 *Arqueología de Cuba.* Novosibirsk Editorial "Nauka" Sección Siberiana. Novosibirsk, Siberia.

Vega, B.

1979 *Los metales y los aborígenes de La Hispaniola.* Ediciones Museo del Hombre Dominicano, Santo Domingo, Dominican Republic.

1987 *Santos, shamanes y zemíes.* Fundación Cultural Dominicana, Santo Domingo, Dominican Republic.

Veloz Maggiolo, M.
1976–1977 Medioambiente y adaptación humana en la prehistoria de Santo Domingo. *Colección Historia y Sociedad 24*. Universidad Autónoma de Santo Domingo, Dominican Republic.
1980 *Las sociedades arcaicas de Santo Domingo.* Coediciones Museo del Hombre Dominicano–Fundación García Arévalo, Santo Domingo, Dominican Republic.
1991 *Panorama historico del Caribe precolombino.* Banco Central, Dominican Republic.
1992 Notas sobre la zamia en la prehistoria del Caribe. *Revista de arqueología americana* 6:125–138.
1993 *La Isla de Santo Domingo antes de Colon.* Banco Central de la República Dominicana, Santo Domingo.

Veloz Maggiolo, M., and E. Ortega
1995 Punta Cana y el origen de la agricultura en la Isla de Santo Domingo. In *Ponencias del primer seminario de arqueología del Caribe,* edited by M. Veloz Maggiolo and A. Caba Fuentes, pp. 5–11. Dominican Republic.

Veloz Maggiolo, M., E. Ortega, and P. Pina
1974 *El Caimito, un antiguo complejo ceramista de las Antillas Mayores.* Fundación García Arévalo, Santo Domingo.

Veloz Maggiolo, M., I. Vargas, M. Sanoja, and F. Luna
1976 *Arqueología de Yuma.* Editorial Taller, Santo Domingo.

Villaverde, C.
1961 [1839] *Excursión a Vuelta Abajo.* Consejo Nacional de Cultura, Havana.

Vincent, J.
1990 *Anthropology and Politics: Visions, Traditions, and Trends.* University of Arizona Press, Tucson.

Watters, D. R.
1993 Recent Initiatives of the Carnegie Museum of Natural History with Cuba. *CLASicos* 33:13–14. University of Pittsburgh.
1997 Bridging the Knowledge Gap about Cuban Archaeology. *CLASicos* 42:13–14. University of Pittsburgh.

Watters, D. R., and R. Dacal Moure
2002 Two-way Traffic on the Bridge. Paper presented at the 14th Annual General Meeting of the Museums Association of the Caribbean, Havana, Cuba.

Weeks, J. M., and P. J. Ferbel
1994 *Ancient Caribbean.* Garland Publishing, New York.

Wheaton, T., and P. Garrow
1985 Acculturation and the Archaeological Record in the Carolina Lowcountry. In *The Archaeology of Slavery and Plantation Life,* edited by T. A. Singleton, pp. 239–259. Academic Press, Orlando, Florida.

Whitley, D. S.
2001 Rock Art and Rock Art Research in Worldwide Perspective: An Introduction. In *Handbook of Rock Art Research,* edited by D. S. Whitley, pp. 7–51. Altamira Press, Walnut Creek, California.

Wienker, C.
2001 Physical Anthropology in Contemporary Cuba. *Physical Anthropology, Official Newsletter of the American Association of Physical Anthropologists* 1(4):2.

Wilkie, J. W., and M. Moreno-Ibáñez
1985 Latin American Food Production and Population in the Era of Land Reform since the 1950s. In *Food, Politics, and Society in Latin America,* edited by J. C. Super and T. C. Wright, pp. 65–105. University of Nebraska Press, Lincoln.

Wilkie, L. A.
1996 Glass-Knapping at a Louisiana Plantation: African-American Tools? *Historical Archaeology* 30(4):37–49.

Willey, G. R., and J. A. Sabloff
1993 *A History of American Archaeology.* 3d ed. W. H. Freeman, New York.

Williams, D.
1992 El arcaico en el noroeste de Guyana y los comienzos de la horticultura. In *Prehistoria sudamericana. Nuevas perspectivas.* Taraxacum, Washington D.C.

Wylie, A.
1999 Why Should Historical Archaeologists Study Capitalism? The Logic of Question and Answer, and the Challenge of Systemic Analysis. In *Historical Archaeologies of Capitalism,* edited by M. P. Leone and P. B. Potter, pp. 23–50. Plenum/Kluwer, New York.

Zucchi, A.
1984 Nuevos datos sobre la penetración de grupos cerámicos a las Antillas Mayores. In *Relaciones prehispánicas de Venezuela.* Acta Científica Venezolana, Caracas.

Contributors

Mary Jane Berman, director, Center of American and World Cultures, and associate professor of anthropology, Miami University, Oxford, Ohio, received her Ph.D. in anthropology from the State University of New York at Binghamton in 1989. She has conducted archaeological research in Arizona, New Mexico, New York, Texas, Malta, Cuba, and, since 1983, the Bahamas (San Salvador, Grand Bahama, and Long Island). She is codirector of the Lucayan Ecological Archaeology Research Project. Her research interests include the emergence of chiefdoms, shamanism, prehistoric island subsistence strategies, material culture studies (ceramics, lithics, basketry), and museum studies. Currently, she is the book review editor for the journal *Museum Anthropology.* Her research on the Bahamas has been published in *Latin American Antiquity, World Archaeology, Journal of Field Archaeology,* and the *Bahamas Journal of Science.*

L. Antonio Curet is an assistant curator at the Field Museum of Natural History of Chicago. He obtained his doctorate in anthropology from Arizona State University in 1992. His main interest is the study of social and cultural changes in precolumbian Puerto Rico, specifically those leading to social stratification. Currently he is conducting an excavation project at the site of Tibes, Ponce, Puerto Rico, one of the earliest ceremonial centers in the Caribbean. He has published several articles in journals and is the author of *Caribbean Paleodemography.*

Ramón Dacal Moure obtained his degree in archaeology from the Department of Anthropology of the Academia de Ciencias de Cuba in 1970. He published a number of articles and books, including *Método experimental para el estudio de artefactos líticos de culturas antillanas no ceramistas* (1968) and *Artefactos de concha en las comunidades aborígenes cubanas* (1978). His book with Manuel Rivero de la Calle titled *Arqueología aborígen de Cuba* (1986) was translated and published in 1996 by the University of Pittsburgh Press.

Shannon Lee Dawdy is assistant professor of anthropology and Social Sciences at the College, University of Chicago. She holds a Ph.D. in anthropology and history from the University of Michigan (2003). Her interests lie in the colonial and creole societies of the Caribbean and U.S. South. Her publications include articles on the archaeology of creolization, Native Americans in the colonial Southeast, and the development of early New Orleans and Louisiana. She has also conducted ethnoarchaeological research on food and farming at a postemancipation site in Cuba. She was the founding director of the Greater New Orleans Archaeology Program (1995–1998).

Lourdes Domínguez has a Ph.D. in historic sciences with concentration in archaeology. She is researcher at the Gabinete de Arqueología de la Oficina del Historiador de la Ciudad de La Habana and adjunct professor at the Facultad de Filosofía e Historia of the Universidad de La Habana and has taught at the Centro de Estudios Avanzados de Puerto Rico y el Caribe (San Juan, Puerto Rico) and at the Universidad de Campinas–São Paulo (Brazil). She specializes in the historical archaeology of Cuba and the Spanish Caribbean. Her publications include *Arqueología del centro-sur de Cuba, Arqueología colonial: Dos estudios,* and *Los collares de la santería cubana.* She has also contributed extensively to Cuban and international publications.

Jorge Febles was awarded a Ph.D. from the Scientific Council of the Institute of History, Philology, and Philosophy of the Siberian Branch of the Academy of Sciences of the Soviet Union in 1987, having first completed a course of study in archaeology offered by the Cuban Academy of Sciences in 1974 and then a Licentiate in History from the University of Havana in 1978. He has directed numerous projects in Cuba and published extensively abroad. His significant publications include *Manual para el estudio de la Piedra Tallada de los aborigines de Cuba* (1988), "Las comunidades aborígenes de Cuba," which he coauthored with Lourdes Domínguez and Alexis V. Rives in *Historia de Cuba: La colonia, evolución socioeconómica y formación nacional; De los orígenes hasta 1867* (1994), *Arqueología de Cuba y de otras áreas antillanas* (coedited with Alexis V. Rives) (1991), and the CD-ROM *Taíno, archaeología de Cuba.* He is a recent recipient of the John Simon Guggenheim Memorial Fellowship.

Perry L. Gnivecki, assistant professor of anthropology, Miami University, Oxford, Ohio, received his Ph.D. in anthropology and a certificate in Southwest Asian and North African Studies from the State University of New York at Binghamton in 1983. He is codirector of the Lucayan Ecological Archaeology Project and director of the Pigeon Creek Site excavations. His archaeological research interests include the emergence of chiefdoms, comparative urbanism and state formation, material culture studies, island ecology, and spatial organization. His research on the Bahamas has been published in *World Archaeology* and *Proceedings of the International Association of Caribbean Archaeology.*

Pedro Godo is the chair of the Department of Archaeology of the Centro de Antropología, Academia de Ciencias de Cuba. He obtained his doctorate in history in 1995 from the Universidad de la Habana. He has participated in a number of field research projects on precolumbian sites, especially those of foraging groups. He has published multiple articles on the early ceramic groups of Cuba and recently has been publishing on precolumbian art and religion, especially regarding the symbolism of designs on late precolumbian ceramics. As chair of the Department of Archaeology, he has dedicated himself to the protection of the archaeological heritage of Cuba.

Gabino La Rosa Corzo is a researcher in the Department of Archaeology of the Centro de Antropología, Academia de Ciencias de Cuba. He obtained his licenciate in history from Universidad de La Habana in 1968 and a doctoral degree in historical sciences with specialization in archaeology in 1994. He has conducted a number of research projects on both precolumbian and historic sites and has published a number of books, including *Los cimarrones de Cuba* (1989), *Costumbre funerarias de los aborígenes de Cuba* (1995), *Arqueología en sitios de contrabandistas* (1995), and *Los palenques del oriente de Cuba: Resistencia y acoso* (1991). This last book was translated into English and published in 2003 by the University of North Carolina Press.

Marlene S. Linville is a Ph.D. candidate in archaeology at the Graduate School and University Center of the City University of New York. She is an adjunct lecturer in the Department of Anthropology at Hunter College, where she has also served as a Graduate Teaching Fellow. In addition to rock art, her research interests includes material culture, symbolism, and the emergence of complex societies among the Amerindian cultures of the Caribbean and northern South America. A specialist in the analysis of marine shell artifacts, she is currently working as both contributor and coeditor of a volume that focuses on marine shell artifacts in the Archaeological Museum of Aruba.

César A. Rodríguez Arce is assistant researcher at the Departamento Centro Oriental de Arqueología, Delegación del Ministerio de Ciencias, Tecnología y Medio Ambiente en Holguín, Cuba. A veterinarian, he specializes in the precolumbian archaeology of Cuba, particularly in zooarchaeology and physical anthropology.

Theresa A. Singleton is associate professor, Department of Anthropology, Syracuse University. Her interests include African diasporas, slavery, and plantation life in the southern United States and the Caribbean. She has edited two books on the archaeological study of African-American life, *The Archaeology of Slavery and Plantation Life* (Academic Press, 1985) and *I, too, am America: Studies in the Archaeology of African Life* (University of Virginia Press, 1999), and has written numerous articles and book chapters on this subject.

Jorge Ulloa Hung received his licienciate in history in 1988 and his master's in 1999, both from the Universidad de Oriente, Santiago de Cuba. He is an assistant researcher of the Casa del Caribe and a coordinator of the journal *El Caribe Arqueológico.* He is a professor in Area de Ciencias Sociales del Instituto Technológico de Santo Domingo. His research has been on the foraging ceramic communities of southeastern Cuba, the *protoagrícola* communities in Holguín, and a historic study of the Hospital de las Minas del Cobre. With Roberto Valcárcel he has published a monograph titled *Cerámica temprana en el centro oriente de Cuba* (2003). He also published a book titled *Arqueología en la iglesia de Macao* with Elpidio Ortega and Gabriel Atiles and a number of articles in volumes including *Santiago de Cuba. La ciudad revisitada, Santiago de Cuba, Trescientos años de historiografía,* and *Las culturas aborígenes del Caribe.*

Roberto Valcárcel Rojas is assistant researcher at the Departamento Centro Oriental de Arqueología, Delegación del Ministerio de Ciencias, Tecnología y Medio Ambiente en Holguín, Cuba. He obtained a licienciate and master's from the Universidad de Oriente in Cuban and Caribbean history and culture, with specialization in the precolumbian archaeology of Cuba.

David R. Watters is curator-in-charge of the section of anthropology at Carnegie Museum of Natural History. He received his Ph.D. in anthropology from University of Pittsburgh (1980). He is particularly interested in the maritime adaptive strategies of human populations in the insular setting and linkages between oceanography and archaeology. A longstanding member of the International Association for Caribbean Archaeology and of the Museums Association of the Caribbean, he is interested in fostering collaborative research and promoting cooperative ventures among colleagues throughout the Caribbean region.

Samuel M. Wilson, professor of anthropology at the University of Texas, has carried out historical and archaeological research on the indigenous people of the Caribbean, with emphasis on the emergence of complex societies in the Greater Antilles. He has also explored issues of indigenous population dynamics, exchange, and political geography in the Lesser Antilles. His publications include *Hispaniola: Caribbean Chiefdoms in the Age of Columbus* and *The Emperor's Giraffe and Other Stories of Cultures in Contact.*

Index

www.ingramcontent.com/pod-product-compliance
Lightning Source LLC
LaVergne TN
LVHW051420090926
847619LV00027B/246
9780817351878